BAPTISTS & BOOTLEGGERS

A PROHIBITION EXPEDITION THROUGH THE SOUTH

...with Cocktail Recipes

KATHRYN SMITH

EVENING POST BOOKS

Our Accent Is Southern!

Published by Evening Post Books, Charleston, South Carolina

Editor: John M. Burbage
Design and composition: Kim Scott/Bumpy Design

A CIP catalog record for this book has been applied for from the
Library of Congress.

ISBN: 978-1-929647-72-9

To Leo,
my partner in life and
on the Prohibition Expedition
and Dad,
who coined the phrase

MAJOR SITES ON THE PROHIBITION EXPEDITION

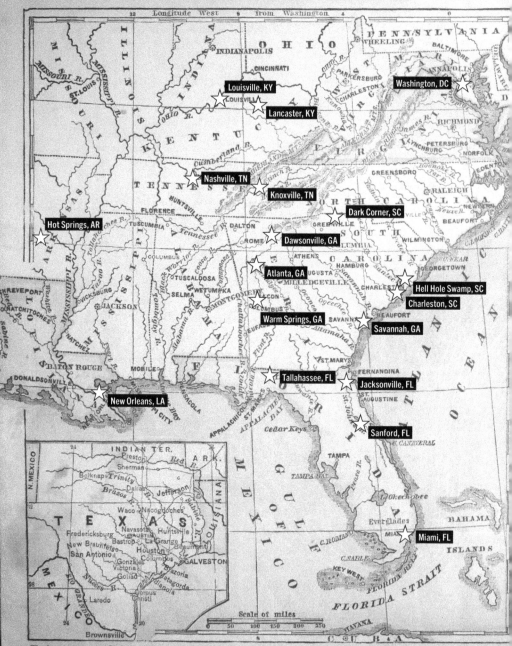

TABLE OF CONTENTS

*I*NTRODUCTION

LATE ONE AFTERNOON, I walked into the Prohibition Bar and Restaurant on Charleston's King Street. It is a welcoming sort of place even before five o'clock, with a long, rustic bar manned by bartenders in quasi-period dress—a pair of suspenders here, a flat cap there—ready to mix up cocktails from the second-largest selection of liquors in South Carolina. Or so I was later told by Ian Farley, one of the mixologists, as he prepared a Ramos Gin Fizz for me.

The young female hostess wasn't busy, and when I told her I was working on a book about the real Prohibition—the period from January 16, 1920 to December 5, 1933, when the Eighteenth Amendment was in force—she offered to show me around the place. Prohibition strives for a rustic-chic look, with Edison lights hanging over the tables in wire cages, Mason jars for glassware, and recycled liquor barrels here and there. The walls are decorated with photographs of Prohibition scenes in sepia hues—revenue agents busting up stills, protestors hoisting signs reading "We Want Beer," and a portrait of the infamous saloon wrecker Carry A. Nation waving her trademark hatchet.

"Oh, there's Carry Nation," I said, walking over to the picture.

The hostess joined me. "I wish I knew something about her," she said.

Right then, the plan for this book began to crystalize in my mind. I had been mulling over a serious history book about women and the Prohibition period, linking brief biographies of women such as Carry Nation; Mabel Walker Willebrandt, the nation's chief enforcer at the Justice Department; and the woman who led the charge to repeal Prohibition, New York socialite Pauline Morton Sabin.

But what were the chances that younger people like the friendly hostess at Prohibition would read that kind of book? Almost zilch. It would only appeal to a bunch of aging history nerds like me. As I sat at the bar chatting with mixologist Ian, I realized there are a lot of people like him who are fascinated by the Prohibition period and its role in birthing cocktail culture. Ian had his shirt sleeves rolled to the elbow, showing his tattoos: a long-stemmed tasting spoon on one arm and a strainer on the other. He referred me to a website where I could peruse vintage cocktail mixing guides and find recipes. When I asked for an appropriate Prohibition cocktail, he produced his foamy and delicious Ramos Gin Fizz, which I later learned was the favorite drink of Louisiana's notoriously corrupt (and "wet") governor and senator, Huey Long, "the Kingfish."

RAMOS GIN FIZZ

- 2 oz. London dry gin (Beefeater suggested)
- 0.5 oz. lime juice
- 0.5 oz. lemon juice
- 1 oz. simple syrup
- 1 egg white
- 5 drops orange flower water
- 4 drops vanilla extract
- Soda water (to top with)

Dry shake all ingredients except soda water for two minutes. Add ice and shake with intent for eight minutes. Strain into an ice-cold Collins glass and top slowly with soda water until the head sits around an inch above the rim.

—Jim McCourt, beverage director, Prohibition Charleston

Over the next few days, I did some more noodling and research and came up with a completely different approach to this book. What I have written is a fun but informative look at Prohibition in the South, tying events to places that readers can visit, should they wish to take a Prohibition expedition of their own, and drinks they can try if they prefer to be armchair travelers. The Southern states—except Louisiana—had all gone dry before national Prohibition, thanks to the influence of Baptists and Methodists and dedicated temperance special interest groups on their legislatures. In practice, it meant these states had flourishing illegal booze networks in place to serve themselves and their Northern brethren long before the nation went dry in 1920.[1]

Southern port cities such as Charleston, Savannah, Mobile, and New Orleans, not to mention most of the coast of Florida, kept much of the Eastern Seaboard lubricated with rum and other illegal liquor imports during Prohibition. Meanwhile, the Appalachian Mountains was a hotbed of illegal liquor production that quenched the thirst—and sometimes killed—drinkers who were less particular about their hooch. Here's a statistic for you: the Southern states accounted for *half* the moonshine still seizures by law enforcement between 1923 and 1924.[2] These moonshiners were loath to give up their lucrative trade and continued making white lightning long after the Eighteenth Amendment was negated by the Twenty-First Amendment in 1933. And incidentally, NASCAR racing was a direct legacy of the drivers carrying loads of 'shine to customers. They honed their skills outracing lawmen down the nearest Thunder Road.

I also realized that all the people I had been thinking of including in my book had some tie to the South. Mabel Walker Willebrandt brought successful cases against infamous rings of rum-runners in Savannah and Mobile. She put the Cincinnati "Bootlegger King" George Remus in prison in Atlanta and came up with the prosecutorial gambit that nabbed Al Capone for income tax evasion some years later. Capone also served time at the Atlanta pen and lived out his final years in Miami Beach. Reformer Pauline Morton Sabin owned a vacation home outside Charleston called The Oaks. Carry A. Nation was born in Kentucky, and though she conducted most of her saloon wrecking in the Midwest, she made tours of the South that led to communities enacting local option dry laws and ended her tumultuous life in Eureka Springs, Arkansas.

My research on Prohibition in the South took me to the birthplace of Carry Nation, the Miami Beach mansion of Al Capone, a haunted hotel, a moonshine festival, Louisville's famed Whiskey Row, and the graves of a temperance leader, notorious bootleggers, and a stock car racer murdered in a dispute over a still. I met mixologists, modern-day distillers, and

Prohibition history buffs, and drank more alcohol than I've ever had in my life. (It's a tough job, but someone has to do it.) In the middle of my research, the coronavirus pandemic hit, upending the bar and restaurant industry. That eventually led to almost everything in the country being prohibited, though, curiously, as states and localities shut down "non-essential" businesses and even churches to slow the spread of the virus, liquor stores were generally classified as essential. Sniffed a writer in the letters-to-the-editor column of the *Wall Street Journal*, "Are we really willing to acquiesce to a government official's decision that buying liquor is more important than receiving the sacraments?"[3] Apparently, we were.

To write this book, I read a lot of history—so you, dear reader, don't have to. Well, just a little, because you need to understand what a serious drinking problem America once had and how the crazy notion of drying up the country came about, barreled through Congress, and was embraced by most of the country's voters to such a degree that it became a constitutional amendment—the only amendment that was ever repealed.

Before we plunge in, a word about the title of this book. My father, Bruce Yandle, is an economist of some note who came up with a theory of government regulation more than thirty years ago that he calls "Bootleggers and Baptists." The Baptists—and Methodists and Presbyterians and other Protestant denominations—who favored Prohibition wanted to dry up sales of liquor to improve the homelives of women and children. They didn't realize that they were playing into the hands of the bootleggers—and moonshiners and rumrunners—who made a fortune by selling illegal liquor during Prohibition. B&B theory applies in countless real-life situations, from climate change legislation to federal dietary recommendations to the labeling of tobacco products.[4] My father and my son, Adam C. Smith, also an economist, co-authored a book in 2014 called *Bootleggers and Baptists: How Economic Forces and Moral Persuasion Interact to Shape Regulatory Politics.*[5] Whenever I mentioned the title of their book, people responded, "Oooh, that sounds like a fun read!" It's definitely an *interesting* read, but we're talking the dismal science here, so I wouldn't exactly call it fun. With their permission, I have inverted their title to minimize confusion and, I hope, produced a book that is more likely to meet the expectations of those looking for a fun read. Hang on, you're about to meet some drinkers and the teetotalers who tried to turn off the taps.

PROHIBITION BAR AND RESTAURANT

547 King Street • www.prohibitioncharleston.com

Jim McCourt, beverage director at Prohibition Charleston, stirs up something delicious at the bar. *Courtesy Prohibition Charleston*

Prohibition was opened on Charleston's King Street in 2013 by Ray Burns and James Walsh, both natives of Ireland, who wanted a restaurant and bar that gave a nod to the 1920s. "It feels like you are stepping back in time, with the vintage style décor, but the cocktails and cuisine are anything but old fashioned," explained events and operations manager Alexa Pavlovski. Besides the enticement of food and drink, Prohibition offers live entertainment, from era-appropriate jazz during dinner on Friday and Saturday nights to free swing and salsa dancing lessons a couple of days a week to a bluegrass band for weekend brunches. A standard event is its Prohibition Repeal Party, held every year on December 5, with drink specials (in 2019 it was Bee's Knees), women dressed as flappers, and live jazz. Burns and Walsh opened a second Prohibition in Savannah, Georgia, in 2017, but renamed it Repeal 33 in 2020. With the rest of the food and beverage industry, both restaurants were hard-hit by the coronavirus pandemic. They closed from March to August 2020, reopened with reduced capacity, and suspended live entertainment until health conditions improved. But like the food and beverage businesses struck by Prohibition itself, the restaurants are learning to adapt in order to survive. "We have seen a drop in sales," Pavlovski said, "but we are happy with the way everything is going." ■

BEE'S KNEES

- 2 oz. gin
- 0.75 oz. lemon juice
- 0.75 oz. honey syrup (2:1 ratio of honey to water)

Add all ingredients to a shaker, add ice, and shake well for ten seconds. Double-strain into a chilled cocktail glass, no garnish.

—Jim McCourt, beverage director, Prohibition Charleston

CHAPTER ONE

A Brief *History*

IT WAS AN UNUSUALLY BALMY winter day even for Charleston when I entered a small, gated courtyard on East Bay Street. It was five minutes to five and the brass door handle of The Gin Joint didn't yield to my touch. A man sitting on a balcony on the building next door yelled down, "Five o'clock!"—obviously something he did with some regularity—and I settled into a chair in the courtyard to wait. A man sitting on a bench on the other side of the black iron fence was deep in conversation on his cell phone. "I watched a hell of a show here last night," he confided, and then a couple of cars passed. I caught the word "drag," but when I realized he was talking about drag racing rather than drag queens, I tuned out.

At exactly five o'clock, the bar door opened, I was ushered to a table for two beside a window, and soon Robert F. Moss arrived. My son-in-law, Nick Dowling, a restauranteur and former distillery manager, had set up our meeting, assuring me Robert would be a fount of information about Southern drinking habits, past and present. A tall, friendly-faced man with

Robert F. Moss is the author of *Southern Spirits. Courtesy Robert F. Moss*

7

curly, red hair, Robert told me that he holds a doctorate in English but earns his living as a computer consultant. It's obvious his real passion, though, is Southern food and beverage. He is the barbecue editor of *Southern Living—* imagine!—and author of *Southern Spirits: Four Hundred Years of Drinking in the American South, with Recipes.* His eyes really light up when he is talking about cooking a pig with famous pitmaster Rodney Scott or Charleston's 100-member strong Brown Water Brotherhood, which he helped to found.

Robert had suggested we meet at The Gin Joint, which is Charleston's oldest craft cocktail bar. The one-room bar is simple and inviting, with low lights and vintage jazz music setting a relaxing end-of-day mood. Single-file rows of bottles were arranged on high shelves on the walls, with chain-link gates guarding more bottles on one side of the room—a nice bootlegger touch, Robert said. Wanting to stick with vintage cocktails, I ordered a simple sidecar—Cognac, Cointreau, and lemon—and Robert ordered something under the menu heading "Strong & Stirred" called Mischief Managed—a Harry Potter reference—composed of Early Times bourbon, Burnt Rose syrup, Madeira wine, Salers aperitif, Cap Corse Rouge, Peychaud's bitters and Palo Santo wood. Obviously, Robert knows his stuff; I had no idea what any of these ingredients were, other than the bourbon and the bitters.

A sidecar is a classic cocktail from the Prohibition era.

James Bolt, owner of The Gin Joint, pours a craft cocktail dubbed "Mischief Managed." *Both pictures courtesy The Gin Joint*

MISCHIEF MANAGED

- 1½ oz. Early Times Bottled in Bond Bourbon
- ¾ oz. Cap Corse Rouge
- ¾ oz. Burnt Rose syrup
- ½ oz. Rainwater Madeira
- ½ oz. Salers aperitif
- 5 dashes Peychaud's bitters

Combine all ingredients in a mixing glass with ice, stir to combine for 15–20 seconds.

Place a small piece of Palo Santo wood on a fireproof surface and light with a torch. Place a rocks glass over the ignited wood to extinguish the flame and smoke the glass for 10–15 seconds.

Pour cocktail into smoked glass and garnish with a dehydrated lemon slice.

—James Bolt, The Gin Joint

When our cocktails arrived, Robert gave me a brief history lesson on Southern drinking habits, beginning with colonial days, when settlers in the South mostly drank a dark, rough rum imported from the Caribbean and fruit brandy they made themselves from their most plentiful crops. From the North Carolina mountains to Virginia, they favored apple brandy, and for the more Southern colonies, like South Carolina and Georgia, they preferred peach brandy. (Georgia, of course, is still called the Peach State, though South Carolina is a much larger producer of peaches.)

Robert said that after the Revolutionary War, it became harder to get rum from the Caribbean because of British trade laws, so Americans started distilling their own whiskey from corn and rye. Bourbon, made primarily from corn, was drunk in Kentucky and to the west, while rye whiskey was favored to the east; it's what George Washington distilled at Mount Vernon in his post-presidency years.

You may recall from your high school history days that distilleries were at the center of one of the greatest crises of Washington's presidency. In order to pay off the young nation's war debts, Washington's secretary of the treasury, Alexander Hamilton—yes, he of Broadway fame—suggested that an excise tax on distilled spirits be instituted. The law passed in 1791 and caused such a ruckus—including an insurrection in Pennsylvania that forced Washington to call out the militia—that it was repealed in 1802 after Thomas Jefferson came into office. Taxing alcohol wasn't attempted

A vintage postcard of George Washington in front of his plantation house, Mount Vernon, doesn't show his still. *Author collection*

again until 1862, when the Union needed emergency funds to pay for its army in the Civil War. President Lincoln was successful in implementing the tax, and a federal excise tax has been in effect ever since—except during Prohibition, when there was no alcohol to tax. (Supposedly.) I read later that the revenue taken in by the federal government through alcohol excise taxes averaged 23 percent of tax receipts each year from 1873 to 1917.[6] Thus the government and the alcohol industry had an interdependency that protected producers from temperance advocates for quite some time.

Robert and I chatted for an hour, until my parking meter ran out. Having suffered under the efficiency of the Charleston Police Department's parking division in various ways over the years, I said goodbye and hurried off. But one thing Robert said stuck in my mind. We were talking about the pride people seem to take in their hometowns' attempts to thwart Prohibition. Everyone seems to have an ancestor who was a bootlegger or a moonshiner, and they are eager to tell you that person supplied Al Capone or knew Al Capone or worked for Al Capone. In fact, Al Capone seemed to have slept more places than George Washington did (hence the chapter called "Al Capone Slept Here" that you'll find later in this book.) Robert grinned and said in every town the Prohibition story is pretty much the same. Only the names and faces change. I found this was also true on the "Baptist" side; each town had its anti-alcohol leaders. I discovered my own grandmother—whose brother owned a string of liquor stores around Macon, Georgia—was a member of the Women's Christian Temperance Union. She was a Methodist, but still . . .

Robert's book is a fascinating and in-depth account of Southern history viewed through the bottom of a glass, along with some modern takes on classic drinks. (This is necessary because many of the ingredients in old drink recipes just aren't available anymore.) I recommend it to anyone who is inspired by this book to learn more. I also delved into some other books, including Daniel Okrent's *Last Call: The Rise and Fall of Prohibition*, as well as re-watching the outstanding Ken Burns/Lynn Novick documentary *Prohibition* that first ran on PBS in 2011.

To recap Okrent and Burns, America by the early nineteenth century was "a nation of drunkards," so great were the quantities of alcohol consumed. Early on, it was because of the iffy nature of water quality; the Pilgrims arrived with the hold of *The Mayflower* loaded with barrels of beer. Beer and hard cider were safer alternatives than water, which might kill you, and because it was pretty low-alcohol stuff, drinking it all day wouldn't knock you out. But by 1763, Okrent says, there were 159 commercial distilleries just in New England, "and by the 1820s, liquor was so plentiful and so freely available, it was less expensive than tea."

Here's the statistic that always floors me: Okrent writes that by 1830, American adults drank seven gallons of pure alcohol a year. Broken down into more comprehensible language, it means each American drank the equivalent of 1.7 bottles of 80-proof liquor per week. And that's per capita, factoring in all the abstainers, and women, who drank far less than men. Robert Moss's book *Southern Spirits* contains an entertaining story about the South Carolina Revolutionary War hero Francis Marion, known as the Swamp Fox. During these times, it was the custom in Charleston to lock the doors of dining rooms when a dinner party was going on, trapping the men inside until they either passed out under the table or were released to stagger home. In 1780, Marion attempted to escape the fate of his fellow diners by jumping out of a second-story window. In doing so, he broke his ankle. Luckily for the Patriots, Marion left Charleston to recuperate—avoiding capture when the British took the city a few months later. From there he organized his band of guerilla fighters in the swamps of the Pee Dee and earned the nickname by which most South Carolinians know him today.[7] (Later on, we'll visit a South Carolina rum distillery named for this hero.)

How do the drinking habits of these early Americans compare to ours today? In the past few years, annual alcohol consumption per capita has been in the neighborhood of 2.3 gallons, so less than a third of what our ancestors guzzled.[8]

The drinking trend could not continue at that pace, and by the early 1820s, the words "intemperance" and "temperance" were coming into vogue. Even the hard-partying South Carolinians realized they had to mend their ways. In 1829, a group of men met in Columbia and formed

A pre-Civil War magazine aimed at children urged temperance, with a barrel of liquor on the cover labeled "Ruin." *Courtesy Steven Lomazow, M.D.*

a task force to study the effects of alcohol on the people of the state. That resulted in the formation of the South Carolina Temperance Society, according to historian, physician, and antique liquor bottle collector Phillip Kenneth Huggins.[9]

Like most temperance organizations at the time, this group swore abstinence among themselves and hoped to use their good example and "moral suasion" to encourage others to do the same. However, it was obvious from the start that the people they were most eager to keep alcohol away from was the slave population, followed by the "laboring classes" of whites. (This was a common thread in the South among temperance organizations, while elsewhere in the country the primary targets were immigrants, Native Americans, and lower-class whites.) The temperance organization soon had almost a hundred local chapters in place, including one in Charleston. In 1842, a national group of former alcoholics who had formed a forerunner to Alcoholics Anonymous called the Washington Temperance Society (apparently unaware of President Washington's distillery) set up a Charleston chapter. The Washingtonian movement gained many adherents, but the nature of alcoholism, with its unfortunate backslides, led purists to begin campaigning for laws that banned alcohol entirely.

Tennessee passed the first temperance law in the country in 1838, making it a misdemeanor to sell alcoholic beverages in taverns and stores.[10] Maine was the first state to ban alcohol entirely, in 1851, and inspired several others to follow suit. But the laws were unpopular among many citizens and they had all disappeared by the time of the Civil War. Wars are expensive, and President Lincoln instituted an excise tax of twenty cents per gallon of distilled spirits in 1862.[11] By the end of the war, the tax had reached a whopping two dollars per gallon. After the war, the former Confederate States got a tax break until 1867, when Reconstruction began, and the Bureau of Internal Revenue went into action demanding the federal excise tax on Southern alcohol producers. As a result, many went underground, making illegal liquor in hidden stills. Because much of the action took place at night in order to avoid detection, the illegal raw corn whiskey was dubbed "moonshine." 'Shine was made virtually everywhere in the South (and the rest of the country) whenever legal alcohol was prohibited, but let's start out in Tennessee, home of the oldest licensed distillery in the country, Jack Daniel's, as well as a town that was founded by the temperance movement as a haven for non-drinkers.

Before we go, one note about Prohibition with a big "P" and prohibition with a little "p." When I write about national Prohibition, the law from 1920 to 1933, I use the big "P." When I write about state and local efforts to limit alcohol, both before and after national Prohibition, I use the small one.

PROHIBITION EXPEDITION

The Gin Joint • 182 E Bay Street #2169 • www.theginjoint.com

This charming small bar was opened in 2010 by Joe and MariElena Raya, becoming Charleston's first craft cocktail bar following the repeal of the South Carolina mini-bottle law in 2006. Under the mini-bottle law, in effect from 1973 to 2006, all liquor sold in bars and restaurants was contained in 1.7-ounce bottles, making it hard to serve a drink more complicated than a martini or a rum and Coke. The repeal of the law to allow free-pouring of alcohol led to the present heyday of cocktail culture.[12]

James and Wells Bolt are the husband-and-wife owners of The Gin Joint, Charleston's first craft cocktail bar. *Courtesy The Gin Joint*

Today, The Gin Joint is owned by James Bolt, who worked there for the Rayas, and his wife, Wells. They focus on Prohibition and pre-Prohibition drinks, as well as James's Gin Joint Originals. True to this time period, they do not carry vodka because it was not brought to the United States until after Prohibition ended, Wells said. James will also custom mix a drink based on a combination of adjectives a customer chooses from a menu of fifteen. For example, my husband, Leo, chose "smoky" and "spicy" for his.

continues on next page

continued from previous page

As for the name of the bar, Wells explains that a gin joint is simply "somewhere you can get a really good, stiff drink." James contributes the two recipes Robert Moss and I enjoyed: a classic Sidecar and a Gin Joint Original called Mischief Managed (see page 9).

GIN JOINT SIDECAR

- 1½ oz. Pierre Ferrand 1840 Cognac
- 1 oz. fresh lemon juice
- ¾ oz. Pierre Ferrand Dry curaçao
- ¼ oz. simple syrup (1:1 ratio sugar to water)

Combine all ingredients into a cocktail shaker with ice. Shake hard for 10–15 seconds. Double-strain into a chilled coupe glass. Garnish with an expressed lemon peel.

CEMETERY SIDE TRIP

Francis Marion, "the Swamp Fox," is entombed at Belle Isle Plantation Cemetery in Berkeley County. The site is managed by the South Carolina Department of Parks, Recreation, and Tourism and is open to the public. Highway 45, Pineville, South Carolina. http://www.schistorytrail.com/property.html?i=7

A vintage postcard features the grave of Revolutionary War hero Francis Marion. *Author collection*

RECOMMENDED READING

Southern Spirits: Four Hundred Years of Drinking in the American South, with Recipes by Robert F. Moss (Berkeley: Ten Speed Press, 2016)

CHAPTER TWO

SHOOT-OUT IN KNOXVILLE

ON A BITTERLY COLD winter morning in Knoxville, Tennessee, I came upon three women gathered in front of a bronze sculpture outside the Museum of East Tennessee History. They were dressed in black, but one was wearing a stunning vintage Persian lamb coat trimmed in fur and a feathered velvet slouch hat. She said they had belonged to her grandmother. Stretched across their chests were purple, yellow, and white sashes reading "Votes for Women."

The shivering trio was drawing attention to the centennial of the Nineteenth Amendment and Tennessee's pivotal role in the women's suffrage movement. They were standing in front of the Burn Memorial, which celebrates a crucial vote for ratification cast by a 24-year-old Tennessee legislator, Harry Burn, at the urging of his mother. On August 18, 1920, Harry, who had been on the anti-suffrage side of the issue, received a seven-page letter from his mother, Phoebe, back home in Niota. She concluded her letter with the words, "Hurrah and vote suffrage! . . . Don't forget to be a good boy and help Mrs. Catt put the 'rat' in ratification. Your Mother." Harry was indeed a good boy, took her urging to heart, and switched sides. Tennessee became the final state needed to achieve ratification of the Nineteenth Amendment. By August 26, it was the law of the land, entitling the women of the United

Marking the centennial of women's suffrage at the Burn Memorial in downtown Knoxville are, from left, Vivian Shipe, Tanya Coats, and Knox County Commissioner Evelyn Gill. *Author photo*

States to vote for the first time in the upcoming presidential election.[13] Sadly, Southern black women were largely excluded from exercising their right, and the women who did vote supported Warren G. Harding in a landslide. But more about him later.

If I were a betting woman, I would bet that Phoebe Burn, known as Miss Febb, was also a supporter of temperance, as the movements for women's suffrage and Prohibition were closely intertwined. The "Mrs. Catt" in Miss Febb's letter was Carrie Chapman Catt, who succeeded Susan B. Anthony as president of the influential National American Woman Suffrage Association and led the final, successful charge. She went on to establish the League of Women Voters.[14] Catt had first gotten involved in the suffrage cause as a member of the Women's Christian Temperance Union, which had a suffrage action arm. In fact, Susan B. Anthony's original cause, a decade before the Civil War, was temperance. She decided to focus instead on suffrage when a men's temperance organization refused to let her address its assembly, but she remained a dedicated dry.

Whether women were working for suffrage or temperance or both, what they wanted was some power and control over their own lives. They were fed up with being unable to own property, get divorces, keep their children should they leave abusive spouses, and have any say in the way they were governed, both at home and outside the home. They wanted to raise the age of sexual consent from ten to at least sixteen. The Women's Christian Temperance Union, which was founded in 1874, tackled all these issues, though its principal cause was ridding the United States of drink, which its members believed was the source of all evil.

There had been previous efforts, generally led by women, that had been at least temporarily successful in limiting drinking. As I mentioned earlier, Tennessee had been the first state in the nation to enact a prohibition law, in 1838 making it illegal to sell alcoholic beverages in taverns and stores. The fines for violating the law were designated for support of public schools.[15] This didn't last, of course, and the Civil War threw everything in disarray. It was the WCTU, with passionate, tireless, and dedicated leaders such as Frances E. Willard that built an army of women who declared, "Lips that Touch Liquor Should Not Touch Ours."

Frances E. Willard was the most consequential member of the temperance movement in the nineteenth century. This engraving appeared in her book *Woman and Temperance.*

Their emblem was the white ribbon and their motto was "For God and Home and Every Land." Women flocked to the cause, and the WCTU grew into a formidable organization with departments that addressed everything from childcare for working women to abolishing tobacco use. One of its most influential departments was education, which eventually won approval over textbooks throughout the country. That led to some pretty outlandish claims being drummed into children's heads, such as that drinking one alcoholic beverage could destroy your stomach lining or cause you to burst into flames.

The Human Body and Its Health, an 1884 elementary school textbook used by Ollie Fant of Anderson, South Carolina, had a three-page section on "Effects of Alcohol and Tobacco." Children were warned that "King alcohol is an enemy to reason and, once admitted, he may dethrone the rightful sovereign at any moment." As for tobacco, "Many boys are throwing away their manly strength, and dwarfing their minds, by the use of tobacco."[16]

Although the WCTU was based in Ohio, by 1882 every state in the South had leaders and multiple chapters, thanks to Miss Willard's astonishing organizing ability, and no end of feisty Southern women joined up.[17]

Lide Smith Meriwether was a temperance leader in Tennessee. *Carrie Chapman Catt albums, Bryn Mawr College Libraries, Special Collections.*

Tennessee's longtime leader was Lide Smith Meriwether of Memphis, who headed both the state WCTU and state Equal Rights Association. "In her suffrage petition of 1895," the *Tennessee Encyclopedia* says, "she argued against the classification of women with minors, aliens, paupers, criminals, and idiots."[18] Meriwether was a crusader in many women's rights fields, including the treatment of "fallen women." She established a home for the rehabilitation of prostitutes and even took some of these women into her own home.

"Protect the home" was a rallying cry of the WCTU, and Meriwether proved herself particularly adept at this when her daughter, Virginia, left her husband, a drug addict. Mother and daughter had gone to a mineral springs resort in Tennessee to recover where they were tracked down by the abandoned husband, armed with a gun. Lide convinced him to lay the gun down and leave, but he returned later with another gun and again threatened his wife. Virginia picked up the first gun and shot him in the stomach. Before he died, he admitted it was his own fault and she shot him in self-defense, sparing her from prosecution. After that, Lide sent Virginia to medical school in New York, and she became one of the first women physicians in that state, practicing into her late eighties.[19]

Meriwether was noteworthy in reaching out to black women, including Lucy Tappan Phillips, a graduate of Fisk University and minister's wife long active in temperance matters within the church. Phillips presided over the Tennessee Black WCTU. National WCTU President Willard had accepted white Southern WCTU leaders' view that because of "tradition"—a word still used in the South today to justify onerous, outdated practices—the races must have separate organizations. Willard controversially wrote that she pitied white women who had to live in a land where "the colored race multiplies like the locusts of Egypt" and raised fears about drunken black men raping white women, a common refrain in the Southern WCTU's messaging. She got into a famous war of words with Memphis's crusading black journalist Ida B. Wells, who demanded the WCTU join her anti-lynching campaign and add equal rights for black voters to its mission.

Another WCTU leader, Silena Moore Holman of Nashville, helped the organization push through a law that made it illegal to sell liquor within four miles of a school. That "Four-Mile Rule" effectively wiped out legal liquor sales in all rural areas of Tennessee. By 1907, liquor sales were legal in only four cities in the state.

Remember that year, 1907. It came up again and again during my Prohibition expeditions while researching this book. It's almost spooky! I'll remind you as the number pops up.

While lobbying and writing letters and giving speeches are all important aspects of passing laws, nothing brings things to a head like spectacular crimes, and Tennessee had some shocking ones in the early twentieth century.

Ida B. Wells fought for many progressive causes, especially an end to lynching, but drew the ire of Frances Willard. *Wikimedia Commons*

Do you remember the scene in the great movie *Butch Cassidy and the Sundance Kid* when the Wild Bunch gang member named Harvey Logan challenges Butch Cassidy to a knife fight? Butch asks about the rules. "Rules! In a knife fight? No rules!" bellows his opponent, after which Butch kicks him in the groin, punches him in the jaw, and leaves him writhing in the dust of their Hole-in-the-Wall hideout. Then they go off and rob a train together.

Logan, also known as Kid Curry, came to Knoxville on the heels of this caper in 1901. Knoxville was an up-and-coming city by then, and like all up-and-coming cities, it had a red-light district. It was called the Bowery, apparently after the corresponding district in New York, and was located along present-day Central Avenue. In addition to saloons and bawdy houses, the district held drugstores where little round tins of morphine and cocaine were sold to "long pale-faced women or girls or boys barely out of their teens, with bloodshot eyes and bloated features showing long dissipation."[20]

Logan, a pitiless murderer, immediately began to carouse in the Bowery with Knoxville's most attractive ladies of pleasure, get drunk, and start fights. On the evening of December 13, 1901, he was in the process of strangling a man in Ike Jones' Resort on Central Avenue when two policemen,

The Wild Bunch (left to right: the Sundance Kid, Will Carver, Ben Kilpatrick, Harvey Logan, and Butch Cassidy) were known as bank robbers but played a role in prohibition too. *Wikimedia Commons*

Robert T. Saylor and William M. Dinwiddie, entered and tried to break up the fight using their billy clubs. While still strangling his opponent with one hand, Logan managed to shoot both officers—he put three bullets into Saylor—and then jump off the back porch and escape to parts unknown. Incredibly, the police officers both survived the shootings for more than a dozen years, though they were seriously damaged by their wounds and considered by their department to have died in the line of duty.

Logan was captured and brought back to Knoxville, where he spent a year awaiting trial. Given the entire second floor of the Knox County Jail, he became a celebrity-behind-bars, visited by everyone from the ladies of the WCTU to the governor, and showered with home-cooked meals and gifts to make his cell more comfortable. The sheriff finally had to limit his visitors to out-of-town VIPs and the Knoxville upper crust. (President Theodore Roosevelt visited Knoxville during his incarceration but didn't call on the outlaw.)

Tried in federal court on charges related to the train robbery, Logan was convicted and returned to jail while awaiting appeal. On June 27, 1903, he overpowered his guard by slipping a noose made from a wire taken from a broom around his neck, finagled a gun, escaped the jail, and galloped off on the sheriff's favorite saddle horse. He never returned to Knoxville, though his life lasted only another year. In 1904, wounded by a posse after robbing yet another train in Parachute, Colorado, he shot himself in the head rather than go to prison. Last words: "I'm hit! I will make an end to it!" The chief of the Pinkerton Detective Agency, William A. Pinkerton, said Curry "is the only criminal I know of who does not have one single good point."[21]

This and other notorious crimes in the Bowery galvanized the WCTU in Knoxville to push for citywide prohibition, and local leaders voted in 1907 for Knoxville to become the first dry city in Tennessee. Notes the *Tennessee Encyclopedia*, "a carnival atmosphere pervaded. Church bells rang each hour of the day, a parade was staged in the morning, and the University of Tennessee students appeared riding a water wagon in support of prohibition."[22] (How things change. A few years ago, a writer for the college newspaper described UT as "a drinking school with a studying problem."[23])

A year after Knoxville went dry, the shocking murder of a newspaper editor in Nashville carried the rest of the state into dry-dom. Legally, at least.

Edward Ward Carmack, former congressman and U.S. senator, became editor of the fledgling newspaper the *Nashville Tennessean* in 1908. A strong proponent of temperance, he used his newspaper as a platform to rail against alcohol, making him the darling of the WCTU. That same year, he challenged the incumbent governor, Malcolm Patterson, a "wet" championed by the liquor industry (remember, Tennessee was home to the Jack Daniel's Distillery and many others) who was endorsed

"HE'S ON THE RUN"

[From The Nashville Tennessean]

Souvenir of Thirty-fourth Annual Meeting of the Woman's Christian Temperance Union, Nashville, Tennessee, November 9-13, 1907

A souvenir postcard from the WCTU's 1907 convention in Tennessee expressed confidence that the saloons would soon be closed.

by another local paper, the *Nashville American*. Carmack lost the Democratic primary and began writing some pretty libelous stuff about the governor and the editor of the rival paper, Duncan Brown Cooper. Coming upon Cooper and his son, Robin, on the streets of Nashville shortly after the general election, Carmack was said to have feared for his life, drew his gun, and shot and wounded Robin. Duncan Cooper then shot and killed Carmack. The two Coopers were convicted of second-degree murder, but Governor Patterson pardoned them.

(As a former newspaper journalist, I find the idea of shoot-outs by political rivals of editors rather shocking, but the same thing happened in Columbia, South Carolina in 1903. In this case, the editor of *The State* newspaper, a sworn enemy of South Carolina's U.S. Senator Ben Tillman, was shot dead in front of the State House by the lieutenant governor, who happened to be Tillman's nephew. Even though there were many witnesses, the lieutenant governor was acquitted on the basis of self defense.[24] You'll be hearing a lot more about Ben Tillman later in this book, but let's get back to Tennessee.)

The people of Tennessee went wild, and the supporters of temperance were galvanized. Silena Holman declared, "The bullet that ended Carmack's life will write prohibition on the statue books of Tennessee." A front-page editorial in the weekly *Nashville Globe* a week after Carmack's murder focused on the bar scene in the capital city, using the WCTU playbook to decry alcohol. "Dens of Vice Breeding Crime. Hash Houses and Saloons Rendezvous for Loafers. Men and Women Throng the Streets Like Flies."[25] The editorial described a Saturday afternoon on Third Avenue: "Men and women, boys and girls, the thoughtless old and the inexperienced young, congregate on the sidewalks and in the streets . . . drinking, carousing, and carrying on all kinds of antics . . . Men draw their wages on Saturday and drift into this mob and there drink up their earnings while in many cases their families are suffering for the necessities of life. Young women are led to destruction."

The WCTU and another powerful temperance organization, the Anti-Saloon League, used Carmack's "martyrdom" as a ramrod to force Tennessee to ban the manufacture of alcohol in Tennessee in 1909, though possession and transportation were still legal.[26] Governor Patterson vetoed the bill, but he was overridden by the legislature. The exceptions for possession and transportation ended with a "Bone-Dry Bill" passed in 1917.[27] Two years later, Tennessee voted to ratify the Eighteenth Amendment.

EDWARD W. CARMACK

Martyr or racist? Edward W. Carmack was a man of very strong opinions, to say the least, and he used the bully pulpit of elected office and the newspapers he edited to put forth his views. Born to a poor family in Sumner County, Tennessee, in 1858, Carmack managed to get a college education and pass the Tennessee bar. He achieved his first elective office, the Tennessee legislature, in 1884.

Edward W. Carmack was both an avowed racist and a martyr to the temperance cause. His statue was pulled down by protestors in the summer of 2020. *Wikimedia Commons*

Five years later, Carmack joined the staff of newspapers in Nashville, including the *Nashville American*, where his mentor was the man who later killed him, Duncan Brown Cooper. From there he went to Memphis, becoming editor of the *Memphis Commercial* in 1892. Another newspaper operating there at the time was the *Free Speech*, edited by crusading civil rights leader Ida B. Wells. One of her most important causes was ending lynching, a tragically common practice. Shortly after Carmack's arrival in Memphis, a particularly ugly lynching took the lives of three black grocers. Carmack viciously attacked Wells over her coverage of the event, styling her "a black wench," and urging retaliation. While Wells was out of town, a crowd demolished her newspaper office. She did not return to the South for thirty years, instead moving to the North where she became a founder and leader of the NAACP.

Carmack rode his popularity to election to the U.S. House in 1886 and the U.S. Senate in 1901, though the Tennessee General Assembly chose not to return him to the Senate in 1907. (Legislatures elected senators at the time; this changed with the ratification of the Seventeenth Amendment in 1913.) He returned to Nashville and journalism, which resulted in defeat at the polls and, a few months later, his death.

As a martyr to the temperance cause, Carmack was memorialized by the legislature with a large bronze statue on the grounds of the Tennessee State House, erected in 1927. This statue was pulled down during demonstrations against racism in May 2020 and taken away for repairs.[28] The public library in Gallatin, Tennessee, was once named for Carmack, but when a new library was built, the name was changed to Gallatin Public Library.[29] ■

Jack Daniel had transferred the ownership of his distillery in Lynchburg to his nephew in 1907—See! There's that year again—who moved it to St. Louis in 1910. The distillery didn't return to Lynchburg until 1938, and, ironically, it operates there today in a county that is still dry.[30] (An exception is made for sales at the distillery, which has a quarter-million visitors a year.) But Tennesseans hardly went thirsty. Like the rest of the South, a thriving bootleg liquor industry had developed in Tennessee after the Civil War. Despite efforts of legendary federal revenue agents like James M. Davis, who racked up fifteen arrests and destroyed twenty-seven stills during his first ten days on the job, the Appalachian Mountains of Tennessee, Kentucky, Georgia, the Carolinas, and Virginia harbored thriving moonshine makers.[31]

With all this history in mind, I spent a night in Knoxville with Leo, my husband and boon companion on the expeditions throughout this book. We stayed at the Hyatt Place hotel on Gay Street, which had opened as the Farragut Hotel in 1919, just as Tennessee's bone-dry prohibition began. The nine-story brick building was one of Knoxville's showplaces for decades,

Farragut Hotel, Knoxville, Tenn.

but it eventually closed and sat empty for years. During its 2017 renovation, Hyatt maintained the hotel's façade, including an elaborate stone tablet displaying its original name, but the interior is all slick and shiny modern surfaces. Thanks to the desk clerk, I found in the basement an illustrated timeline that shared some of the hotel's storied history.

First of all, it was named for General David Glasgow Farragut, a Knoxville native who is considered the greatest naval hero of the Civil War on the Union side. In 1864, he famously ordered, "Damn the torpedoes! Full speed ahead!" and won the Battle of Mobile Bay. Famous guests have included New York Yankees Babe Ruth and Lou Gehrig, Prime Minister David

The Farragut Hotel has a storied history and maintains its historic facade, as shown in this vintage postcard. *Author collection*

Ben-Gurion of Israel, and entertainers Fanny Brice, Tom Mix, Glenn Miller, and Desi Arnaz, Jr. The Southeastern Conference was founded there in a meeting in December 1932, and James Brown set up a radio station, WJBE (James Brown Enterprises), on the lower level in 1969. The Farragut was one of the first hotels in Knoxville to desegregate.

A few blocks from the Farragut on Union Avenue is The Oliver, a boutique hotel in a building that once housed the bakery of a man named Peter Kern. We heard it had a speakeasy inside, accessible from an alleyway beside the hotel or through a sliding door in the lobby. There was a single red light hanging over the entrance in the alley, but the passageway was so dimly lit we decided to enter via the lobby. A man standing beside an innocuous sliding door asked us if we were staying at the hotel. Even though we weren't, he slid the door open and we stepped into an enchanting one-room bar. There was a fireplace with gas logs at one end of the room and the bar at the other, with shelves of books and other curiosities everywhere we looked. Over the bar hung a portrait of the library's namesake, Peter Kern.

We settled on stools and examined the menus, which were bound into old encyclopedias. There was a mix of standard and specialty drinks, some of which were named for literary figures. One of the most popular is the Holly Golightly, a fizzy concoction of strawberry- and raspberry-infused vodka, lavender liqueur, fresh lime juice, and house-made strawberry bitters, topped with prosecco and a single raspberry.[32]

Josh Burchell was one of two bartenders on duty under Kern's watchful eye. He told me he had started out as a dishwasher at the hotel, then studied

Under the watchful eye of Peter Kern, bartenders mix up drinks in the speakeasy at The Oliver hotel. At left is Josh Burchell. *Leo Smith photo*

bartending books and worked with the experienced staff to become a bartender himself. When I told Josh I was writing a book about Prohibition and wanted a vintage drink, he suggested a Martinez, an early version of the martini. He then shared the story of Peter Kern with great enthusiasm. I have augmented his story with my own research on the industrious Mr. Kern.

MARTINEZ

The first known published recipe was in 1884's *The Modern Bartender's Guide* by O.H. Byron

- 1.5 oz. Old Tom gin
- 0.75 oz. sweet vermouth
- 0.25 oz. Maraschino liqueur
- 1 dash Angostura bitters

Stir with ice to chill and serve straight up, in stemware with no ice, with an orange twist.

—Josh Burchell, bartender, the Peter Kern Library

Kern was a German immigrant, born in 1835, who immigrated to New York in the early 1850s. By 1857 he was in Georgia, where he joined the Confederate Army at the outbreak of the Civil War. He was wounded fighting in Virginia and sent home to recover. On his way back to the front in 1863, his train stopped in Knoxville, which had just been captured by Union forces under General Ambrose Burnside. Burnside, who established his command post in a private home on the site of the present-day Hyatt Place hotel, was said by Civil War historian Bruce Catton to have had "what was probably the most artistic and awe-inspiring set of whiskers in all that bewhiskered Army." Later, his name was bastardized to create the word "sideburns" to describe the facial hairstyle.[33]

Union Civil War General Ambrose Burnside's distinctive facial hair is now known as sideburns. *Author collection*

Kern was briefly held as a POW and then was released and allowed to stay in Knoxville as long as he promised not to rejoin the Confederate Army. So, he and another German immigrant started a bakery at the corner of State Street and Main Avenue, selling cookies to the Union forces. After the war, he prospered enough in the bakery business to construct a three-story brick building on Market Square. Kern continued his bakery—which is, in fact, still in business today as Kern's Bakery, part of the Sara Lee company[34]—expanding it to include an ice cream parlor, confectionary shop, and meeting hall for the Odd Fellows fraternal organization. He served as an alderman and mayor of Knoxville and was a founder of the city's Society for the Prevention of Cruelty to Animals. (Josh found this last accomplishment particularly endearing.)

Whether Kern had any interest in books or booze isn't clear from his biography, though as a German you would expect he enjoyed a beer now and again. He died just short of his 72nd birthday in 1907—See? There it is again!—shortly after Knoxville became the first city in Tennessee to ban alcohol.

After our pleasant respite at the Peter Kern Library, we walked down to Market Square, a lively space ringed with restaurants, bars, and shops. At a place called Stock & Barrel—which touted its bourbon and burgers—I had a glass of Angel's Envy bourbon and a huge hamburger, sitting elbow-to-elbow with guests at the tables on either side. (This was a pre-Covid-19 night out!) Miraculously, the subject of Prohibition came up at the table to the left. One of the diners mentioned that exceptions were made for buying alcohol needed for "medicinal purposes." His friend laughed and said, "I'd need it a couple of times a week."

We walked back to the Hyatt, passing a bar where a crowd of Bernie Sanders supporters was having a noisy gathering on the patio, and gratefully tumbled into bed at the Hyatt. The next morning, it was on to Kentucky, birthplace of the hatchet-wielding temperance warrior Carry A. Nation.

Harriman, Tennessee

Harriman, Tennessee was established in 1891 as "The Town that Temperance Built," the brainchild of a Methodist minister and land developer from New York who envisioned a utopian community centered around sober industry where "no manufacture, storage, or sales of intoxicating liquor or beverages" would take place. The Rev. Frederick Gates and a like-minded group of investors—including the publishers Isaac Funk and Adam Wagnalls, whose company became known for its dictionary and encyclopedias—created the East Tennessee Land Company. They purchased several thousand acres of land on the Emory River and laid out the town in a grid pattern of wide streets, unusual for mountain communities. Their land sale in 1890, heavily advertised in the temperance press, was a runaway success. In just three days, three thousand people from eighteen states bought 573 lots, bringing $600,000 into the company's coffers. Their deeds had an unusual clause that stipulated if the owner ever violated the founding temperance principles, the land would revert to the East Tennessee Land Company.[35]

The town took its name from the father of the managing director of the company, Walter Harriman, who had traveled the area as a Union Army officer during the Civil War and was a former governor of New Hampshire. The founders erected as the company's headquarters a handsome Queen Anne-style building of brick and stone, with four Norman towers. Industrialist/philanthropist Andrew Carnegie endowed the town's library. By mid-1891,

The Temperance Building, former home to American Temperance University, now houses the Harriman Heritage Museum. *Wikimedia Commons*

Harriman had grown to encompass three hundred homes, several factories, fifty retail establishments, four churches, and two chapters of the WCTU.[36] Despite its high-minded principles, Harriman seemed snake-bit. A national financial panic in 1893 and an economic depression that followed wiped out the land company. The abandoned headquarters became home to American Temperance University, which attracted hundreds of students from many states, including two future members of Congress, but it closed in 1908. (The building is still referred to as The Temperance Building and is now home to the town's history museum.[37]) A tornado in 1895 and a flood in 1929 caused serious damage to the town and a bitter strike by textile workers in 1933 divided Harriman for years.[38] However, no landowner ever violated the temperance agreement—or at least, no land was ever reclaimed by the company for that reason.[39] Nevertheless, according to the city's website, "The temperance heritage was slow to depart. There was no liquor store in Harriman until 1993." ▧

PROHIBITION EXPEDITION

Hyatt Place, the old Farragut Hotel, 530 S. Gay Street. https://www.hyatt.com/local/tennessee/knoxville

Museum of East Tennessee History, 601 S. Gay Street (kitty-corner to the hotel), housed in the building where Kid Curry was tried. http://www.easttnhistory.org/museum-east-tennessee-history

Burn Memorial, corner of Clinch Avenue and Market Square.

The Oliver Hotel, 407 Union Avenue, and Peter Kern Library speakeasy. https://www.theoliverhotel.com/

Stock & Barrel, 35 Market Square, Knoxville. (There is also a Stock & Barrel at 901 Gleaves Street in Nashville.) https://thestockandbarrel.com/

The Old City, Central Street, formerly Crozier Avenue, once home to the notorious Bowery and various saloons, including the one where Kid Curry shot the police officers. 100 North Central Street was the home of the Patrick Sullivan Saloon, now part of a "western bistro" chain called The Lonesome Dove. Specialties include rattlesnake-rabbit sausage. https://lonesomedoveknoxville.com/

CEMETERY SIDE TRIP

Knoxville's **Old Gray Cemetery** was established in 1850 and is the resting place of some of the city's most prominent leaders. These include speakeasy namesake Peter Kern, whose distinctive family marker looks like a chess piece.[40] 543 N. Broadway, www.oldgraycemetery.org/home

Policeman **Robert T. Saylor** is buried in Oaklawn Cemetery in Knoxville, 4500 Woodlawn Pike. His partner, **William M. Dinwiddie,** lies in Pleasant Grove-Fielden Cemetery, 910 Churchview Street, in New Market, Tennessee. Both WCTU leader **Silena Moore Holman** and murdered newspaper editor **Edward Ward Carmack** rest in Rose Hill Cemetery, 511 W. Edison Street, Fayetteville, Tennessee. Holman's gravestone is decorated with a ribbon chiseled in the stone, the emblem of the WCTU; Carmack's bears a bronze martyr's crown of leaves.

WCTU and suffrage activist **Lide Smith Meriwether** and her husband, Niles, lie under a joint stone inscribed with the words "He giveth his beloved sleep" in the historic Elmwood Cemetery in Memphis. This is a fascinating cemetery, established in 1852, full of haunting Victorian and gothic statuary. Elmwood offers themed tours such as "Scandals and Scoundrels" and an occasional outdoor movie night in the cemetery. 824 S. Dudley Street. https://www.elmwoodcemetery.org/events-calendar

Lucy Tappan Phillips rests at Mount Ararat Cemetery, Orr Avenue at Elm Hill Pike, in Nashville. Mount Ararat was established in 1869 as the first African American cemetery in middle Tennessee.

Distiller **Jack Daniel** is buried in the Lynchburg City Cemetery, Cemetery Street at Church Street, in Lynchburg, Tennessee. His gravesite includes two decorative iron chairs where mourners can rest while they visit. Interestingly, the chairs are turned away from the headstone.

RECOMMENDED READING

Dead Distillers: A History of the Upstarts and Outlaws Who Made American Spirits by Colin Spoelman and David Haskell (New York: Abrams Image, 2016), recommended by Josh Burchell. This book not only gives you great mini-biographies of distillers, both legal and illegal, but tells where they are buried.

CHAPTER THREE

IN SEARCH OF CARRY NATION

CARRY AMELIA NATION, the pit bull–faced, Bible-thumping, hatchet-wielding crusader for temperance and women's rights, was described as "America's foremost lady hell-raiser" and "the apostle of reform violence, prime dragoness on a field strewn with the bones of sinners," in Robert Lewis Taylor's riotous biography *Vessel of Wrath*. He continued, "Stated loosely, Mrs. Nation was against alcohol, tobacco, sex, politics, government (national, state and local), the Masonic Lodge, William McKinley, Theodore Roosevelt, and William Jennings Bryan, in approximately that order."[1]

Add to that list corsets and fancy women's clothing, especially feathered hats, but I'm not sure about the sex part. In her autobiography, Nation lamented, "The bitterest sorrows of my life have come from not having the love of a husband." Not that she didn't try. She was married twice, first to an alcoholic doctor who died shortly after their daughter was born, second to a lawyer who she believed God had put in her path when she was widowed and destitute. Of her union with David Nation, she simply said, "My married life with Mr. Nation was not a happy one." He would probably have said the same. They divorced after twenty-four years once Carry's hatchet-wielding escapades had made her an international celebrity.[42] David Nation's petition cited "extreme cruelty and desertion." I think he was just worn out.

Carry admitted to being bitter about the divorce, but throughout her life she exhibited what biographer Taylor called "armor-plated indifference to censure . . . She was denounced as a quack, a humbug, a fourflusher [braggart], a felon, a bully, a busybody, a common scold, a secret drinker, a man in woman's clothes, a nymphomaniac, an Amazon-gone-amok, a sub rosa traveler in bar fixtures, a reincarnation of Lucrezia Borgia, a possible werewolf, and a professional peddler of cheap souvenirs."[43]

This last, at least, is true. To fund her activities, Nation sold brooches shaped like tiny hatchets with mother-of-pearl blades, and miniature portraits, suitable for pinning on one's bosom, showing her with a Bible in one hand and a hatchet in the other. Written on the portrait in tiny letters are the words, "Carrie Nation Your Loving Home Defender."[44] She was not particular about how her first name was spelled, but we'll go with Carry here, as she spelled it in her autobiography.

Carry Nation sold pins like these to finance her hatchetations. *Author photo*

She was born in 1846 to George and Mary Moore, in a ten-room farmhouse in Garrard County, Kentucky, about two hours north of Knoxville. On my drive with Leo toward Lancaster, the county seat, we traveled through rolling hills dotted with silos and barns, some ancient ones collapsing under the weight of their metal roofs, but most well kept. We passed neat white churches every mile or so, many with inspirational messages on their sign boards: "A clean conscience is a soft pillow," "God enters through a broken heart." One advertised an upcoming Bible study on the theme "The Bait of Satan."

I felt sure there would be a sign as we entered Lancaster saying, "Birthplace of Carry A. Nation," but there was no mention of its native daughter, and the coordinates for her home that I was using took us into the parking lot of a bank in the middle of the town's thriving and attractive business district. Leo is a banker and felt perfectly comfortable going inside to ask for assistance. The tellers there gave us some vague directions "near the lake, out Carry Nation Road," and showed off their beautiful antique Mosler safe manufactured in—you guessed it—1907.

With fresh directions downloaded, about fifteen minutes later we turned down Carry A. Nation Road, a narrow lane that eventually dwindled to a cowpath, and found the house. Although it is on the National Register of Historic Places, the wood-sided house is in great disrepair, with broken windows and a partially caved-in roof. It sits on the edge of a working cattle farm. Looking at it, the word *hardscrabble* came to mind, though Nation's memoir paints a fond picture of the homestead where she lived with her parents, various relatives, and slaves, who she described as "servants."

A true "daddy's girl," Nation says almost nothing in her autobiography about her mother, except that she was "very handsome" and "an aristocrat in her ideas." It went way beyond that. According to biographer Taylor, Mrs. Moore suffered under the delusion that she was Queen Victoria, swished around the house wearing a purple velvet dress with a train and a crown made of chandelier crystals and cut glass and only saw family members, including her husband, by appointment.

The family left the homestead when Carry was five and lived on farms near Danville and Midway, Kentucky, before setting out for Missouri when she was nine. Carry suffered from poor health for most of her childhood as her father repeatedly uprooted the family, finally recovering when she was in her late teens and they settled in Cass County, Missouri. By then,

Carry Nation's birthplace is in this modest farmhouse, now fallen into disrepair, on the edge of a cattle farm. *Author photo*

the Civil War had ended, the family "servants" had fled to the North, her mother had become even more useless than before, and Carry became the maid-of-all-work and caregiver to her younger siblings.

Salvation appeared to come when a young physician, Charles Gloyd, arrived at their door, seeking the position of schoolmaster at the local schoolhouse, which her father was in a position to influence. Gloyd became a boarder in their home and waged a surreptitious but effective courtship of Carry, using a volume of Shakespeare on the parlor table to pass her notes. "Queen Victoria" was not amused, either because she deemed the young doctor not aristocratic enough for her daughter, or because she sensed he had a drinking problem. Nevertheless, Carry married him in 1867 and realized within days that her mother was right. Gloyd was a hopeless alcoholic.

The seed was planted for the cause that would rule Carry's life. After Gloyd died and Carry married the much older David Nation, the household—including daughter Charlien, a stepdaughter, and her first mother-in-law—eventually wound up in Medicine Lodge, Kansas. She organized a local chapter of the Women's Christian Temperance Union, serving as its "jail evangelist," and came to believe, she wrote in her autobiography, that "almost everyone in the jail was directly or indirectly there from the influence of intoxicating drinks."[45] Statewide prohibition had been implemented in Kansas in 1881, almost twenty years before, yet seven backroom bars in Medicine Lodge did business without much concern about the law. Carry called these places "dives" and the owners "dive-keepers" or "jointists." Divine inspiration struck and she teamed up with her WCTU co-founder, the wife of Baptist minister Wesley Cain, and planned their first assault.

Carry Nation's home in Medicine Lodge, Kansas, depicted in a vintage postcard, became the base for her temperance activities. *Author collection*

CARRY A. NATION AND HOME

One Saturday afternoon in 1899, they parked themselves outside the establishment of a noted jointist, Mrs. Cain lugging a hand organ and Carry armed with an umbrella. As Mrs. Cain played, Carry began loudly singing a temperance song, "with tears running down my face." A tremendous crowd gathered and cheered the women on as they burst through the swinging doors of the saloon. In the melee that followed, Carry and the bar owner got into a tussle that knocked him down, and the local constable admonished her, saying he wished he could keep her off the streets. Carry reported his behavior to the mayor and council, arousing "great indignation." The dive-keeper was sent packing, and Carry had scored her first victory and discovered her life's work.[46] You might even think of it as an addiction.

At this point, you need to form a good mental picture of fifty-four-year-old Carry Nation. The sepia-tone photographs present us with a barrel-shaped, gray-haired woman, jaw set in determination, dressed in a black alpaca dress with a big white bow at the neck—emblem of the WCTU, remember—and Bible in hand. She seems stern but fairly harmless, a little old lady in button-top shoes. But the reality, according to most accounts, was quite different. Carry Nation was almost six feet tall at a time when the average man of her age was five-foot-six.[47] Her weight was 175 pounds. She was accustomed to manual labor—chopping wood, carrying pails of water, kneading bread—and had formidable upper body strength and a flawless aim. When she came into a dive, towering over most of the men, bellowing prayers, or singing hymns at the top of her voice, she was nothing short of terrifying.

In the months that followed, Carry Nation and Mrs. Cain cleaned up Medicine Lodge, closing down every establishment that sold alcohol. Carry, however, was not satisfied with singing and praying to accomplish her tasks. One February day in 1899, with her WCTU sisters, she planned a visit to a druggist in Medicine Lodge who sold liquor. Discovering a ten-gallon whiskey keg behind the counter, she rolled it out into the street as her confederates fought off the men who sought to stop them. She sent one of the women to the hardware store for a hatchet, but the proprietor refused to sell it. Another WCTU member ran to the blacksmith's and returned with a sledgehammer. "I struck with all my might," Nation recalled. "The whiskey flew high in the air." The druggist was driven out of business and left town.

The women suffered some reprisals—murdered chickens, sabotaged carriages, vandalism of their homes—but eventually won the respect of the

The saloon at the Carey Hotel in Wichita, Kansas, received two visits from Carry Nation. *Author collection*

people of Medicine Lodge, at least the nondrinkers. It was time for Carry to widen her arena. Biographer Taylor describes her raid on Kiowa, Kansas, on June 6, 1900, when she "smashed one saloon's Venetian mirror with brick-bats, flung stones through a second saloon's windows, leveled a half-brick at the head of a boy attempting to sweep up (missing him by inches), ripped some candid and stimulating prints from the walls, powdered the bric-a-brac and glasses, separated the rungs from all chairs, drop-kicked a cuspidor over a pot-bellied stove and threw a billiard ball at what she mistakenly took to be 'Satan' lounging behind the bar. (It was in fact the bartender, who dove to the floor and scuttled rapidly out of sight.)"

Carry Nation's life as a celebrity had begun. She was hailed as a heroine by her WCTU sisters in Medicine Lodge, written up in major newspapers across the country, and inundated by requests to speak. She quickly made herself available to the press—one reporter described her as "a motherly type gone wrong"—and plotted her next move. Two days after Christmas 1900, she arrived in Wichita and unleashed her one-woman tornado in the luxurious bar of the Carey Hotel. Among other things, she threw two sharp-edged rocks through the painting of a naked Cleopatra preparing for her bath and destroyed a mirror that covered one wall of the bar. She was hauled off to jail. Flocks of temperance warriors soon arrived, disrupting operations at the jail with their loud singing and prayers. Carry used her time behind bars to convert the inmates, who helped her answer the mail bags of correspondence dumped in her cell each day and jointly penned an ode to her called "Solemn Thoughts."

Upon her release a few weeks later, Carry hand-picked four lieutenants who armed themselves with tools in the basement of a Mrs. Evans—including, for the first time, a hatchet—and went back to smashing saloons, even visiting the Carey Hotel for another round. She was arrested again, returned to jail, and her elderly husband, having reached his limits, filed for divorce.

Unencumbered by wifely duties, Nation traveled widely, smashing as she went. In her autobiography, she proudly listed all the places she had been jailed. Besides three times in Wichita, they included seven stays in Topeka, one each in Kansas City, Los Angeles, San Francisco, Philadelphia, and Bayonne, New Jersey and three in Pittsburgh. With a few other scattered places factored in, she had been jailed twenty-three times by the time she wrote her autobiography in 1905. In between creating mayhem and cooling her heels in jail cells, she appeared on Broadway in the temperance play *Ten Nights in a Barroom*, and on a visit to Washington tried, and failed, to get an audience with President Theodore Roosevelt and sold dozens of miniature hatchets in the Ladies Gallery of the U.S. Senate. Eventually, she spent far more time lecturing and publishing temperance propaganda than smashing, traveling across the country and even abroad. (She will pop up in the chapter on Florida.)

CARRY NATION PUNCH

- 8 oz. pineapple juice
- 8 oz. simple syrup
- 56 oz. ginger ale
- 32 oz. orange juice
- 24 oz. lemon juice
- 3 lemon slices
- 3 orange slices

Mix simple syrup and fruit juices together and chill in the refrigerator for several hours. Pour into a punch bowl. Slowly and gently mix in the ginger ale, using ax handle to stir if you wish. Garnish with the fruit slices.

—*Barnonedrinks.com, except for the ax handle part*

Although Nation's monster demolition tour of saloons was relatively short-lived, she retained the hatchet as her emblem. She published a newspaper called *The Hatchet*, which printed the opinions of the opposition under the heading "Letters from Hell," and in her last years operated a home for destitute women in Eureka Springs, Arkansas, called Hatchet Hall. Both her mother and her daughter, Charlien, spent time in insane asylums; a lot of folks thought Carry belonged in one too. She died in 1911 and was buried in an unmarked grave in Belton, Missouri. The WCTU stepped in and erected a handsome stone with the epitaph, "Faithful to the Cause of Prohibition, She Hath Done What She Could." It would be another seven years before Kentucky's legislature voted the entire state dry, 1919 before the law was implemented. By then, national Prohibition was on its way to ratification.

As my husband and I drove away from her birthplace, we came upon a historical marker. The front side is titled, "Birthplace of Carry A. Nation." The reverse side is titled "Lady with the Hatchet." We were headed to the place that Carry would certainly consider a den of iniquity, to visit "murder mills" she would have loved to smash, and sample the "devil's poison": Louisville, Kentucky, and its famous Whiskey Row. But for the purposes of historical continuity, I'm going to take us on a detour back to South Carolina, which came up with its own, peculiar method for keeping liquor under control: the state dispensary.

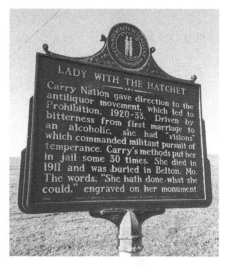

A historic marker is one of the few clues that the notorious Carry Nation began her life in Kentucky. *Leo Smith photo*

Carry Nation edited several newspapers about her crusade, including *The Hatchet.* This one carries her autograph. *Courtesy Steven Lomazow, M.D.*

PROHIBITION EXPEDITION

Carry A. Nation Birthplace, west of Lancaster, Kentucky, off Fisher Ford Road

Historical Marker #1733. Coordinates N 37° 41.141 W 084° 40.719 will point you in the right direction. If you use the Google Maps directions, you'll wind up in a bank parking lot in downtown Lancaster.

It's a natural progression to drive from Garrard County to Louisville, but if you get a hankering for a taste of bourbon along the way, there are two well-known distilleries in Lawrenceburg, about halfway between Lancaster and Louisville.

Four Roses Bourbon • https://fourrosesbourbon.com

In 1884, before Carry Nation picked up her first brickbat, a man named Paul Jones Jr. established this distillery in Louisville. Over the next 120 years, the company changed hands several times, and moved its distillery operations to Lawrenceburg (1224 Bonds Mill Road) and its bottling facility to Cox's Creek (624 Lotus Road). Both are open for tours.

Wild Turkey • https://wildturkeybourbon.com • 1417 Versailles Road

Wild Turkey has even deeper roots, extending to the Ripy Family, who opened a distillery in 1869 on Wild Turkey Hill in Lawrenceburg. However, the bourbon only got its name in 1945 when a distillery executive shared some of his product with friends on a hunting trip. You can guess what their quarry was. Tours are given six days a week year-round, and from March to December they are also offered on Sundays. Wouldn't Carry Nation be fit to be tied?

CEMETERY SIDE TRIP

It would be *quite* a side trip (612 miles), but if you happen to be in Cass County, Missouri, you could visit the grave of Carry Nation at Belton Cemetery, on Cambridge Road just west of South Scott Avenue. She is buried beside her mother, Mary Moore, aka Queen Victoria. http://beltoncemetery.com/default.aspx

RECOMMENDED READING

Robert Lewis Taylor's *Vessel of Wrath: The Life and Times of Carry Nation* is long out of print, but used copies are plentiful and cheap on the internet. Treat yourself to this rollicking read!

Carry Nation's autobiography *The Use and Need of the Life of Carry A. Nation* is also out of print, but used copies are available online. You can also read the book for free at http://www.gutenberg.org/ebooks/1485

CHAPTER FOUR

THE SOUTH CAROLINA DISPENSARY

WHEN SOUTH CAROLINA SECEDED from the union in 1860, prominent attorney James L. Petigru famously declared, "South Carolina is too small for a republic and too large for an insane asylum." This observation has been proven accurate many times since then, especially as it applies to the state's politics.

A case in point was the state government's unique solution to the question of prohibition, for which South Carolina's dominant Baptist and Methodist populations and the Women's Christian Temperance Union were pushing in the 1880s and 1890s. The leader of this movement was a Charleston widow, Sallie F. Chapin, who had made such a strong impression on national WCTU President Frances E. Willard—she described her as among the "noble women 'to the manor born'"—that Willard made her superintendent for the WCTU for the entire South.

Chapin, born in Charleston, reared and educated in Abbeville, had been as good a Confederate as any woman in the South, nursing wounded soldiers during the war and memorializing the "lost cause" with a children's

Sallie F. Chapin of Charleston led the WCTU charge in the South. This engraving appeared in Frances Willard's book *Woman and Temperance.*

book she wrote, *Fitzhugh St. Clair, the South Carolina Rebel Boy, or It Is No Crime to Be Born a Gentleman.* Her brother, killed in the war, had been a leader in the secession movement and she was the proud owner of the pen with which the Ordinance of Secession had been signed.[48] But by 1881, the "lost cause" was losing steam as a political movement, and Chapin came to see the WCTU as a vehicle to unite the women who had been torn apart by the Civil War in a common war on alcohol.

Like other Southern WCTU organizations, the one Chapin headed in Charleston was segregated, but she worked closely with a black bishop, visiting his congregations and getting members to sign a petition asking for prohibition. Also like other Southern temperance advocates, Chapin focused on the evils of drink among African Americans, insisting that enslaved people had been religious prior to the war, but now "they are demoralized; taught by barroom teachings they speak flippantly of sacred things, and they say they want whiskey and more of it." She insisted that alcoholism was a far worse form of slavery than the kind abolished by the war. Her principled stands led her to be the subject of ridicule and attack in booze-loving Charleston, including by writers for the wringing-wet Charleston *News and Courier* newspaper.[49]

Like many states during this period, South Carolina offered a local option wherein counties could vote themselves dry.[50] Generally, rural and more conservative regions—the South Carolina Upstate was one—took the dry option, while counties with large cities, such as Columbia and Charleston, voted to remain wet. That set the stage for South Carolina's unique solution to the problem of regulating alcohol, the South Carolina Dispensary. I learned more about it during a walking tour of Charleston.

I met my tour guide Valerie Stow at the pineapple fountain in Charleston's waterfront park on a warm Saturday afternoon in mid-March. The coronavirus had raised its ugly head by then and the city had canceled its St. Patrick's Day activities, but sheltering-in-place orders had not been issued yet, so people were walking about in kelly-green hats and Irish-themed T-shirts, and two bridal parties took photos in front of the fountain while Valerie and I got acquainted.

She began by talking about the Dispensary Act of 1892, which was the response of Governor Benjamin Ryan Tillman to a statewide referendum in favor of prohibition. Tillman, a one-eyed firebrand farmer from Edgefield County, was among a wave of Democrat populists who came to office in the latter part of the nineteenth century. (A state history textbook used in South Carolina eighth grades for many years opined that he was the first in a long line of "Dixie Demagogues."[51] The book's description of Tillman's stump meetings brings to mind Donald Trump's rallies.) In his case, that meant taking on the elite urban "Bourbons," as he styled them—most from Charleston—who had been elected after federal Reconstruction ended. A member of a boisterous and violent clan of brothers given to duels, murder, and domestic violence, he hated Charlestonians and all they stood for.

The feeling was mutual. The *News and Courier* styled him as the leader of a people "who expectorate on the floor, who have no toothbrushes, and comb their hair with their fingers."[52] He later earned the nickname "Pitchfork Ben" for declaring that President Grover Cleveland was "an old bag of beef and I am going to Washington with a pitchfork and prod him in his old fat ribs."

The only people Tillman hated more than Charlestonians were black people. In his first address after being elected governor in 1890, he said, "The whites have absolute control of the state government, and we intend at any and all hazard to control it." At the time he was elected, almost 60 percent of South Carolina's residents were black.[53] Under his leadership as state political boss, Jim Crow law was written into the state's new constitution in 1895, effectively disenfranchising black male voters, while also continuing to deny women the right to vote. The WCTU was gratified, however, that it raised the age of sexual consent from ten to sixteen.

"Pitchfork Ben" Tillman tried to satisfy the temperance lobby by creating a state liquor monopoly. *Library of Congress*

Despite all this, Tillman was in some ways a progressive reformer, with a great respect for education. His achievements as governor included shepherding the establishment of a men's agricultural college in Clemson and an industrial college for women in Rock Hill. The Clemson University website offers a frank appraisal of Tillman, including the wry observation, "Tillman's legacy for South Carolina and the nation is complex and often disturbing."[54] Both Clemson and Winthrop universities renamed their iconic main buildings "Tillman Hall" in the mid-twentieth century, a source of no little controversy in the racially charged climate of 2020. That spring, both universities petitioned the legislature to allow them to revert the buildings to their original names—the rather prosaic but non-controversial "Old Main Hall." Like the racist politician and newspaper editor Edward W. Carmack in Tennessee, Tillman is memorialized with a large bronze sculpture on the Capitol grounds in Columbia. A few years ago, a weekly newspaper in Charleston ran a cover with a photo illustration of the poop-encrusted sculpture, a pigeon on its shoulder, being yanked off its pedestal. "Down With Tillman," the headline said. "Ben Tillman was a racist, terrorist, and murderer. It's time to remove his statue from the Statehouse grounds."[55] In the summer of 2020, a man and woman were arrested for allegedly planting an "incendiary device" at the base of Tillman's statue.[56]

But I digress.

In 1892 Tillman was re-elected and a referendum on prohibition was held, finding support for the banning of alcohol in all but eight counties. (One of them was, of course, Charleston.) Tillman was a teetotaler but a pragmatist. He believed it was impossible to ban liquor entirely and that by giving all control of production and distribution to the state government—and shutting down all saloons—he could appease the temperance crowd while at the same time reaping vast funds for the state treasury. Prior to passage of the new state constitution, he also saw state control of liquor as a method to further limit the political power of black voters. He was convinced that Republican organizers doled liquor out on election day as an inducement for blacks to vote for GOP candidates.

Tillman's idea was to do away with all private purveyors of liquor in favor of a state-operated dispensary system that bottled and sold alcohol. Such a system had been tried with some success elsewhere, including Athens, Georgia, where a University of Georgia student had to get a letter from the president of the university in order to buy whiskey. (This got me to thinking about my UGA undergraduate days in the 1970s, when even liquor could be purchased legally by an eighteen-year-old freshman and our dorm council regularly sponsored parties featuring punch made from grain alcohol filched from the botany department. If the president had to write letters for every student who drank at UGA, he wouldn't have had time for many of his important duties, such as attending football games.)

Mrs. Chapin and the ladies of the WCTU were thrilled, and initially, the "dry" press was supportive of Tillman's idea. *The Yorkville Enquirer* in York County opined that "if South Carolina is successful in her efforts to control the liquor business in the way she has blocked out, other states will soon follow suit and all over the land the greatest evil of the land will be under government control."[57] These were prophetic words but in all sorts of unexpected ways.

Tour guide Valerie continued her briefing by telling me that on Christmas Eve, 1892, the legislature passed the dispensary law, which became known as "Ben Tillman's Baby." The following July, the South Carolina Dispensary Board was in operation, bottling corn liquor and whiskey. Fifty dispensaries, or state-run liquor stores, were set up around the state, ten of them in Charleston and environs. That was supposed to replace 613 saloons, plus 400 drugstores that had dispensed whiskey for "medicinal purposes."[58]

Charleston alone had 248 state-licensed barrooms. There was a huge liquor "fire sale" as the bars closed, and barkeepers tried to unload their booze.

Valerie noted that some of the rules governing the dispensary echo in today's regulation of alcohol sales. Alcohol could only be sold from sunup to sundown. Today's ABC stores close at 7 p.m. It had to be sold in sealed packages, hence the term "package shop" still used today.

The dispensary's glass bottles were either embossed with a palmetto tree with crossed logs at its foot or bore a paper label with a similar emblem. In order to buy from the dispensary,

A bottle from the South Carolina Dispensary still bears its paper label. *Courtesy Art Gose*

customers had to fill out an application, which limited the number of bottles they could buy and supposedly banned sales to habitual drunks and underage people. (The lower age limits still apply, though it's hard to imagine one of today's liquor stores turning away a "good" customer who was known to have a drinking problem.)

Tillman enforced his new dispensary law with a battalion of constables. They could go into a business or even a private dwelling with or without a search warrant, and the constable could seize contraband and force the suspect outside, then make an arrest. Although the local law enforcement was supposed to assist, in many communities the leadership turned a blind eye and the often hotheaded constables shot and sometimes killed their suspects. Tillman, of course, pardoned all such constables. Soon Charlestonians complained that the constables were "insulting our women and shooting and killing our sons," Valerie said.

Illegal alcohol sales quickly began, if they had ever ended. One of the main scofflaws was an Italian immigrant named Vincent Chicco, who opened a saloon in the old city market area in 1892. "You could write a book on Vincent Chicco," Valerie said, noting that her search of his name from a digital collection of South Carolina newspapers turned up eighty-two articles between 1893 and 1917—and that didn't even include the Charleston newspapers. Shortly after the dispensary law went into effect, Chicco sold a beer to an undercover constable named R. H. Pepper and a brouhaha ensued.[59]

Later I looked up the full account as told in the *Yorkville Enquirer.*[60] Three constables presented evidence against Chicco and were given a warrant for his arrest. When they arrived at his saloon, they found only a little wine and beer behind the bar. Sure that he was hiding more contraband, they pounded on the door of his residence, which was next door. Told that Mrs. Chicco was sick, and they couldn't come inside, they threatened to break down the door. They were admitted and found that Mrs. Chicco was indeed sick—and harboring $100 in liquor, which they seized and took outside for impoundment.

"While the raid on the establishment was going on, hundreds of people gathered on the street in front of the door," the article said. "They hooted and jeered and even threatened violence. Several photographers were present with [K]odaks.[61] They took snap shots at the constables and afterwards distributed their pictures over the city in order that everybody might know them." So much for working undercover! The jeering crowd followed the

Vincent Chicco's grocery store and saloon were located in the area of Charleston's Old Market, shown in this 1915 postcard. *Author collection*

arrested Vincent Chicco to the chambers of the trial judge. Chicco "was beside himself with rage. He raved and cursed like a madman, and at the office of the trial justice, he began to apply insulting epithets to R. H. Pepper." The constable withstood the insults as long as he could, then drew his revolver and aimed it at Chicco. "The crowd scattered like magic. Somebody caught Pepper's hand and prevented him from firing." Chicco's lawyer posted bail of $500 for him, and the Italian swore out a warrant on Pepper, charging him with "assault and attempting to draw a deadly weapon."

I couldn't find out how Pepper's trial turned out, but Chicco continued to sell illegal liquor and Pepper continued to try to enforce the dispensary law. He and another constable were killed during an anti-dispensary riot in Darlington in March 1894 that was characterized as South Carolina's "whiskey rebellion." Two citizens also died, and a constable and the Darlington chief of police were wounded. Governor Tillman put down the uprising with difficulty—several companies of the state militia, including the one based in Charleston, refused to go to Darlington—but ultimately restored order with a mob of his supporters, and the dispensary system continued. Shortly after the Darlington rebellion, the three-member state Supreme Court ruled the system was unconstitutional and must be shut down. When one of the justices subsequently retired, Tillman simply appointed a justice who thought like he did and, after a short break, the dispensary system was restored.

THE TWO DETERMINED

One of Vincent Chicco's marketing ploys was to devise a label for his "house brand" of whiskey featuring his profile facing Governor Tillman's under the heading "The Two Determined." He also used this label for his house brand of cigars. Despite the repeated raids of his business by Tillman's "spies," Chicco and Tillman did not meet face-to-face until years after Tillman left the governor's office for the U.S. Senate, and it was apparently a most cordial meeting. Chicco greeted Tillman with a handshake and a complimentary cigar when he visited Charleston in 1901. According to an account in the *Lancaster Ledger*, Sen. Tillman joked that Chicco "had never sent him that famous brand of Tillman-Chicco whiskey which he had promised." Chicco said he would dispatch a bottle immediately, along with a box of cigars. Tillman quickly reminded him that he never indulged in drink. "'You look like a man who takes a drink,' Chicco responded. The members of the party laughed heartily and passed on through the market."[62] Chicco sent a complimentary box of his Two Determined cigars to Tillman as a Christmas gift each year.

Vincent Chicco nettled his rival Ben Tillman with a brand for his whiskey and cigars featuring their photographs. *Courtesy Robert F. Moss*

THE TWO DETERMINED

Tillman had stopped laughing five years later when someone gave him a paper fan—like a funeral home fan—bearing the Tillman-Chicco double portrait when he was preparing to speak in Columbia. *The State* newspaper, which was rabidly anti-Tillman, reported that the senator's outrage was obviously "feigned cholera" that "reveals his utter insincerity in dealing with the people of South Carolina. Do we care for that kind of dictator?" ∎

Chicco continued selling booze, getting raided, and vehemently denying he sold booze when brought to court. He became something of a folk hero in Charleston, eventually winning a seat on the city council, where he served five terms. [63] "He was like Robin Hood," Valerie said.

THE NEGRONI

In a tip of the hat to Italian bootlegger Vincent Chicco, this classic Italian cocktail was said to have been first mixed up in Florence in 1920, a couple of years before Chicco's death, so it is just conceivable that he may have enjoyed one. Or six. This recipe comes from *The Savoy Cocktail Book*, a collection of recipes compiled by bartender Harry Craddock at London's Savoy Hotel, first published in 1930.

- ¾ oz. dry gin
- ¾ oz. Campari
- ¾ oz. sweet or dry vermouth

Stir with ice and strain into cocktail glass, over ice cubes, with or without a splash of carbonated water. Add twist of lemon peel.

By this time, Valerie and I were walking past the Old Exchange and Provost Dungeon at the corner of East Bay and Broad Street. It dates to 1771 and is the site of some of the most historic moments in South Carolina history, including a visit by President George Washington in 1791. Next door is another historic building, The Tavern, which touts itself as "America's Oldest Liquor Store" and a survivor, like the city itself, of "pirate attacks, the Revolution and Civil War, earthquakes and hurricanes, Prohibition, and the Great Depression." Established in 1686, it has been a purveyor of liquor in one form or another ever since. During the state dispensary and Prohibition years, a dentist's office operated in the front room and liquor for "medicinal purposes" was available in the back. Valerie said there is also a tunnel with access through a trap door in the second room, probably dating to pirate days, when booty and booze could be hidden and moved to sites such as speakeasies, which in Charleston were called "blind tigers." Today it is a state-licensed ABC store, advertising its staff as "friendly, knowledgeable, sober."

"Do we have time to go over there?" I asked.

"Sure," Valerie said, and we crossed the street. However, an employee of the store was blocking the door, explaining a tasting was going on inside

Todd Vick, market manager for Palmetto Distillery, touts his products at The Tavern. *Author photo*

and we would have to wait for the next one to start. The tasting was provided by Palmetto Distillery of Anderson and a heavily tattooed man wearing overalls but no shirt was conducting it with plenty of redneck gusto.

When our time to enter came, we were ushered inside and handed tiny plastic cups, the type in which Baptists and Methodists serve communion. "Free liquor in Jesus cups!" bellowed Todd Vick, the man in the overalls, who later confided that he works as a charter boat captain in Murrells Inlet near Myrtle Beach during the week and does tastings at The Tavern on the weekends. Todd laid it on thick with his audience, repeatedly referring to an attractive young lady in the crowd as "pretty lady" and promising us as he served up shots of Palmetto Moonshine, from the high-octane, 105-proof White Lightning to the lower-proof moonshine flavored with blackberry and apple pie, "No hangovers with this stuff." Then he taught us the proper way to do a shot. You take a breath, swallow the whole thing, then blow your breath out hard enough to ruffle "this lovely lady's hair." (I was the lovely lady.) That way, he explained, you don't feel a burn in your chest.[64]

Pertinent to the conversation Valerie and I were having, Todd explained that Palmetto Distillery's whiskey—"the most awarded small batch whiskey in South Carolina"—was based on the 1893 dispensary recipe. The front of the bottle is painted with a replica of the palmetto tree and crossed logs on the earliest South Carolina Dispensary bottles and bears the words, "Southern Tradition 1893." He explained that Palmetto Distillery produced the first legal moonshine in the state since Prohibition ended in South Carolina in 1935. It opened in 2012. (We'll visit there in the chapter on moonshine.)

Buoyed by six "Jesus cups" of whiskey, moonshine, margaritas, and Bloody Marys, Valerie and I continued up Broad Street, stopping at a building that she said had housed a dispensary in 1908. That was the intermediate step South Carolina took after the state dispensary closed and before total statewide prohibition was implemented in 1916. Counties were given the option of opening their own dispensaries, which enabled them to keep most of the liquor tax revenue. The one in North Augusta in Aiken County, for example, did a land office business selling booze to residents of Augusta, Georgia after Georgia went dry in 1908. In just a few years, Aiken County raised enough money from its dispensaries to build twenty-one new schools, lengthen the school year, and raise teacher pay above the state average. It also built an interurban road connecting Aiken and Augusta and paved a larger percentage of its roads than all but three counties in the state.

THE PRESBYTERIAN

- 1½ oz. Palmetto Whiskey, based on the 1893 dispensary recipe
- 2 oz. club soda
- 2 oz. ginger ale

Pour ingredients into a tall Collins glass and stir. Add ice.

—Courtesy Palmetto Distillery

Valerie and I crossed the street to the Blind Tiger Pub, which took its name from the Southern version of the speakeasy. She said restaurants began putting their bars in the back instead of the front of their service areas and sheltering them from view. A thirsty patron would inform someone in the restaurant, "I want to see a blind tiger," then he would pay for the spectacle and be provided free refreshment while he waited for the exotic animal to appear. And waited and waited. "There's never been a native tiger in North America but in Charleston there were hundreds of them," Valerie said. "Why they were blind I don't know; maybe from drinking the moonshine."

The St. Patrick's Day pre-party was in full swing at the Blind Tiger Pub, which opened in 1992. Whether it was the site of a bar in the past isn't stated by the pub's website, but it certainly pays tribute to the heritage: "If you're lucky, you may catch a glimpse of the often whispered, seldom seen, and NEVER tamed 'blind tiger' rumored to be wandering within these historic walls."[65] The souvenir shirts sold there are emblazoned with a tiger, but its eyes appear functional. Vincent Chicco, who came to be known as the King of the Blind Tigers, went so far as to distribute metal advertising token coins that showed a tiger wearing a blindfold on one side, and "Good for 5 c [cents] in Trade at Chicco's Café" on the other. Wink, wink.

The blind tigers in Charleston definitely had a dark side. As we continued down Broad Street, Valerie told the story of a shoe salesman from Pennsylvania who visited one even though he wasn't much of a drinker. He demanded two shots and then had a couple more with some men he met at the bar. He quickly became staggering drunk and bumped into a large man, who took great umbrage. After a few more drinks, the salesman accepted the invitation of some fellow imbibers to visit another blind tiger. At the corner of Market and Church streets, he met the big man he had jostled at the bar. The big man pretended to be overjoyed to see him and enveloped him in a hug. When he let go, the salesman fell at his feet. He had been killed with an ice pick stabbed in his jugular vein.

Near this gruesome scene is the former site of Henry Hasselmeyer's grocery store and bar, the site of today's Henry's-on-the-Market restaurant and bar. I remembered Robert Moss telling me a story about revenue agents raiding Henry's while his wife, Maria, sat on a beer barrel, covering it with her wide skirts to fool them. They weren't fooled.[66] After Prohibition ended, Henry and Maria opened a beer parlor where they served deviled crabs. The food side of the business expanded over the years but Hasselmeyer continued to have trouble obeying the liquor laws. Nevertheless, his family ran the business until 1985, building a reputation as the best place to eat in Charleston. Henry's touts itself today as the oldest continuously serving restaurant in South Carolina.

A vintage postcard advertises Henry's, which began as a German immigrant's grocery store and bar. *Author collection*

The saga of Ben Tillman's Baby predicted what would happen on the national stage. The dispensary made huge amounts of money—some $9.7 million in profits during its 14-year run, eventually bringing in 64 percent of the state's revenue—but it was rife with corruption. Its officials took bribes from liquor companies and legislators took bribes to appoint people as officials. Large numbers of the constables were paid to turn a blind eye to the blind tigers. An investigation was launched, and the system closed in 1907. (See? There's that year again.)

Most counties in the state voted to go dry and some operated their own dispensaries, but the whole legal liquor-selling practice came to a halt in South Carolina in 1916, four years before national Prohibition. That didn't mean the liquor stopped flowing, ever. The city of Florence broke ground for a new jail in 1916, "[s]purred by the city's growth and the recent upturn in prohibition-related crime," according to a display at the Florence County Museum.

Valerie quoted a man who recalled his childhood days when a pint of milk and a pint of whiskey were left on the back doorstep every morning. "I don't know how Daddy did it," he said.

PROHIBITION EXPEDITION

The Tavern • 120 E. Bay Street • http://www.charlestonspirits.com/

Henry's on the Market • 54 N. Market Street
https://www.henrysonthemarket.com/

Blind Tiger Pub • 36-38 Broad Street • https://blindtigerchs.com/

CEMETERY SIDE TRIP

There are several historic cemeteries on Huguenin Avenue in Charleston, two of which are the resting places of people pertinent to this story. The graves of **Vincent Chicco** and his wife **Mary Ann** are in Saint Lawrence Cemetery, 60 Huguenin Avenue. The city's third Catholic cemetery, it was established in 1854. Their monument, just inside the gate, is large and impressive, capped with a cross, and a later generation of Chiccos has a grand marble mausoleum with a stained-glass Jesus window inside. A plaque on the mausoleum wall proclaims the "ancient origin" of the Chicco family, whose members in Italy numbered among them "merchants, doctors, and landlords." There is no mention of bootleggers.[67]

You can't miss Vincent Chicco's grave, located just inside the gate at Saint Lawrence Cemetery. *Author photo*

Much larger and peopled with more prominent Charlestonians is Magnolia Cemetery, established in 1850 on a former rice plantation beside the Cooper River. This is where **Sallie F. Chapin** is buried under a marker erected by "her sisters of the National WCTU" after her death in 1896, age 66. Magnolia is the resting place of 2,000 Confederate soldiers, including 85 who fought at Gettysburg, and the crews of the ill-fated *H.L. Hunley*, a submarine deployed in Charleston harbor in 1863 to help break the stranglehold of the Union blockade. In three separate outings, it drowned 21 sailors, leading Confederate General P. G. T. Beauregard to say, "It is more dangerous to those who use it than to the enemy."[68]

Magnolia Cemetery is full of twisty old oak trees hung with Spanish moss and has a large pond in the middle. (A disconcerting sign at the entrance asks that you not feed the alligators, but fortunately I didn't see any.) At the office, which was once the plantation house, an efficient clerk provided me with two maps and a schematic drawing of the Chapin grave. She traced the path with a yellow highlighter and pointed out the Bird monument as a landmark. "It's huge, you can't miss it," she said. Apparently, you could. Embarrassingly map-challenged, I drove the cemetery's lanes—paved and unpaved, and the map didn't give the "road" names that are posted—for almost an hour before I noticed the Bird monument, which wasn't that huge. Along the way I found the Hunley graves as well as a life-size stone bassinette that marked the grave of Rosalie White, who died in 1882 at age seven months. Under the hood, there is a bronze death mask of the baby's face, turned green with age.[69] I think it's the saddest monument to a life cut short that I have ever seen. This cemetery is well worth an afternoon of your time. www.magnoliacemetery.net

Benjamin Ryan Tillman's large (and very wordy) tombstone is located in the Ebenezer Baptist Church Cemetery in his native Edgefield County. The inscription hails him for his achievements in providing education to the children of the "common people" of South Carolina at Clemson and Winthrop colleges, but does not mention his "baby," the dispensary system. 275 Samuel E. Diggs Road, Trenton.[70]

RECOMMENDED READING

The South Carolina Dispensary: A Bottle Collector's Atlas and History of the System by Phillip Kenneth Huggins (Orangeburg, SC: Sandlapper Publishing Company, 1977). Out of print, but copies are plentiful on-line.

The Coming of Southern Prohibition: The Dispensary System and the Battle Over Liquor in South Carolina, 1907–1915 by Michael Lewis (Baton Rouge: Louisiana University Press, 2016)

Wicked Charleston Volume 2: Prostitutes, Politics, and Prohibition by Mark R. Jones (Charleston: History Press, 2006)

CHAPTER FIVE

*F*LORIDA'S
*D*RY-*W*ET *W*AR

FLORIDA, THE SUNSHINE STATE, projects a vibe of unrestrained fun: golden bodies on golden beaches, cruise ships with groaning buffet boards and fully stocked bars, citrus trees—which produce a major ingredient of so many delicious fruity cocktails—and a casual native population that goes about year-round in T-shirts, shorts, and sandals, sipping tall drinks decorated with tiny paper umbrellas as they loll about under the palm trees. In central Florida, The Villages, a gargantuan retirement community covering three counties, hosts nightly parties on its village "squares," with live music and outdoor bars fueling the good times.

But in the late nineteenth and early twentieth centuries, Floridians were as divided over alcohol as the rest of the nation. Generally, the northern part of the state, where the capital, Tallahassee, is located, was more conservative and prohibitionist. The morals loosened as you traveled downstate, though even "wicked" Miami had gotten bitten by the dry bug by 1907—See? There's that year again—when a referendum on making Dade County dry was defeated in a close vote.

Capitol Bldg. Tallahassee, Fla.

The 1845 Capitol building, shown in an old postcard, was in use when
Floridians went to war over prohibition. *Author collection*

The following March, our friend Carry A. Nation arrived in Miami to
rally the troops. Nation based her activities in a large revival tent near the
county courthouse downtown, urging the tremendous crowds—said to be
record-setting—to not only clean up Miami but to petition their representatives in Congress to "do the right thing" for the country. She had left her
saloon-wrecking hatchet at home but sold $300 of the miniature type to
fuel her activities, which by then had taken her across the United States and
even to Europe.

When she wasn't holding forth on the evils of liquor, tobacco, and
impure sex, Nation and two of her WCTU hostesses were out gathering
evidence of Miami vice, visiting saloons, a gambling den, and a brothel. Not
surprisingly, she found plenty. In a particularly dramatic moment, she was
challenged to produce evidence of her findings by the skeptical local prosecutor. She pulled from "the mysterious confines of her dress" two bottles
of liquor she claimed she had purchased on a Sunday, in violation of state
liquor laws. The official's angry response was drowned out by the audience
bellowing "Onward, Christian Soldiers."

Two of Miami's daily newspapers dismissed Nation as a nut, but she
was supported by the anti-wet *Miami Daily Metropolis*, at that time the city's
largest circulation daily, which said she had won over "disinterested people"
who had earlier "thought Mrs. Nation simply a sufferer from a certain form
of dementia Americana." By the time she left town, even the governor had

joined her on the stage at her tent. In the months to come, both stricter laws and stricter law enforcement followed, though Dade County did not go dry until 1913.[71] It followed Leon County, where Tallahassee is situated, by one year. The *Tampa Bay Tribune* facetiously suggested that lobbyists coming to the capital "arrange to conceal a barroom somewhere in luggage, or have trousers made with special reference to deep and roomy hip pockets—about one quart capacity." Liquor was available in Tallahassee on the black market and local stills churned out moonshine, while enforcement of the dry law was practically nonexistent.[72]

Tallahassee's version of Carry Nation was Luella Pugh Knott, a former schoolteacher married to Florida's longtime state treasurer. Though not a pugilist in the Nation mold, she led the first attempt to make Leon County dry in 1904 and was involved in the successful effort eight years later. Her husband, William, ran for governor in 1916, but was defeated by Sidney J. Catts, the nominee of the Prohibition Party, whose campaign posters featured a fearsome black cat, tail bristling and teeth bared, with the message, "What is this cat mewing for? To be Governor of Florida! . . . Register

Luella Knott may look demure in this portrait, but she was a firebrand when it came to temperance. She and her husband, William, died within days of each other in 1965. *Left, State Archives of Florida. Right, Collection of the Knott House Museum.*

Mr. Voter—Kill the Rats—Pay Your Poll Tax and Vote for CATTS!" In later life, Mrs. Knott continued to be active in progressive causes and attained some fame as a poet. The home she and her husband shared in downtown Tallahassee, now a museum, became known as "The House That Rhymes" because she tied her own verses to pieces of furniture. The Knotts died within eight days of each other in 1965. The following year, Tallahassee's first legal post-Prohibition bar opened. One wonders if they rolled over in their graves at the Oakland Cemetery.

To get a feeling about what Florida was like between its northern and southern extremes, Leo and I visited the central Florida city of Sanford, founded in 1877 by Henry Shelton Sanford, who had been Lincoln's ambassador to Belgium during the Civil War. He had operated as a sort of rogue CIA agent in Europe, running the Union's covert intelligence service and spending more than a million dollars on war materiel.[73]

Ambassador Sanford was an urbane man with expensive tastes, bad luck, and dreadful business sense. He established the new city and an orange-growing empire with the help of a former Confederate spy and saboteur, Judge Joseph Wofford Tucker. While the groves flourished for some years, his trees turned out to be too far north for the long haul, and freezes destroyed his crops, leading his Belgian wife, Gertrude, to compare Florida to "a vampire that . . . sucked the *repose* & the beauty & the *dignity* & cheerfulness out of our lives." Sanford died bankrupt in 1890, leaving his wife to rely on the charity of her daughter, Ethel, who had been married off to a wealthy cousin. Eventually, Ethel Sanford lived in a twenty-eight-room New York mansion on the Upper East Side and entertained the Prince of Wales (the future Edward VIII) and other guests. There was never any shortage of alcohol in the Sanford domain.[74] Judge Tucker, however, remained in Sanford as a

Henry Shelton Sanford was the founding father of Sanford, Florida. *Library of Congress*

devoted Methodist and temperance rabble rouser. In a letter to the editor of a Jacksonville newspaper, he suggested that anyone wishing to make a living off booze should just "ship it to Savannah." In other words, over the state border to Georgia.

The center of Sanford's historical activities is the Sanford Museum, a charming structure with columns shaped like celery plants—Sanford was once dubbed "Celery City" because it grew so much of the stuff—located downtown near scenic Lake Monroe and the St. Johns Riverwalk. It contains not only Henry Sanford's archives and a scaled-down version of his private library but many other artifacts and papers documenting the small city's history.

Curator Brigitte Stephenson is an enthusiastic interpreter of local history who enjoys making and wearing period costumes ranging from Victorian widow's weeds to an Edwardian day dress complete with bustle, and finding creative ways to bring the past alive. Her investigation into an old saloon in Sanford led to the Smith's Barroom Challenge, a fundraiser for the Sanford Historical Society that resulted in fifteen local bars and restaurants devising specialty drinks using a stock list from Smith's Barroom, circa 1882. To launch it, she gave a lively presentation on the history of the war between wets and drys in Sanford.[75]

Sanford Museum curator Brigitte Stephenson and Sanford Historical Society board member Amber Babcock toast the success of the Smith's Barroom Challenge. *Sanford Historical Society*

On the dry side, Sanford had a very large and active chapter of the WCTU, Stephenson said, which allied itself with the Woman's Club of Sanford and various churches, especially Judge Tucker's First Methodist Church. On the wet side, besides individuals who wanted to drink, Sanford had a German beer supplier, Joseph Zapf, an immigrant who had settled in Jacksonville in the late 1880s and became a bottler for St. Louis-based Anheuser-Busch. Adolphus Busch was among a large number of German immigrants who brought the craft of beer-making to the United States in the late nineteenth century, eventually leading drinkers' tastes from whiskey to beer. In 1850, Americans consumed 36 million gallons of beer. The population had tripled by 1890, but beer consumption had increased 24-fold, to 855 million gallons.[76]

Zapf's Florida enterprises included a bar with a billiard room and both wholesale and retail beer sales in Sanford. The marquee at Zapf's saloon touted beer as "liquid bread," which Adolphus Busch and his fellow brewers presented as an alternative to "unhealthy" whiskey, but Zapf also bottled and sold wine and whiskey as he touted his company as "the best known and largest liquor house in the state."[77] Nationally, the trend of immigrant brewers and bottlers drove much of the anti-alcohol activity at this time, which mixed

A vintage postcard depicts the First United Methodist Church of Sanford, a hotbed of temperance activity. *Author collection*

hatred of drunkenness with distrust of immigrants and their "foreign" customs. The hatred mingled with nationalism and patriotism when World War I broke out in 1914, making it tough to have a German name in America.

Another leading wet in Sanford was R. A. Wheeler, whose Wheeler's Exchange Saloon on 1st Street was advertised with handbills reading, "Admit Bearer to Any Insane Asylum in the United States or Canada." Both Wheeler and Zapf were part of an organization called the Liquor Dealers Protective Association, which tried to influence lawmakers on all levels to lay off their business, Stephenson said.

The WCTU members were not saloon wreckers like Carry Nation, but they were not above guerilla warfare. When a petition circulated in Sanford by the wets asked for signatures in support of saloons, the ladies got hold of it, had large leaflets printed with the names of all the petitioners and dropped them in every yard in town, hoping to shame the signers. Stephenson

Joseph Zapf, a German immigrant, kept central Florida wet with both beer and whiskey. *Sanford Museum* said the tug of war lasted from 1887 to 1911, during which time the town voted itself wet and dry six times. The frequency and closeness of the elections are clear indications of the divisiveness of the issue.

The day Sanfordites voted themselves dry the first time in November 1887, a stray ash from a bakery set the town on fire, though prohibitionists darkly speculated it was the act of vengeful "saloonists." By 1889, Sanford was wet again. The vote was reaffirmed in 1898 by a three-vote margin. (That election day, temperance supporters provided free lunches near the polls to sweeten voters' appetites, and it's fair to assume the wets were offering something to wash down the lunches.) Nevertheless, in October the vote was countermanded by the county commission and the entire county went dry. By 1902, the tide had turned again, and the county went wet by a two-thirds vote. Five years later, the wets managed to keep control, but

Sascha Webber and Mary Montalvo operate a lively wine and beer bar, with retro speakeasy, in Sanford. *Courtesy Luisa's Cellar*

the margin had narrowed to eleven votes. In 1911, Sanford went dry again with a vote of 125 to 119. That prevailed until state prohibition began in 1919, followed by national Prohibition in 1920.

Today, Sanford's downtown is a walkable, lively place, with restaurants, bars, cafes, and specialty shops lining its streets. On a pub crawl one night with my sister-in-law Anna Culp, a longtime resident, I met Yellymary Montalvo, an exuberant Puerto Rican–born sommelier and owner, with her German husband Sascha Weber, of Luisa's Cellar. The "wine bar with a beer problem," as she calls it, also has a second-floor speakeasy called Wolfgang's Lounge. (Luisa was Mary's grandmother, and Wolfgang is Sascha's father.) Sascha has a working knowledge of more than 300 beers, Mary confided, and is also the cocktail craftsman, specializing in drinks that were popular in Germany between the wars. Mary said the cocktails are too time-consuming for her to manage, cheerfully admitting that she can't make anything more complicated than a rum and Coke.

Both the upstairs and downstairs are a mishmash of furniture and funky accessories procured at estate sales. There are big, lumpy couches, an upright piano draped in white Christmas lights, and lamps with beaded shades. Anna and I settled down on one of the couches, over which hung the framed front page of a Chicago newspaper heralding the end of Prohibition in 1933.

When Mary joined us from behind the bar, she said the building itself has been home to a casket shop, a printshop, and a nondenominational church. At the time she and Sascha took it over, the landlord and his family lived upstairs, with their eight children sharing two bedrooms and the landlord using what is now Wolfgang's Lounge as his man cave. The lounge is indeed a cave, dimly lit, with a bar accented with vintage glassware and cocktail accessories and Frank Sinatra music playing on the jukebox. Mary apologized that we couldn't stay, as a private poker party had booked it for later that night, but she and Sascha shared a Prohibition-era recipe for this book.

MARY PICKFORD

- 1½ oz. white rum
- 1½ oz. pineapple juice
- 1 tsp. grenadine
- 6 drops maraschino liqueur

Pour first four ingredients into a cocktail shaker and shake vigorously. Pour into a chilled cocktail glass and garnish with maraschino cherries if you wish.

—Sascha Weber, Luisa's Cellar and Wolfgang's Lounge

SMITH'S SAGE ADVICE

- ½ oz. brandy
- ½ oz. blackberry liqueur
- Club soda to top
- Orange slice

Place an orange slice in a glass and top with ice. Pour brandy and blackberry liqueur into the glass, then top off with club soda. Garnish with a fresh blackberry and a sprig of sage.

—Dave Lengert, Hollerbach's Willow Tree Café
Winner of the 2019 Smith's Barroom Challenge

THE VILLAGES

The Villages, the largest gated retirement community in America, began in the early 1980s when a developer had trouble selling lots in his mobile home park, Orange Blossom Gardens. The new concept of building a planned community to appeal to aging Baby Boomers took off like a rocket. Today The Villages has more than 132,000 residents, most of them 55 years of age or older, the threshold age for owning property. The Villages has been called "America's Friendliest Hometown" as well as "Disneyland for Adults." It has amenities ranging from championship golf courses to an acute-care hospital. Its numerous recreation centers offer everything from pickleball and tennis to yoga and bridge, plus classes on a spectacular array of subjects. In addition, The Villages has more than two thousand special interest clubs and associations, including one for African violet enthusiasts, a golf cart drill team, and twenty chapters of Alcoholics Anonymous.[78]

Of course, if you know one thing about The Villages, it's the story that came out in 2006 in which a gynecologist said she had seen more cases of STDs—specifically herpes and HPV—from patients in The Villages than in her big-city practice in Miami. That was followed a few years later by an article in the *New York Post* about all the wild sex going on at a place where women outnumber men ten to one and no one has to worry about birth control. There was an incident in 2014 of a couple being arrested and serving time for having sex at one of the three public squares and another couple arrested for doing the nasty on a utility box.

But c'mon, with 132,000-plus residents, you are bound to have some bad apples, right?

Residents of The Villages gathered for a campaign stop by President Donald Trump in October 2020. *Wikimedia Commons*

The Villages is also famous for its nightly live entertainment outdoors at its public squares, Spanish Springs, Lake Sumter Landing, and Brownwood Paddock. This last is named for William G. Brown, founder of Brownwood, Florida, who established a large cattle ranch in 1879. He was quite successful, to the degree that he could eventually spend his leisure time pursuing hobbies such as hot air ballooning—yes, The Villages has its own balloon festival—and, after barely surviving a crash and swearing off that hobby, golf because it was something he could do on solid ground. But even that turned out to be too dangerous for Brown, who caught a cold on the golf course early in 1929 and died of pneumonia. His last words were memorable. Sitting up in bed, he said, "I didn't order milk! Bring me a Scotch whiskey!"[79]

This seems to have been adopted as a motto by many of the denizens of The Villages.

After giving a talk at one of the recreation centers about my book on Henry S. Sanford's adventurous granddaughter, Gertrude Sanford Legendre, I drove with Leo to Lake Sumter Landing (where the couple got caught in the act) to check out the scene. About 150 people had attended my book talk, and I soon discovered where everyone else was. They were grooving to the tunes of a rock group called Chasing Amy, which was the evening's free act at the square. The squares are like little downtowns, surrounded with shops, bars, restaurants, and a movie theatre, and the performance arena is anchored on two sides by a drinks bar. Most of the people appeared to have driven over on their golf carts—one of them had a name, "Goody Two-Shoes and the Filthy Beast," a reference to the Cary Grant-Leslie Caron film *Father Goose.*

I figured that with all this drinking going on, a golf cart was a much safer way to get home than a car. But I learned that even golf carts can be problematic. According to The Villages' newspaper, a resident was arrested a couple of weeks after my visit when she tried to drive her cart the wrong way on a one-way street. She admitted to having consumed a few at the World of Beer but wasn't cooperative with the police and was hauled off to the pokey. The other problem is the politicizing of golf carts. The Villages was Trump territory in 2020 and his fans demonstrated their support with golf cart parades. Not everyone was a fan. The same week I visited, a resident named Ed McGinty showed up at a parade with his cart decorated with anti-Trump signs such as "Hitler and Trump Exactly Same DNA," "Trump Is a Sexual Predator" and "Trump Compulsive Liar." His display

In The Villages, even golf carts get political. *Wikimedia Commons*

was followed by a visit from the local sheriff's office because so many people had complained. He even got a handwritten note attached to his door reading, "Be very careful if the well-being of your family is of importance."

Ah, well, in a community of 132,000 people, you're bound to have a few bad apples.

Leo and I found a bistro that seemed to be hopping and settled into a booth. The hostess told us the entertainment would start in a few moments. About the time we ordered, a chrome-domed musician in Lycra sportswear—looking like a bald Richard Simmons—began performing hits from the 1970s and 1980s, from Kenny G to the Rolling Stones. Three women soon hit the dance floor, along with a couple who immediately demonstrated they were accomplished dancers. She was dressed like a contestant in "Dancing with the Stars." Soon a trim man with only slightly graying hair joined the trio, singling out the woman with the waist-length blonde hair. The next time I looked up, they were gone. The singer began belting out "Miss You" with a voice that was a fairly good imitation of Mick Jagger:

Hey, what's the matter, man?
We're gonna come around at twelve
With some Puerto Rican girls that's just dyin' to meet you
We're gonna bring a case of wine . . .

Except instead of Puerto Rican girls he said, "Some Village girls," which drew a roar of approval from the crowd. Too bad they didn't get to know Yellymary Montalvo, a real Puerto Rican girl with many cases of really fine wine. But they would have to go to Sanford to meet her.

PROHIBITION EXPEDITION

Knott House, the home of Luella and William Pugh, is preserved as it was in 1928, complete with Mrs. Knott's poetry tied to the furniture.

Knott House • 301 E. Park Avenue, Tallahassee
https://www.museumoffloridahistory.com/about/the-knott-house-museum/

The Knott House is a
Tallahassee landmark.
Author photo

For a contrasting view of home life in the state capital, visit **Goodwood Museum and Gardens**, once the home of Florida senator William Hodges and his wife, Margaret. From the drinks tray in the front hall to the library where the senator conducted much business over a glass, Goodwood presents a walk on the wet side. 1600 Miccosukee Road. www.goodwoodmuseum.org.

Sanford Museum
520 E. 1st Street, Sanford • https://www.sanfordfl.gov/visitors/sanford-museum

Luisa's Cellar and Wolfgang's Lounge
206 Sanford Avenue, Sanford • https://www.luisascellar.com/

Hollerbach's Willow Tree Café
205 E. 1st Street, Sanford • www.hollerbachs.com.
German restaurant and winner of Smith's Barroom Challenge.

CEMETERY SIDE TRIP

Luella Pugh Knott, Tallahassee's leading temperance advocate, and her husband **William Knott** are buried at Oakland Cemetery, 838 N. Bronough Street, in Tallahassee. While you are there, look for the grave of **James E. Bowdoin**, a federal Prohibition law enforcement officer nicknamed "Pistol Pete," who was gunned down during a still raid in 1925. He will come up in a future chapter. **Judge Joseph Wofford Tucker**, one of Sanford's founding fathers and most ardent prohibitionists, rests in Lakeview Cemetery, 1975 W. 25th Street, Sanford.

CHAPTER SIX

*M*EANWHILE,
IN *W*ASHINGTON

BY THE SECOND DECADE of the twentieth century, it was getting hard to buy a legal drink in much of the United States, especially in the South. Georgia was the first Southern state to go dry, partly in reaction to the Atlanta Race Riot of 1906, which had been triggered by alleged (and never substantiated) assaults by black men on white women reported by two racist newspapers, the *Atlanta Georgian* and the *Atlanta News.*

The riot, instigated by white vigilantes, resulted in the destruction of many black-owned businesses and the deaths of dozens of African American men and women as well as two whites, one of them an elderly woman who had a heart attack after seeing a mob outside her home. It had been stoked by two gubernatorial candidates with ties to the major Atlanta newspapers who were trying to prove who was the bigger white supremacist.

The stereotype of the drunken black man defiling white womanhood was a driving force behind the Southern temperance movement. Georgia passed its state-wide prohibition law in 1907—see, there's that year again— and in 1908 enacted black suffrage restrictions, stripping blacks of their political power and further codifying the Jim Crow system.[80]

A temperance cartoon urged
women representing "wet"
states to join Georgia and other
"dry" states under an umbrella.
*Author photo taken at American
Prohibition Museum Library of
Congress.*

"COME IN OUT OF THE WET"

The other Southern states fell into line, passing progressively tighter restrictions on alcohol sales and manufacture, until by 1919 every state in the South except Louisiana had banned the manufacture and sale of alcohol, most with what were called "Bone-Dry" laws,[81] as had many states in the Midwest and West. Local option laws had dried up large portions of other states across the country.

That didn't mean people weren't drinking. The well-to-do ordered booze from makers in states that had looser rules, liquor was purchased legally in the Caribbean and smuggled to the east coast, and stills by the tens of thousands were churning out moonshine for those less particular (or wealthy). Enforcement of dry laws was mixed at best: Tennessee found it necessary to pass a law enabling the ouster of any official found negligent in enforcing prohibition. But by and large, the work of the first wave of the WCTU had been successful. The original leaders of the organization—President Frances Willard, the hatchet-wielding Carry Nation, Sallie Chapin in Charleston, Silena Moore Holman, Lide Parker Meriwether, and Lucy Tappan Phillips in Tennessee—had all died by then, but their work was carried on by an enthusiastic second wave exemplified by Luella Pugh Knott of Tallahassee. (Even in death, however, Frances Willard had pull. Her birthday was a school holiday in four states, including South Carolina, and the state of Illinois donated her statue to the U.S. Capitol's National Statuary Collection in 1905. It was the first figure of a woman to be added to the collection.)

Drunk on success, the WCTU, the Baptists, and Methodists, and the rest of the dry coalition set their sights higher: they wanted the entire nation to go dry. They were part of a rising national movement—indeed, an international movement—called the progressives. Activists wanted to improve the human condition and increasingly saw a role for government in this, such as regulating everything from industrial safety to food and drug purity to corporate mergers, and extending the right to vote to women. Targets of their wrath included political bosses in the big cities, who built their power with immigrant support, for the Progressives were largely a God-fearing lot of WASPs from middle America. Writes historian Jackson Lears, "Offended or frightened by the unseemly

FRANCES E. WILLARD, STATUARY HALL, U. S. CAPITOL.

The statue of Frances Willard, shown in a vintage postcard, was the first one representing a woman placed in the U.S. Capitol's National Statuary Collection. *Author collection*

pleasures of the sporting crowd (which, according to common assumption included free blacks as well as liquored-up Irishmen and beer-swilling Germans), Protestant moral reformers embraced Prohibition as a means of allying racially inflected fears of social disorder—of keeping the unwashed classes sober, self-disciplined, and on time for work."[82]

In the second decade of the twentieth century, four amendments to the Constitution were passed, all of them carrying out progressive aims; the last two of them were the amendments banning alcohol and extending the right to vote to women. As I have mentioned before, the WCTU's members were generally allies in the women's suffrage movement, though less so in the South, where suffrage was often regarded as an overreach of states' rights. Women had long recognized that to have any meaningful power they had to have the right to vote. By 1918, all but twenty states—most of these in the South and on the east coast—had extended the vote to women.[83]

The progressive movement crossed party lines. Theodore Roosevelt, who was a Republican, was part of it. So was his niece, Eleanor Roosevelt,

Josephus Daniels, while secretary of the Navy, banned anything stronger than coffee from Navy bases and ships. *Library of Congress*

Wayne B. Wheeler was the extremely effective leader of the Anti-Saloon League. *Library of Congress*

a Democrat, favoring both women's suffrage and national Prohibition. (Her husband, Franklin, was a nominal dry, but he enjoyed his martinis in private.) Democratic President Woodrow Wilson's secretary of the Navy, Josephus Daniels of North Carolina, knew very little about ships—he called them all "boats"—but he knew sin when he saw it and the Navy was full of it. He quickly banned anything stronger than coffee from Navy bases and ships, which is why we still refer to a cup of coffee as "a cup of joe."[84] Wilson's secretary of state was William Jennings Bryan, a three-time candidate for president and a passionate advocate for temperance. On Long Island, a wealthy socialite named Pauline Morton Sabin, who became the first female member of the National Republican Committee, believed "a world without liquor would be a beautiful thing." She later changed her mind—to a startling degree.[85]

The progressive prohibitionists had an essential ally in the Anti-Saloon League, an organization started in Ohio in 1893. It was one of the first organizations to successfully use a wedge issue in politics, and its de facto chief, Wayne B. Wheeler, a homely little man with a push-broom moustache, became the most feared man in America—if you were a politician. After converting the Ohio legislature and governor's mansion into dry believers by routing all the wets at the ballot box, Wheeler turned his attention to other states and then to Congress. The only issue he cared about in supporting a candidate or ousting him was his position on alcohol. And he didn't care about what politicians did in their private lives. He famously said, "I don't care how a man drinks, I care how he votes." Tireless and pitiless, Wheeler was described as "a locomotive in trousers."

Wheeler and his supporters had their work cut out for them. The number of saloons in the country had tripled between 1870 and 1900, according to Prohibition historian Daniel Okrent, largely because of the efforts of beer barons such as Adolphus Busch. (Eighty percent of the bars in the country were owned or affiliated with German brewers.) Carry Nation, asked why she had not brought her hatchet to Cincinnati, said, "I would have dropped from exhaustion before I had gone a block."[86]

But Wheeler also knew how to harness the energy of disparate groups—even some that openly despised each other—into a coalition against alcohol. In addition to the WCTU and the Methodist and Baptist denominations, Wheeler's ASL coalition included racists, nativists, women's suffragists, industrialists John D. Rockefeller and Henry Ford, social worker Jane Addams, evangelist Billy Sunday, and the Ku Klux Klan. The Klan, incidentally, was resurrected in 1915 after decades of inactivity by William J. Simmons of Atlanta. (According to Okrent, Simmons "spent his later years in an Atlanta movie house, smelling of bourbon and cloves, as he watched *Birth of a Nation* over and over.") The principal targets of the "new" Klan's hatred were Catholics and Jews, both of whom use wine in their rites, as well as

A cartoon in a pro-KKK publication depicts Klansmen attacking a tree representing the Catholic Church. *Wikimedia Commons*

THIS TREE MUST COME DOWN

immigrants, making the white-robed members natural allies for the ASL. In the 1920s, it became primarily a white supremacist organization, and in 1923 it began admitting women, many of whom had cut their activist teeth in the temperance and women's suffrage movements![87]

Wheeler also gathered up populists, such as William Jennings Bryan and Tennessee Senator Cordell Hull, who had been clamoring for an income tax on the wealthy to take the tax burden off the "little man." Southerners largely saw this as a way to put the finger in the eye of the North, and their instincts were correct: in the first year of collection, 44 percent of the income tax was paid by residents of New York. Indeed, eight of the first nine states to ratify the Sixteenth Amendment were Southern states.

The ratification of this amendment in 1913, conveniently, gave the federal government a source of income to replace the excise tax on alcohol, which then accounted for almost a third of federal revenue.[88]

An amendment to the Constitution banning the production, sale, and transportation of "intoxicating alcohol" was introduced for the first time that year by Alabama Congressman Richmond Hobson. It went down in defeat, 197 for and 190 against—a two-thirds majority of both houses was required for passage—but the wets were encouraged by the close vote. Hobson lost his House seat over another issue—he had expressed moderate views on race—but went on the national lecture circuit, thundering his message of temperance all over the country. The ASL's adherents and financial sources multiplied. History was on their side.

The outbreak of World War I in Europe in 1914, which the U.S. entered in 1917, made all things German very unpopular. Dachshunds were so despised as a breed that the American Kennel Club tried to rebrand them as "badger dogs," the German translation of their name. People named Schmidt changed their name to Smith. On top of everything else, the war pretty much put the nail in the coffin of the German brewers. With public sentiment changing—remember those millions of school children raised on the WCTU's propaganda?—the Eighteenth Amendment to the Constitution was once again introduced as a joint resolution in Congress in 1917, this time by Texas Senator John Morris Sheppard, and it passed in December. It was ratified in just thirteen months, with every state on board except Connecticut and Rhode Island. Mississippi was the first state to ratify and the state that banned alcohol the longest. It remained (legally) dry until 1966, when the legislature passed a local-option law.

RICHMOND P. HOBSON AND THE USS *HOBSON*

A handsome Navy hero of the Spanish-American war—his penchant for kissing adoring women earned him the sobriquet "The Most Kissed Man in America"— Richmond P. Hobson was the highest paid speaker on the Anti-Saloon League circuit, giving a lecture called "Alcohol the Great Destroyer" throughout the 1920s and 1930s.[89] After his first sobriquet wore off, he became known as "the Father of American Prohibition." Hobson was born on his family's plantation, Magnolia Grove, near Greensboro, Hale County, Alabama, in 1870.

A Democrat, Hobson was a dedicated progressive who favored women's suffrage and expanded educational opportunities. He served four terms in Congress, supporting all four constitutional amendments that passed between 1913 and 1919. With national Prohibition achieved, Hobson went on to advocate restrictions on narcotic drugs, particularly heroin, which became his lifelong passion.

Prohibition was repealed during the first year of the Roosevelt administration, 1933, but Hobson got a consolation prize: shortly after his inauguration, FDR presented him the Congressional Medal of Honor for his heroism during the Spanish-American War. In 1941, four years after Hobson's death, a Navy destroyer was launched at the Charleston Naval Shipyard and christened the USS *Hobson*.[90] The *Hobson* participated in some of the most storied battles of World War II, including Operation Torch, D-Day, and Okinawa, where she was hit by a kamikaze bomber. Stationed in Charleston after the war, she was involved in maneuvers in the Atlantic prior to deployment to Korea in 1952 when her commanding officer gave orders that caused a collision with the aircraft carrier she was escorting. The ship went down in four minutes, and 176 men lost their lives. The commander threw himself overboard—or fell accidentally—and was among those who drowned. ▪

Left, Richmond P. Hobson of Alabama was a temperance leader. *Wikimedia Commons*

Right, The striking memorial to the USS *Hobson* is located in Charleston's White Point Garden on the Battery. *Author photo*

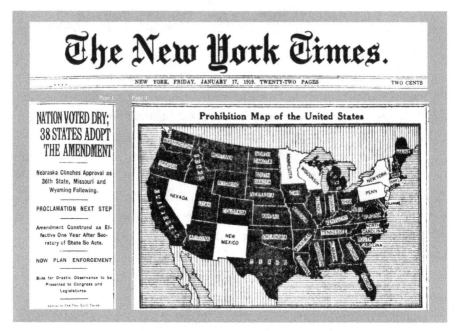

A map on the front page of the *New York Times* on January 17, 1919, told the story of the speedy ratification of the Eighteenth Amendment. *Wikimedia Commons*

The language in the Eighteenth Amendment was simple: "After one year from the ratification of this article the manufacture, sale, or transportation of intoxicating liquors within, the importation thereof into, or the exportation thereof from the United States and all the territory subject to the jurisdiction thereof for beverage purposes is hereby prohibited." Section two of the amendment gave the states and the federal government joint authority to enforce the amendment, and section three stipulated that ratification had to be completed within seven years. (At the time, most wets considered section three a victory, never believing that the states would ratify within that timeframe.)

The old saying about the devil being in the details was certainly true about the legislation Congress passed in 1919 to enforce the Eighteenth Amendment. Drafted by the ASL's Wayne B. Wheeler himself, the National Prohibition Act became better known as the Volstead Act after its sponsor, Minnesota congressman Andrew Volstead. The act defined an alcoholic beverage as anything containing more than a half a percent of alcohol—what we sometimes call "near beer" today. This came as a surprise to many people who had supported the amendment, who had assumed "intoxicating liquors" meant liquor, not beer or light wine. Anyone suspected of making, selling, transporting, bartering, or giving away alcohol could have their premises searched without warrant and, on first offense conviction, could be fined up to $1,000 (almost $13,000 in 2020 money) or jailed for up to a year—or both.[91] As the writer Pete Hamill observed in the Ken Burns film *Prohibition*, "Here were all these evangelical Christians . . . who decided to pass a law that would imprison Jesus if he turned water into wine. They'd say, 'There he goes, lock him up.'"

The country's fifth largest industry ground to a halt. According to Mabel Walker Willebrandt, who became the Justice Department's top Prohibition enforcer, January 17 ushered in the closing of 507 distilleries, 1,217 breweries and 178,000 saloons. And these were just the legal ones. Two hundred million gallons of intoxicating beverages were stored in warehouses under federal lock and key, but just as illegal speakeasies and blind tigers replaced the legal saloons, somehow many of those gallons disappeared.[92]

There were some loopholes in the law, such as allowing people to keep alcohol they had on hand on January 17, 1920, the day Prohibition went into effect, and to transport it between their residences. This enabled Warren G. Harding to move $1,800 worth of liquor from his Washington residence to the White House when he took office as president in 1921.[93] Another loophole allowed physicians to prescribe alcohol for medicinal purposes (and some distillers to sell it to them for the same) and pharmacy companies to use it in medicines. A third allowed use of alcohol for religious rites. The American public would make full use of these loopholes, and create their own illegal ones, in the months leading up to the deadline and over the next thirteen years, until the Eighteenth Amendment was repealed by the Twenty-first.

Depending on how you came down on the wet-dry issue, January 16 was either a day for quiet jubilation or deep mourning (and perhaps getting legally drunk for the last time). Up until the deadline, liquor stores did a steady business as customers took advantage of the provision in the Volstead Act allowing them to keep on hand any alcohol they had in their homes as of midnight. They needn't have panicked; liquor and beer would flow freely to anyone who didn't mind breaking the law—though it would be quite a bit more expensive and of decidedly inferior quality.

Atlanta's drys celebrated with a huge parade and bonfire, with a still and barrel of confiscated moonshine fueling the flames.[94] Throughout the nation, funerals for "John Barleycorn," the fictitious embodiment of alcohol, were held. In Washington, Josephus Daniels and William Jennings Bryan attended a service at the First Congregational Church where dry speakers orated for hours. Daniels proclaimed that "The saloon is as dead as slavery"—an interesting comparison for an unrepentant racist—and predicted no Congress would ever lessen enforcement of Prohibition. Bryan was the final and most anticipated speaker, and at midnight he bellowed, quoting the gospel of Matthew, "'They are dead, they are dead who sought the young child's life.' Those who would kill us and who would destroy us, we have destroyed them."[95]

MOCKTAIL

- 1 cup sweet cider
- ½ cup cherry juice
- ½ inch preserved ginger

Chop the ginger, mix with the cider, cherry juice (homemade or commercial) and ice in a cocktail shaker. Shake well and strain into a cocktail glass.

—*From* What to Drink: The Blue Book of Beverages: Recipes and Directions for Making and Serving Non-alcoholic Drinks for all Occasions *by Bertha E. L. Stockbridge, first published in 1909 and still in print*

The women who had fought for both temperance and suffrage had another reason to be happy that night. The resolution for the Nineteenth Amendment, giving women the vote, had passed Congress in June 1919, and was rapidly racking up state ratifications. Remember the Burn Memorial I talked about in Knoxville? Young Harry Burn heeded his mother, voted for ratification, and Tennessee became the final state needed to amend the Constitution. This happened in August 1920, in time for women to vote in the upcoming presidential election, but even before that, the Democratic Party welcomed women as delegates to its national convention. (The GOP followed suit in 1924.)

Democratic presidential nominee James M. Cox and his running mate Franklin Delano Roosevelt campaigned in 1920. Both would play roles in the repeal of Prohibition. *Franklin Delano Roosevelt Presidential Library and Museum*

Kentucky sent two women as delegates-at-large, both veterans of the suffrage and temperance movements, Laura M. Clay and Cora Wilson Stewart. Mrs. Stewart, whose main cause was adult illiteracy, was asked to second the nomination of James M. Cox for president—his running mate was Assistant Secretary of the Navy Franklin D. Roosevelt—and, as a courtesy, the chairman of the Kentucky delegation put both women's names into nomination for the presidency and the delegation gave them each one vote. They were the first women in American history to receive a vote in nomination for president by a major political party.[96]

Which brings us to our next stop on the Prohibition trail, Kentucky, home of bluegrass music, thoroughbred racing, and what some say is the best bourbon whiskey on the planet.

PROHIBITION EXPEDITION

ALABAMA • Magnolia Grove, Richmond Hobson's birthplace, is a house museum operated by the Alabama Historical Commission. The Greek Revival mansion and grounds are open for tours three days a week.

Magnolia Grove • 1002 Hobson Street, Greensboro
https://ahc.alabama.gov/properties/magnoliagrove/magnoliagrove.aspx

---

SOUTH CAROLINA • There is a **monument to the USS *Hobson*** and its lost crew on the Charleston Battery above White Point Garden.[97] The granite obelisk sits on a platform paved with 38 stones, one from each state that that lost a sailor in the tragedy.

Monument to the USS *Hobson* • 251 ½ King Street

WASHINGTON, D.C. • Not everyone considers Washington, D.C. to be part of the South, but if you happen to be there, visit the **Temperance Fountain** at 678 Indiana Avenue, at the intersection with 7th Avenue. At the turn of the century, it was popular to assume that people drank because they didn't have access to cold fresh water. A San Francisco philanthropist, Dr. Henry Cogswell, paid for the installation of sixteen identical Temperance Fountains across the country. The one in Washington, put in place in 1884, is the last intact fountain, though it no longer serves water. It features a pavilion with the words *faith*, *hope*, *charity*, and *temperance* chiseled into the lintel, and a bronze sculpture of a heron on top. Often criticized for its ugliness, the Washington fountain has somehow endured, though it was moved in 1987 from its original location on Pennsylvania Avenue where, ironically, a liquor store had opened a few steps away.[98] In the Capitol building, you can also see the **statue of Frances Willard** in the National Hall of Statuary.

The temperance fountain has been described as the ugliest monument in Washington, D.C. *Leo Smith photo*

CEMETERY SIDE TRIP

Rear Admiral **Richmond P. Hobson's** grave is at Arlington National Cemetery. His wife, Grizelda, who cracked the bottle of Champagne on the USS *Hobson* at the Charleston Naval Yard, rests beside him. **Josephus Daniels** is buried under an imposing obelisk at Oakwood Cemetery, 701 Oakwood Avenue, Raleigh, North Carolina, the marker shared with his wife, Addie. Oakwood is another of the garden cemeteries begun in the Victorian era. Many deceased governors, Congress members and senators are buried there, as well as famed N.C. State basketball coach **Jim Valvano** and **Elizabeth Edwards**, whose marital problems with her husband, Sen. John Edwards, blew up his bid for the presidency in 2008.

More information and virtual tours of the cemetery are available at https://www.historicoakwoodcemetery.org/[99]

RECOMMENDED READING

Daniel Okrent's book *Last Call: The Rise and Fall of Prohibition* (New York: Scribner, 2010) was featured in the Ken Burns/Lynn Novick film *Prohibition*, which debuted on PBS in 2011. Historian Geoffrey Ward wrote the script, which won an Emmy. It is a fascinating and highly entertaining history of the noble experiment that failed.

CHAPTER SEVEN

For Medicinal Purposes Only

IF AL CAPONE AND F. SCOTT FITZGERALD walked into the lobby of the Seelbach Hotel in Louisville, Kentucky today, they probably would not notice much amiss. The lobby has the same marble columns topped with gilded Corinthian capitals, curved mahogany registration desk, chandelier dripping with crystals, and sweeping staircase as when it was opened in 1905 by the Bavarian-born Seelbach brothers. Al would immediately head to the private dining room on the second floor where a blackjack game would be in progress. Scott would quickly glance at the grand staircase, perhaps visualizing Daisy Buchanan, adorned with her quarter-million-dollar pearl necklace, tossing the bouquet after her wedding reception in *The Great Gatsby*. Then he would hurry downstairs to the vaulted and ceramic-covered ceilings and Tiffany stained-glass windows of the fabled Rathskeller. At that point, as the thirsty author wandered among the columns decorated with life-size ceramic pelicans, he might be a bit nonplussed. The bar where he drank himself senseless as a lieutenant at Camp Zachary Taylor—getting thrown out three times in four weeks—is empty.[100]

The curved staircase of the Seelbach Hotel was descended by Daisy Buchanan, the fictional heroine of F. Scott Fitzgerald's novel *The Great Gatsby. Wikimedia Commons*

It is said that Fitzgerald met the inspiration for his most famous character, Jay Gatsby, in the Rathskeller. But more about that later.

The Old Seelbach Bar, to the right of the registration desk, is the current watering hole at the Seelbach, now a Hyatt hotel. That's where Leo and I were one cold winter night, sharing drinks with bourbon enthusiasts Linda and Fred Ruffenach. Linda, a caramel blonde with a dazzling smile, is the author of *How to Be a Bourbon Badass* and founder and head chick of the Whisky Chicks, a women's bourbon appreciation group. The Chicks had just held a sold-out 1920s-themed party in the Rathskeller marking the hundredth anniversary of Prohibition. Fred, her tall, dark-haired, dimpled husband, runs Thievery Spirits LLC, a promotional products company serving the distillery industry. He has also written a book, *The Bourbon Badass Training Manual*, a guide to getting the most from bourbon tasting. Between the two, they are a fount of bourbon knowledge.

Leo and I ordered Seelbach Cocktails, the hotel's signature drink, while Linda perused the five and a half pages of bourbons and ryes on the menu and ordered a bourbon pour with a separate glass of ice. She plunked a fresh ice cube in her drink from time to time as we talked, enabling her to enjoy the bourbon flavor without watering down the drink too much. Linda, who grew up in Louisville, likes to tell the story of an early bourbon experience. Her grandparents had a tradition of making frozen whiskey sours each Christmas Eve. As a tiny girl, "I spotted that bright red maraschino cherry on top of that sweet frozen concoction, and before anyone noticed, I had downed the entire drink," she said. She has become such a connoisseur that today she teaches workshops on "wild and wacky whiskey pairings," such as beef jerky, cotton candy, and peanut butter and jelly.

The Seelbach's Rathskellar was a popular gathering place for drinkers. Author F. Scott Fitzgerald was regularly asked to leave. *Wikimedia Commons*

THE SEELBACH COCKTAIL

Into a mixing glass filled with ice, pour:

- 1½ oz. Old Forrester bourbon
- 1 oz. Cointreau
- 7 dashes Angostura bitters
- 7 dashes Peychaud's bitters

Stir until well chilled. Strain into a Champagne flute and top with Champagne. Garnish with a section of orange peel, its oils expressed over the top of the drink.[101]

In boom times before Prohibition began, Louisville was the seat of the Kentucky bourbon industry, although bourbon was first produced in distilleries throughout the state. Linda and Fred said that in the 1990s, as bourbon began to reclaim its popularity from vodka among American drinkers, the idea of bourbon tourism took hold. The Kentucky Distillers' Association started the first Kentucky Bourbon Trail in 1999 and today there are eighteen distilleries on the trail, including six in Louisville. Several of these are located in a section of Main Street that became known as Whiskey Row

THE WHISKY CHICKS

Although Linda Ruffenach grew up in Louisville in a family of light bourbon drinkers, it was her Philadelphia-born husband, Fred, who started her on her bourbon journey. After they married, Fred began a serious study of bourbon and joined a Louisville appreciation group called the Bourbon Society. Linda accompanied him to a society party that marked Prohibition Repeal Day, December 5. She writes in her book *How to Be a Bourbon Badass*, "I knew little about bourbon and proceeded to blindly taste

Whisky Chicks founder Linda Ruffenach, right, celebrates Mother's Day at Churchill Downs with her mother, Mary Rabenecker, center, and sister Anna Rabenecker. They are enjoying mint juleps, of course. *Courtesy Linda Ruffenach*

and sample the selections available." She also met some interesting people at the party and came home with a revelation: "Now I wanted to understand more about this fascinating spirit that has brought together Kentucky's finest for decades and sparked interest in people from all over the world."

Linda held her first Whisky Chicks event—the dropped "e" is intentional—on a freezing night in 2014 at a speakeasy-style bar in Louisville. Thirty-five women braved the cold to be warmed by a special cocktail and friendly conversation. Her second event, a bourbon tasting, was almost a disaster. The guests, most of whom weren't accustomed to strong spirits, were initially turned off by the straight shots they were given. The bartender quickly regrouped and made bourbon Old Fashioneds, a good gateway drink for the novice.

Linda's Whisky Chicks group holds regular gatherings throughout the year, the one common characteristic of its members being a curiosity about bourbon and the desire to begin a journey to become a Bourbon Badass.[102] "When you go to a Whisky Chicks event, you just leave it at the door," she explained as we sipped our drinks at the Seelbach. Members range in ages from their 20s to their 90s. They don't talk about politics, but they do support causes. Their events over the years have raised $160,000 for the Coalition for the Homeless in Louisville.

The Whisky Chicks has a website, www.whiskychicks.com, and a Facebook page. ■

when it was home to eighty-nine bourbon distilleries.[103] A separate bourbon trail focusing on nineteen craft distilleries situated in four regions of the state was introduced by the Kentucky Distillers' Association in 2012.

We followed our pleasant happy hour with the Ruffenachs by walking down the street to the Brown Hotel, opened in 1923 and, like the Seelbach, lovingly preserved, and having dinner in the famous Lobby Bar. During dinner, we were entertained by live piano music and a couple of inebriated literary types holding forth at a nearby table; some sort of poetry conference was being held at the hotel. The Brown's signature dish is a turkey sandwich drenched in gravy called the Hot Brown. I couldn't face all the grease, but I did enjoy a slice of delicious, tooth-achingly sweet chocolate Derby Pie for dessert. (Remember that Louisville is the home of the Kentucky Derby. Linda Ruffenach's book includes a recipe for Derby Pie, which, naturally, is flavored with a couple of tablespoons of Kentucky bourbon.)

Afterward, Leo and I wandered around in the lower level of the Brown, where we were invited into a poetry reading. It seemed rude to refuse, and we tried to pay attention, but it was hard with poets falling asleep all around us and with the subject matter of the first poem seeming to be tedious instructions for making indigo dye. We headed back to the Seelbach to get some sleep before our all-day tour of Louisville distilleries.

Louisville's Brown Hotel maintains much of the Prohibition-era charm evidenced in this vintage postcard. *Author collection*

Bourbon, for the uninitiated, is whiskey made with at least 51 percent corn—moonshine, basically—water and yeast, and must at least touch wood before being sold. Better bourbons are aged in charred oak barrels, and to be labeled a "straight bourbon" requires aging in the barrel for at least two years.[104] Every distillery has its own way of doing things, with particular ingredients and processes that give their bourbons distinctive tastes. When Prohibition began, Louisville lost 6,000 to 8,000 distilling jobs, an economic disaster for the city that was echoed in small distillery towns across Kentucky.[105] Distilleries that couldn't unload their stock before Prohibition went into effect either had to lock it up in federal bonded warehouses, where guards would supposedly be on duty twenty-four hours a day, or

An advertisement for the dispensary in the Brown Hotel offers a drinker's delight of options. *Author collection*

attempt to wiggle through one of the loopholes in the Volstead Act. The largest of these allowed distilleries to be certified as suppliers of whiskey for medicinal purposes to pharmaceutical companies and drugstores. Alcohol was and still is an essential ingredient in certain medicines, such as cough syrup. Have you ever heard a doctor prescribe "rock and rye" for a cough? I have.

The first tour we took the next morning was the Stitzel-Weller Experience, located at what was once a thriving distillery and warehouse complex on the edge of Louisville. Our tour guide was Tim Delonjay, a tall, deep-voiced, long-haired, bearded man wearing a cowboy hat; most of the people on the tour were under age forty. (Leo and I were among the oldest people on tours all that day.) Tim explained that Stitzel-Weller's roots go back to the mid-nineteenth century, but the company is now owned by Bulleit Bourbon and all production except a tiny demonstration operation on the Stitzel-Weller grounds takes place at the company distillery in Shelbyville. As Tim took us around the grounds and into various buildings, such as the cooper or barrel builders' workshop, he shared that Stitzel, which built its distillery in 1872, was one of six companies in Kentucky and just ten in the nation that could sell medicinal whiskey during Prohibition. That meant that every doctor and dentist could write a prescription for a pint of whiskey for every American man, woman, and child every ten days. "And I'm sure those children never got their medicine," he joked.

At the end of the tour Tim took us into a tasting room where he taught us about the "Kentucky chew," in which you swirl the bourbon in the glass, smell its aroma, sip it, roll it around on your tongue and then swallow it. That way you can appreciate all the flavors—caramel and vanilla are the most common, though Tim pointed out one bourbon we tasted had a bit of banana Laffy Taffy flavor in it. We also learned how just a drop of water can "open up" the taste of the bourbon, which is why most people drink it with a little water or ice if they aren't using another mixer. Tim also explained to us that a "Kentucky hug" is the feeling you get in your chest when you chew on your bourbon before you swallow it, versus a "Kentucky burn," which is what you get when you down a shot quickly.

Tour guide Tim Delonjay leads a tour at the Stitzel-Weller Experience. *Author photo*

There's no reason to be a snob about bourbon, he added. "There's no bad bourbon, only better bourbon."

Over the next few hours, we toured the Whiskey Row visitors' centers of Old Forester and Evan Williams and the ultra-modern operation of Rabbit Hole, which does all its distilling and bottling in a former tire factory on Jefferson Street. Old Forester is part of the Brown-Forman Corporation, which also owns the Jack Daniel's Tennessee Whiskey brand.[106] Founder George Garvin Brown was a stickler for quality and was the first distiller who sold his bourbon in sealed glass bottles only, twenty-five years before Congress passed the Bottled-in-Bond Act. That way it supposedly couldn't be watered down by unscrupulous proprietors of bars and liquor stores. In a vain attempt to fight off Prohibition, Brown published a book in 1910 called

GEORGE G. BROWN,
Pres. Brown-Forman Co., Distillers.

A cartoon depicts Brown-Forman founder George G. Brown, who used Bible passages to argue against Prohibition. *Courtesy Brown-Forman Archives*

Barrels of bourbon age at the Old Forester visitor center on Louisville's Whiskey Row. *Leo Smith photo*

The Holy Bible Repudiates Prohibition, in which he quoted every verse in the Bible that mentioned imbibing alcohol. While he insisted that he abhorred drunkenness, in the introduction to his book he thundered, "I am undertaking to expose what I conceive to be the most dangerous propaganda against civil and religious liberty that has ever confronted the American people—'Prohibition'."

Brown died in 1917 but his company survived Prohibition as one of the lucky distilleries licensed to produce spirits for medicinal purposes.

Shortly after Prohibition was put in place, a Chicago attorney named George Remus figured out a way to get rich by exploiting the medicinal alcohol loophole. His fabulous rise and fall over a period of three years may have inspired Fitzgerald's development of Jay Gatsby, and lore from the Seelbach Hotel even claims the author and the bootlegger met in the Rathskeller, though Fitzgerald scholars scoff at that. Still, there are plenty of Gatsby-Remus similarities, and the story of his criminal career and trial was heavily covered in the press. There is no way Fitzgerald—or anyone living in America at the time—could have been unaware of it.

The Remus story has inspired full-length books, including Karen Abbott's fascinating *Ghosts of Eden Park: The Bootleg King, the Women Who Pursued Him and the Murder That Shocked Jazz-Age America*. If you are a fan of HBO's *Boardwalk Empire*, you will recognize some of the names in the convoluted tale from Abbott's book that I am attempting to distill into a few paragraphs.

George Remus was born in Germany and emigrated to the United States as a small child. His first career was in a pharmacy, working under the tutelage of an uncle. He went on to complete law school and set up a criminal-defense practice in Chicago, where he became famous for his courtroom histrionics. His fans called him "the Napoleon of the Chicago Bar." Meanwhile, George fell in love—shades of *Seinfeld!*—with a cleaning woman in his building. Imogene was a voluptuous, dark-haired woman who seems to fit the description of Myrtle, Tom Buchanan's mistress in *The Great Gatsby*: "a thickish woman . . . she carried her surplus flesh sensuously as some women can . . . there was an immediately perceptible vitality about her as if the nerves of her body were continually smoldering." Remus adored her beyond reason. They divorced their spouses and married in June 1920 in Newport, Kentucky and settled in nearby Cincinnati.

By then, the couple had embarked on a new business model that George called "the Circle." He had begun 1920 defending Prohibition offenders and was astounded by the kind of money they were making. Determined to get rich, Remus drew on his experience as a licensed pharmacist to buy wholesale pharmacy companies and drugstores—under fictitious names—and idled distilleries, beginning with one in Covington, Kentucky. He bribed local Prohibition officials to ignore his activities as he "milked" the distilleries of booze and replaced the good stuff with water and ethyl alcohol. In 1921, he was able to get genuine federal withdrawal permits through bribes paid to an official at the Harding Justice Department, so he could legally sell his

Even from the grave, King of the Bootleggers George Remus inspired a line of bourbon. *Courtesy George Remus Bourbon* liquor. But the real genius of the Circle was that he hired men to high-jack his own trucks of booze and take them to an isolated farm he bought near Cincinnati. The road to the warehouse was so heavily guarded that it became known as Death Valley. Soon, the business George and Imogene ran employed three thousand men (doubtless many of whom had held legal jobs in the distillery industry before Prohibition) and controlled more than a third of the liquor in the country.

The money didn't just roll in, it cascaded in. Even with the bribes he was paying—and they included hundreds of thousands doled out to a close associate of Attorney General Harry Daugherty—even Remus couldn't account for it all. It has been estimated that his net worth grew from $8,000 to more than $3 million in just thirteen months—$51 million in current value.[107] He began dressing in silk shirts and bespoke suits, eschewed underwear, and referred to himself in the third person: "Remus was in the whiskey business and Remus was the biggest man in the business." He covered his beloved Imogene in furs and jewels and indulged her every wish. As a wedding gift, he bought her a thirty-one-room mansion in Cincinnati, decorated in vul-garly opulent style—including a solid gold piano—and added an indoor swimming pool that he dubbed the Imogene Baths. Gatsby, whose fortune seemed to be built on bootlegging, illegal gambling, and confidence games, said that it took him just three years to earn the money to buy his spread on Long Island; it took Remus less than two.

Gatsby's famous summer parties were outshone by the one the Remuses threw on New Year's Eve 1921. Remus lighted his guests' cigars with hundred-dollar bills, put a thousand-dollar bill under each dinner plate, and presented diamond stickpins to the male guests and brand-new Pontiacs to the women. When the center of the festivities shifted to the Imogene Baths, Remus dove into the pool in his tuxedo, but then bid his guests good night and retired, Gatsby-like, to his handsomely appointed library, to enjoy a bowl of ice cream as he read a biography of Abraham Lincoln. Unlike his guests, Remus never drank.

Even as Remus saw out the year in gaudy fashion, the net was closing in on him. Mabel Walker Willebrandt, the U.S. assistant attorney general for Prohibition enforcement, had targeted him for her first case. The "Portia of Prohibition," as she was called in the press, was earnest and relentless, and Remus's last hope, the Justice Department official he had bribed who had repeatedly assured him he would never serve time, blew his brains out in Attorney General Daugherty's Washington apartment in June 1923. The following January, Remus began serving a two-year sentence at the federal penitentiary in Atlanta. He later admitted, "Not one scruple [an apothecary measurement equal to about a tenth of an ounce] of liquor prescribed by physicians is ever used for medicine."

There is more to this story—much more—but I will take it up in the next chapter, which involves some rum-running brothers in Savannah.

Mabel Walker Willebrandt's net also scooped up a supposedly "bone dry" Republican Kentucky congressman, John Wesley Langley, who was convicted under the Volstead Act of getting millions of gallons of "medicinal" whiskey released and selling it to New York bootleggers, as well as trying to bribe a Prohibition official. The character witnesses at his trial included the current and former Kentucky governors. Willebrandt wrote to her parents, " . . . if a Congressman is sent to the penitentiary it will do more to clean up Prohibition enforcement in this country than anything else." She won the conviction—the only conviction of a member of Congress during Prohibition. Langley appealed his case all the way to the Supreme Court—winning re-election in the process— then in 1926 resigned from office and presented himself at the Atlanta pen (where George Remus had recently vacated his cell) for a two-year stretch. His wife, Katherine, won his congressional seat on a sympathy vote and served two tumultuous terms. Langley tried to make a comeback after publishing a political memoir, *They Tried to Crucify Me or the Smokescreen of the Cumberlands*, but his wife issued a statement from her Washington office that she would not step aside "for John or anyone else."[108] Her husband backed down, but she lost to a Democratic challenger in 1930. The Langleys rest in peace in Pikeville, Kentucky—in separate cemeteries.

Assistant Attorney General Mabel Walker Willebrandt was dubbed "the Portia of Prohibition." *Library of Congress*

John Wesley Langley was convicted of Volstead Act violations. *Collection of the U.S. House of Representatives*

THE KENTUCKY MULE

- 1½ oz. bourbon
- ½ oz. Rose's Sweetened Lime Juice
- Ginger beer to top

Build the drink in a copper mug, beginning with lots of ice. Add the bourbon and lime juice, then top with ginger beer. Stir, and squeeze a fresh lime wedge over the drink for an extra kick of flavor. You've probably figured out that this is the Kentucky version of the classic Moscow Mule, which is made with vodka. Author's tried-and-true recipe.

THE OLD FASHIONED

Tom Bullock, an African American man born in Kentucky shortly after the Civil War, was a popular bartender in some of the most exclusive clubs in Louisville and St. Louis. He was the first black man to publish a cocktail recipe book, *The Ideal Bartender*, in 1917, that contained 150 pre-Prohibition drinks, including his orange-less version of the Old Fashioned. He called it simply "The Old Fashion Cocktail." Here is his recipe, just as he presented it:[109]

Master mixologist Tom Bullock. *americantable.com*

Use a Toddy glass.

- 1 lump of Ice.
- 2 dashes of Angostura Bitters.
- 1 lump of Sugar and dissolve in Water.
- 1½ Jiggers of Bourbon Whiskey.

Twist piece of Lemon Skin over the drink and drop it in. Stir well and serve.

Back in Louisville, Leo and I wound up our day of bourbon-tasting at a speakeasy on the backside of Whiskey Row called Hell or High Water. A white globe light with the words "Hello Curio" was the only indication there was anything of interest inside. We walked into a small reception room, its walls decorated with old postcards and oddities as well as a 1921 map of Louisville, where an unsmiling young man eventually led us down a nondescript corridor into the speakeasy.

As you know, Prohibition speakeasies ran the gamut, from dingy backrooms with a board laid across two barrels to serve as the bar to posh night clubs with live entertainment. Hell or High Water is of the latter type. The first room contained a long bar and deep red velvet-covered banquettes arranged in cozy corners. Recordings of period music, including the standard "Happy Days Are Here Again," played throughout the speak, but in a low-key way, emanating from vintage radios wired into the sound system. Our waitress took us upstairs to a table for two on a balcony overlooking the main room, which was arranged as a library, complete with walls of old books. A nook beside our table also held shelves of books, accented with vintage items like box cameras and art deco bookends, and while waiting for our drinks, I slipped over there and perused an authentic copy of the *Anti-Saloon League Yearbook* for 1930, which included President Herbert Hoover's recommendations to Congress for tightening enforcement of the Volstead Act. Among them was expanding federal prisons, about a third of whose inmates were Prohibition offenders.

I ordered the night's drink special, Moon River, mostly because it was gin based and my tongue was worn out by all the bourbon tasting I had done that day. As Leo and I sipped and took in the scene, we noticed waiters slipping into an armoire behind our table, and realized it was a speak within the speak. Of course, we thoroughly inspected the private room after the party inside decamped.

The ladies' room had a list of rules posted, including one reminding guests that there are "no cells in hell, so keep electronics in your pocket." The final rule reminded guests to say their good-byes indoors, "so you can slip away into the night quietly."

Drinks at Hell or High Water speakeasy in Louisville were as tasty as they were attractive. The reading material was interesting too. *Author photo*

That is just what we did, walking back to the Seelbach through the Fourth Street Arcade, where a Mardi Gras party was apparently gearing up or winding down—it was hard to tell which. On the corner outside the hotel, a young man with a Bible and a mic was preaching at a high volume. He had just gotten to the part about Jesus dying on the cross for our sins when I walked past him.

I had spent the day consorting with "bootleggers." It was fitting that I should end it with a Baptist.

PROHIBITION EXPEDITION

Seelbach Hilton Hotel and **Old Seelbach Bar**
500 South 4th Street, Louisville • www.seelbachhilton.com

The Brown Hotel and Lobby Bar
335 West Broadway, Louisville • www.brownhotel.com

Frazier History Museum
829 W. Main Street, Louisville • www.fraziermuseum.org

The **Frazier History Museum** is the starting point for the Kentucky Bourbon Trails, with a welcome center, activities, and special exhibits such as the Bourbon Bottle Hall, which displays bottles of every bourbon whiskey currently being produced in Kentucky. One of its regular programs is a monologue by a "teaching artist" portraying the bartender at the Seelbach, telling the story of the rise and fall of George Remus.

Stilzel-Weller Distillery
3860 Fitzgerald Road • https://www.bulleit.com/visit-us/stitzel-weller-distillery/

Old Forester Bourbon Distilling Company
119 West Main Street, Louisville • www.OldForester.com

Evan Williams Bourbon Experience
528 West Main Street, Louisville • www.evanwilliamsbourbonexperience.com

Rabbit Hole • 711 E. Jefferson Street, Louisville • www.rabbitholedistillery.com

Hell or High Water Bar
112 W. Washington Street, Louisville • www.hellorhighwaterbar.com

Kentucky Bourbon Trail helps you map out your own tours in Louisville and other regions of Kentucky. www.kybourbontrail.com

CEMETERY SIDE TRIP

George Garvin Brown, founder of the Brown-Forman Distillery, is buried in Cave Hill Cemetery in Louisville.[110] Another nineteenth century gem of a cemetery, studded with ornamental graves and mausoleums and shaded with 6,000 trees, Cave Hill has so many distillers among its "residents" that its heritage foundation periodically schedules a Bourbon Distillers of Cave Hill Wagon Tour. In addition, Cave Hill is the resting place of Colonel Harland Sanders, founder of Kentucky Fried Chicken, and Meriwether Lewis Clark, grandson of explorer William Clark, who started the Churchill Downs racetrack and the Kentucky Derby. 701 Baxter Avenue. https:// www.cavehillheritagefoundation.org/

RECOMMENDED READING

How to Be a Bourbon Badass by Linda Ruffenach (Bloomington, IN: Red Lightning Books, 2018) is a blast. Besides the drink recipes, it's full of recipes for dishes that, naturally, call for a little bourbon, and are especially delicious when eaten with bourbon.

Bourbon Empire: The Past and Future of America's Whiskey by Reid Mitenbuler (New York: Viking, 2015) is a comprehensive and myth-busting examination of the bourbon business, from colonial times to modern day. Be sure and read page 141, which tells you which of the mid-priced brands are actually much better values than the high-priced stuff.

CHAPTER EIGHT

*R*UMRUNNERS

ON A BALMY SATURDAY AFTERNOON in late summer, I settled on a bar stool at Swamp Fox Distilling on the historic village green of Pendleton, South Carolina and ordered a classic Cuba Libre, better known as a rum and Coke. After one sip of the drink served over crushed ice by distiller Ernie Wagner, I knew I wasn't drinking the rotgut stuff swilled by colonial sailors. Two sips and I thought, *If the real Swamp Fox, Francis Marion, had been offered this stuff, he might not have jumped out of that second-story window and broken his ankle and become a guerilla leader in the Revolutionary War.* That led to all sorts of "what if" thoughts about America still being a British colony. But the more I sipped, the more I thought it was a good thing that Prohibition gave rum a second chance in America.

Whiskey and bourbon had long been the favored spirits here, with beer becoming a more dominant player in the alcoholic beverage market during the decades before Prohibition. Once the legal tap was turned off, moonshine began flooding out of home-made stills and rum from the Caribbean was smuggled into ports all up and down the east coast. Although the smugglers also brought bottles of French brandy and Scotch whiskey picked up in Nassau—exports of Scotch to the Bahamas rose from 25,000 gallons in 1920 to nearly six million gallons a decade later[111]—the practice of liquor smuggling became known as rum-running. At the peak of the rum-running period, it was estimated by a Coast Guard historian that ten million quarts of booze of all kinds passed through the Bahamas in a single year. The formerly hard-up colonial government took full advantage of the boom, slapping on a tariff and using it to fund public projects ranging from an improved harbor to paved roads to a sewer system for Nassau. Writes Daniel Okrent in *Last Call*, the colony's British governor said it would be appropriate to erect a monument to Andrew J. Volstead near those honoring Christopher Columbus and Queen Victoria.[112]

Gertrude Cecilia Lythgoe, nicknamed "Cleopatra" because of her dark hair, eyes, and complexion, and exotic clothing, was an American woman who brokered alcohol sales for two London export firms out of Nassau in these early "rum rush" days. She was the only woman in the business, and proud of it, telling a reporter from the *London Daily News* that her stuff was the best, no matter what he heard on the street. She also pointed out that what she was doing was quite legal; it wasn't her fault if the people buying her booze were smuggling it to America. (The reporter was apparently quite smitten, describing her as a "charming and romantic figure . . . who would grace any London drawing room."[113]) However, she knew how to be tough when the situation demanded it. When she heard a man had been bad-mouthing the quality of her liquor, she confronted him at his barber shop—his face covered with lather—hauled him off to her office and warned him she would "put a bullet through him as sure as he sat there. He went away mighty quick."[114]

This is a portrait of Gertrude Lythgoe that appeared in the book *With the Whiskey Smugglers* by H. De Winton Wigley. He was the *London Daily News* "secret service agent on the American Coast."

In her memoir *The Bahama Queen*, Lythgoe wrote that the earliest smugglers were small operators, many of whom had previously used their boats for fishing. One of these was the celebrated rumrunner Bill McCoy, who became her good friend and took her along on one of his smuggling adventures.[115] A teetotaler whose Jacksonville, Florida-based boatyard had hit on hard times, he recognized a good opportunity for a seasoned captain like himself and turned to smuggling with his

brother, Ben, in 1920. McCoy was known
for his insistence on quality booze—none
of the stuff "stretched" with additives
such as prune juice or distilled water or
worse. Tall, tanned, and handsome, he
ran a clean operation and charged top dol-
lar for his goods. Eventually he had five
smuggling boats under his command and
moved an estimated two million bottles
of booze.[116] McCoy said in his autobiography that he went into rum-running for the
cash and stayed for the fun.

McCoy takes credit for establishing
the congregations of smugglers' boats
three miles offshore, outside the jurisdiction of the Coast Guard, dubbed "Rum
Row." Smaller, swifter motorboats, some
manned by individuals looking for just
a bottle or two, others by bootleggers
seeking large quantities for distribution,

Bill McCoy, one of the earliest rumrunners, was known for the quality of his
products. *U.S. Coast Guard*

buzzed around the large schooners, comparing prices and making deals.
There were Rum Rows located in international waters off Southern ports
as well as Montauk, New York, and Atlantic City, New Jersey, where large
schooners like McCoy's two-masted ship the *Tomoka* transported liquor
from the Caribbean as well as Canada and Europe. Eventually, "anything
with a bottom that could float and a hold that could be filled with booze," as
McCoy put it, formed a wall of liquor warehouses from the Gulf of Mexico
all the way to Maine, stocked by deliveries from rumrunners.[117] McCoy is
also credited with inventing the "ham," six bottles stacked pyramid-style,
wrapped in straw and sewn into burlap bags, which squeezed every inch of
available space from a ship's hold.

Some landlubbers got into the smuggling trade too. In his book *Southern
Spirits*, Robert F. Moss points out that many German grocery store owners ran saloons as an adjunct to their food business. Once saloons became
illegal, they converted them into blind tigers, using the legitimate grocery store as a cover and money laundry. This is what Vincent Chicco of
Charleston did, first flouting the state dispensary system, then statewide

and national Prohibition. His counterpart in Savannah, Georgia, was Frederick Haar, who had emigrated from Germany in the 1880s and opened a grocery store-cum-saloon.

"He and his son, William, were arrested several times between 1909 and 1916 for violations of state prohibition laws, and they stepped up their activities once Prohibition became nationwide," Moss wrote in his book. And how! Fred, Willie, and Fred's other two sons, Carl and Fred Jr., controlled a fleet of schooners that smuggled in booze not only from the Caribbean but from as far away as France and Scotland. Then, they put the bottles in grocery boxes and sent them off via train and truck to points near and far, adding bootlegging to their services. They were so cavalier about their activities that they fielded a recreational baseball squad called the Bootlegger Team.

Enter Mabel Walker Willebrandt, the determined and utterly incorruptible assistant U.S. attorney general for Prohibition enforcement. Willebrandt is the author of the then-novel concept of prosecuting people who did not pay taxes on illegal income, which she successfully argued before the Supreme Court in 1922. (In 1932, not long after she left office, a U.S. attorney in Chicago used this strategy to finally put Al Capone behind bars.) In 1923 Willebrandt and her staff pursued the Haars and members of three other families in business with them for income tax evasion, proving through study of the grocery business's confiscated financial records that they couldn't possibly have achieved their fabulous income through the sale of humble flour and potatoes.

"The number of millionaires created by violation of the Prohibition law is amazing," Willebrandt wrote in her acerbic 1929 book *The Inside of Prohibition*. She said that the ringleader in the Savannah Four, Willie Haar, had in three years "derived such profits from the importation of liquor and other illegal operations that he was reassessed income taxes in the sum of $1,243,254.29. Another owed $301,816.09. Lesser fry in the organization had dodged taxes ranging from $245,000 to $53,000."[118]

The case was a sensational success, sending all four Haars and many of their cohorts to prison, though the government collected just a fraction of the income tax they owed. At the Atlanta federal penitentiary, Willie Haar's next-cell neighbor was George Remus, with whom he no doubt commiserated about their treatment by Willebrandt and Franklin Dodge, Willebrandt's fair-haired boy in the Prohibition Bureau, who had been instrumental in getting them both arrested. Remus would soon have an even better reason to hate Agent Dodge.

The legendary Bill McCoy's days as a rumrunner were numbered by then. He was finally caught red-handed in 1923, pled guilty, and served nine months in prison. Upon his release, he returned to his boatbuilding business in Florida and lived quietly until his death in 1948 at age seventy-one. Big operators and organized crime had muscled in on the "business"—for gangsters indeed used accepted business methods, coupled with bombs and tommy guns as incentives—and brought efficiency to their operations. McCoy probably would not have continued to have fun (or breathe) had he not been arrested, for rum-running had taken a very dark turn. Meyer Lansky, whose New York gang made his first fortune during Prohibition with associates Bugsy Siegel and Lucky Luciano, said they chartered their own ships to bring Scotch directly from Scotland to America, cutting out Bahamian tariffs and middlemen like McCoy. "By the middle twenties we were running the most efficient international shipping business in the world," Lansky said in a late-in-life interview.[119] About this time "Cleopatra" Lythgoe left the trade too, eventually living in Detroit, where she became a pioneer in the rental car business and lived a long, peaceful life.[120]

Once criminal gangs got involved in rum-running, the stakes got high and most of the fun McCoy had so enjoyed went away. Gangs fought over territory, hijacked each other's booze, and left piles of bodies in their wake. Willebrandt eventually turned the focus of her rum-running prosecutions to Florida, which she termed the "leakiest" state in the country, with mixed success. She went after a female rumrunner known as "Spanish Marie" Waite, who took over her husband's illegal enterprise in 1926 after his body washed ashore at Miami's Biscayne Bay, apparently after a run-in with one of his competitors. Writes Sarah Baird in *Saveur* magazine, "Standing six feet tall and with a personality that ran notoriously hot and cold, she swiftly and single-handedly built a boozy empire. Waite used a fleet of four convoy-style boats to move her liquor between Havana and Key West, then a flotilla of fifteen radio-capable speedboats to distribute the wares to various ports along Florida's southern tip."[121]

Although Willebrandt's arsenal included a ramped-up Coast Guard and expansion of the three-mile limit to twelve miles, Waite was able to elude capture and by 1927 she was said to have earned close to $1 million in illegal gains. Finally, in a crackdown begun in January 1928, Willebrandt coordinated her office's efforts with the Coast Guard to saturate the south Florida waters with eleven destroyers, almost a hundred smaller boats, and two amphibian planes, along with over a thousand Coast Guard members. This armada started picking up rumrunners left and right, and in March, Spanish Marie was caught overseeing the unloading of cargo from her flagship *Kid Boots* at Coconut Grove. Playing the mother card, she pled to be allowed to return home where she said she had left two small children sleeping and posted a $500 bond. She was never seen again, a fact Willebrandt did not include in her self-congratulatory account of the case.[122]

Nevertheless, Willebrandt considered her four-month-long Florida campaign a great success, bragging that over a hundred liquor-running vessels were seized, temporarily driving up the price of illegal booze in Florida from $35 a case to $125.

One of the most difficult challenges Willebrandt and her "Mablemen" faced was the downright disdain large swaths of the public had for the Prohibition laws. In his book *Rum Row: The Liquor Fleet that Fueled the Roaring Twenties*, Robert Carse stated bluntly, "A Coast Guard picket boat that pulled alongside a suspect craft could not fire. Mayors, judges, lawyers, doctors, businessmen were at the rail, exhibiting rods and the day's catch, threatening demotion or transfer to distant, isolated stations for the Coast Guard crew if the boat were stopped and searched."[123] In South Jacksonville, Carse continued, the mayor, police chief, president of the city council, county commissioner, and fire chief were all indicted for Volstead Act violations.[124]

Willebrandt recounted the case of a "dry" Republican congressman, Magne Michaelson of Illinois, who was caught smuggling a barrel of rum and a dozen bottles of assorted liquors in his luggage when returning home from a trip abroad through a Florida port. He was acquitted by a Florida jury when his brother-in-law, who was traveling with him, took the fall.[125]

The congressman's assumption of privilege was echoed by the activities of another prominent politician, Franklin Delano Roosevelt, while spending several winters in the early 1920s on a ramshackle houseboat off the Florida coast, his private secretary Marguerite "Missy" LeHand serving as his hostess. FDR had been stricken with polio in 1921 and hoped swimming and sunning would restore his legs. When a friend sent him a flag for the boat, FDR enthused, "I will take it south with me and some day . . . 'hist' the old rag to the mast-head and salute it with 17 rum swizzles." The guests on

Franklin Delano Roosevelt, with his private secretary Missy LeHand and friend Maunsell Crosby, relaxes on a Florida beach during one of his grog-soaked winter cruises in the early 1920s. Note the condition of his legs after his bout with polio. *Courtesy Steven Lomazow, M.D.*

his houseboat ended each day with supper, often the fish they had caught that day, and "grog." One of his guests wrote an ode to the boat, saying its "cargo was gin and rye."[126]

With bootleggers plying the halls of Congress and large swaths of public officials and police on the take, it's no wonder the public took advantage of situations that came its way. When a rumrunner's boat loaded with fine wines and whiskey foundered off the coast of Myrtle Beach, South Carolina, and the crew abandoned ship, the news spread "as if flares had been lit or rockets fired," wrote Blanche Floyd in *Sandlapper* magazine. People in small boats unloaded the cargo and took it to shore, where anyone who could commandeer a cart, wheelbarrow, or even a child's wagon arrived to haul off the loot. The investigation that followed turned up nobody who knew anything.[127]

BERMUDA RUM SWIZZLE

- 2 oz. dark rum
- 1 oz. lime juice
- 1 oz. pineapple juice
- 1 oz. orange juice
- Generous dash of falernum syrup

Shake well and strain into a highball glass filled with ice. Garnish with a slice of orange and a cherry.

—From Jean Edward Smith's FDR *(New York, Random House, 2007)*

SWAMP FOX DISTILLING

128 Exchange Street, Pendleton, South Carolina
www.swampfoxdistilling.com

Ernie Wagner had thirty years of home brewing beer and an abiding love of rum under his belt when he decided to open a rum distillery in Pendleton. He and his wife, Peg, were attracted to the town when their daughter, Stefanie, graduated from nearby Clemson University, married, and presented them with a grandchild. Today, Peg, Stefanie, and their other two daughters, Jenna and Kristen, all pitch in at the family business, along with their ambassador dog, Berkeley, a huge Bernese mountain dog named for the county where Francis Marion lived.

Wagner's research took him to distilleries around the country and the Caribbean. He eventually bought a hundred-year-old building in Pendleton that had once housed a grocery store and a 250-gallon copper still made in Portugal. His ingredients are simple: sugar cane from a family-owned plantation in Louisiana, blackstrap molasses, and a rum yeast from Barbados. "Knowing our rum would be bolder than most, we wanted to name the rum brand to reflect the character," he said. "'Pure Corruption' became that name and fits the rum perfectly."

The distillery opened in November 2019 and despite the unexpected hit it took due to the coronavirus pandemic a few months later, Ernie sold all the rum he could make. (He also made lavender-scented hand sanitizer, which he gives to his patrons.) The distillery is his only sales point.

Berkeley, a Bernese mountain dog, is the official canine ambassador at Swamp Fox Distilling in Pendleton, South Carolina. *Author photo*

Swamp Fox Distilling offers both pure Naked Rum and six flavored rums. The Naked Rum, with its pleasant notes of vanilla, is a good mixer with anything, including the North Carolina soft drink Cheerwine, which Ernie and Peg have combined in a cocktail they dubbed the South Carolina Special. Before I had left the bar, I had also tried a drink they call the Dreamsicle, made of their orange-flavored All In rum, a tip of the hat to Clemson Tigers "All In" football coach Dabo Swinney. It was like drinking a liquid version of the childhood ice cream treat. Cream soda is also the mixer with their coconut-flavored rum, which tastes like a Mounds bar with a kick. Like moonshine and vodka, rum can be consumed right out of the still, but Ernie has also put some aside in white oak barrels to age.

Because of South Carolina licensing laws, Swamp Fox operates under liquor store hours and is limited in how much unbottled product it can serve as samples or in mixed drinks. The restrictions, which the South Carolina legislature has loosened a bit with the advent of the distillery business, are one of the many legacies of Prohibition. ■

The public's sympathy for the felons who supplied their adult beverages was fully evident in 1928 when Jacksonville's "Whiskey King" John Batson Hysler Sr., a supplier for Al Capone, was involved in a shoot-out with a Prohibition agent on the city's St. Johns River expansion bridge. In the exchange of gunfire, Hysler died and the agent was badly wounded. Mabel Willebrandt was still outraged when she wrote about the case a year later. "While the agent lay at the point of death in the hospital," she fumed, "the state authorities, as the result of sensational and unwarranted press reports which inflamed the public mind, and following threats of death from the deceased's associates, endeavored to obtain an indictment for murder against an officer who had risked his life in the performance of a legal duty, and who had not shot until after being thrown in the road, wounded, and then only in self-defense."[128]

Even in this environment, law enforcement had some unqualified successes. J. E. McTeer of Beaufort County, South Carolina, became, at twenty-three, the youngest sheriff in the country when he succeeded his late father in the early years of Prohibition. In his entertaining memoir *High Sheriff of the Low Country*, he recounts the capture of a ship out of Nassau that held "eight hundred cases of high-grade liquor." The local court ordered him to destroy it all.

"With the help of the county chain gang," he wrote, "all eight hundred cases of bottles were broken and drained into the Beaufort River. The entire town turned out to watch, and the Associated Press covered the story for the nation's newspapers. Headlines across the country read, 'Fish Get Drunk as Contraband Liquor is Destroyed.' One reporter even had a drunk trout chase a porpoise up onto the bank."[129]

J. E. McTeer became the youngest sheriff in the country and a dedicated foe of bootleggers and rum-runners in Beaufort County, South Carolina.

Tragedy was narrowly averted when McTeer and his deputies captured a convoy of trucks loaded with liquor and were driving it back to Beaufort. As they rounded a curve, armed men came running out of the woods shouting, "Stop! Don't move or we'll shoot." It was only by chance that one of the men recognized McTeer and called out, "For God's sake, don't shoot! It's Sheriff McTeer!" The ambush squad were federal Prohibition agents from Savannah.[130]

That Keystone Kops moment brings us back to George Remus and Willie Haar, who we left sitting in adjoining cells in the federal pen in Atlanta in 1924. While his Volstead Act conviction was being appealed, Remus, his wife, Imogene, and some other bootleggers had purchased the Jack Daniel's distillery in St. Louis. (It had relocated from Tennessee in 1910 to dodge the newly enacted state prohibition law, but its warehouse was locked down ten years later under national Prohibition.) Their plan was to very gradually "milk" the whiskey out of the barrels, replacing the good stuff pumped out with water and ethyl alcohol so federal inspectors wouldn't suspect anything was amiss. Remus soon learned his partners had gotten greedy and were pumping whiskey around the clock. Worse, he wasn't getting any of the money, and his appeals in his original case had been exhausted. Remus presented himself at the prison in January 1924, and Mabel Willebrandt sent a team of Prohibition agents, included her pet, Franklin Dodge, to St. Louis to investigate the activity at Jack Daniel's.

Federal Prison, Atlanta, Ga.—4

A vintage postcard depicts the federal penitentiary in Atlanta where George Remus and Willie Haar became acquainted. *Author collection*

The prison in Fulton County, which is still in use today, was one of the first federal prisons in the country. Opened in 1902, it had 330 cells meant to hold three times as many prisoners and was considered very modern, with amenities such as electric lights and sanitary plumbing. Its early "guests" included scammer Charles Ponzi, notorious bank robber Roy Gardner, labor leader Eugene V. Debs (who ran for president as a socialist while incarcerated), and black activist Marcus Garvey.[131] Later inmates would include Al Capone and con artist and forger Frank Abagnale, who inspired the movie *Catch Me If You Can.*

The warden was a political hack appointed by President Harding's famously corrupt attorney general, Harry Daugherty, and was, naturally, susceptible to bribes. Haar and his cronies paid to get cushy jobs and cozy cells in the prison, and Remus's "donations" to the warden enabled him to equip his cell with a fine new mattress and bedding and a refrigerator. He was even allowed to eat his meals apart from the prison population. According to Karen Abbott in *The Ghosts of Eden Park*, George would have Willie over to dinner where they feasted on catered meals at a table laid with snow-white linen, then whiled away the evenings playing high-stakes poker. Imogene Remus stayed at the posh Georgian Terrace Hotel on Peachtree Street, and daily visited her husband with fresh flowers and tasty dishes, even scrubbing the floor of his cell for him. Nevertheless, Remus was restless and angry, and sometimes took his frustrations out on Imogene.

And that brings us back to Assistant Attorney General Willebrandt's fair-haired boy, Franklin Dodge. He and a team of Prohibition agents had been gathering evidence in the Jack Daniel's distillery case, and in May 1924, Willebrandt lowered the boom. She issued indictments for both George and Imogene Remus and their bootlegger partners. Imogene feigned ignorance, saying she had no idea what "Daddy" had been up to. Having gotten wind that Remus was living like a king behind bars and intimidating potential witnesses in the Jack Daniel's case, Willebrandt dispatched Dodge to Atlanta. Remus willingly met with him, feeling sure he could charm the agent and bribe him onto his team, as he had with countless other law enforcement officials. Just to be safe, he urged Imogene to "Play up to him, because he is the last chance to help me get out of jail."[132]

Willebrandt's focus on the Atlanta pen had widened considerably beyond George Remus. Discovering the corruption of the warden, she demanded his resignation and launched an investigation; ultimately, he would become an inmate of the prison himself. Meanwhile, Willie Haar had heard stories about just how much Imogene had been playing up to Franklin Dodge and shared them with his buddy George. At first Remus focused his anger on Haar, but eventually he realized the hard truth that Imogene was indeed having an affair with Dodge. Willebrandt, too, began hearing rumors and sent another Mableman to spy on him. She complained, "I found that there were scores of Prohibition agents no more fit to be trusted with a commission to enforce the laws of the United States and to carry a gun than the notorious bandit Jesse James." In August 1925, Dodge joined the ranks of more than 750 agents Willebrandt dismissed for misconduct.

When Remus was released from prison a few weeks later, he discovered his wife and Agent Dodge had cleaned him out, including removing all the furnishings from his Cincinnati mansion. On the way to his divorce hearing, he came upon Imogene and her daughter in a car, ran them off the road and chased his estranged wife into a public park. He shot her dead. At the murder trial, in which he served as his own attorney, he pled temporary insanity and was acquitted. He spent a short time in an asylum and then was released, living out his life in relative peace in Covington, Kentucky. He was seventy-nine when he died, and his third wife erected a sculptural grouping of a woman hoisted on the shoulders of two angels to watch over his grave. At some point, a vandal knocked the angels' wings off.

As we are fond of saying around my house, "You can't make this stuff up." Except we don't use such a polite word.

Regarding Willie Haar, my cursory internet search found mentions of him as a "wealthy Savannah businessman" who owned an entertainment complex. The jazz singer Thelma Terry and her Playboys performed there in the summer of 1928 and after the gig ended, Thelma quit and married Haar. They had a daughter, Patti, but divorced after five years of marriage.[133] Some members of the Haar family are buried at Savannah's famed Bonaventure Cemetery, but Willie's is not among the graves. Another member of the Haar gang, Johnny Harris, opened a tavern in 1924 that morphed into one of Savannah's favorite restaurants. The Johnny Harris Restaurant, famous for its barbecue and fried chicken, closed in 2016.

SCOFFLAW

- 1½ oz. Canadian whisky
- 1½ oz. French vermouth
- Juice of half a lemon
- 2 tsp. grenadine
- 1 dash orange bitters

Shake well with ice and strain into a cocktail glass.

—Adapted by the author from The Savoy Cocktail Book
(Reprint edition Mansfield Centre, CT: Martino Publishing, 2015)

AMERICAN PROHIBITION MUSEUM

The activities of the Haars and their fellow smugglers earned Savannah a new sobriquet, "The Spigot of the South." The title is celebrated today at the American Prohibition Museum, a vastly entertaining for-profit enterprise located in Savannah's City Market, a few blocks from the harbor. There visitors can get their pictures taken with a life-size wax mannequin of Carry Nation complete with hatchet, watch a short film of the dry evangelist Billy Sunday, who once ranted that "Savannah is the wickedest city in the world!" and pick up a few bartending skills at a cocktail-making class from the staff of the in-house speakeasy, 220 Congress Street Up. The museum is owned by Historic Tours of America, which also operates the Shipwreck Treasure Museum in Key West and the Boston Tea Party Museum. The staff at its Potters Wax Museum in St. Augustine, Florida creates the astoundingly realistic figures that bring exhibits to eerie life.

Leo and I arrived arrived at the Savannah museum on a stormy day in early summer. Stepping inside, we were propelled back into time to a city neighborhood in 1918, where women of the temperance movement waved signs reading "Bread Not Beer" and a Ford delivery truck piled high with beer barrels made a delivery to an Irish saloon, complete with a sodden drunk on the sidewalk. Above the display hung a sign with an anti-Prohibition quote from none other than Abraham Lincoln. (It was fictitious propaganda used after Lincoln's death by the wets in Atlanta.)

Visitors to the America Prohibition Museum step into the past as spirited temperance crusaders picket a saloon in a typical city street. *Leo Smith photo*

Other exhibits in the two-story, 5,500-square-foot museum include the lurid scene of a gangland slaying, an open car full of women cheering the enactment of the Eighteenth Amendment, and a display devoted to Anti-Saloon League leader Wayne B. Wheeler, including his quote "I don't care how a man drinks; I care how he votes." Visitors are encouraged to pose for selfies with the wax mannequins and are guided by "actors" in period dress. The museum opened in 2017, according to its Creative and Production Manager Travis Spangenburg, and had just shy of 100,000 visitors in 2019. It had taken a hit from the Covid-19 pandemic and when we visited during the summer it had just reopened, with signs about social distancing and hand washing everywhere, all cleverly designed to fit into the period theme.

The speakeasy in the heart of the museum is one of its most popular features. In a room full of vintage glassware and furniture and a tremendous bar, patrons to 220 Congress Street Up can enjoy drinks such as the Brown Derby and the Aviation. The bar is open during the day to museum visitors and after hours a couple of nights a week from a nondescript entrance in back. That's where Leo and I entered that evening when we came for our two-hour cocktail-making class.

Paul Rabe demonstrates his craft behind the bar at 220 Congress Street and Up, the speakeasy at the American Prohibition Museum. *Leo Smith photo*

Our very entertaining teacher, Paul Rabe, welcomed us with a cup of Chatham Artillery Punch, Savannah's oldest known cocktail, and introduced us to various bartending tools. As he led us through the steps of making several cocktails, he taught us tricks such as using two metal cups as a shaker, using the most expensive ingredients last so you waste less money if you have to start over with the drink, and shaking vigorously back and forth rather than up and down. (When I was successful in pulling my frozen cups apart and pouring my drink into a cocktail glass without spilling a drop, I was as proud as if I had just given birth!)

About Chatham Artillery Punch, Paul said, "This drink is the unofficial drink of Savannah because it was the official drink of the Chatham Artillery Regiment during the colonial era all the way through the Civil War. You have to think of the Chatham Artillery Regiment less as an organized militia and more as a group of drinking buddies that could shoot really well." Francis Marion, you have been warned! "This recipe is the oldest recipe that the American Prohibition Museum could find which is the simplest, strongest, and best version."

If you can't get to the museum, make a habit of visiting its Facebook page, which is full of pictures, videos, and trivia. You'll learn a lot about the "noble experiment."

American Prohibition Museum • 209 W. St. Julian Street, Savannah
www.americanprohibitionmuseum.com

CHATHAM ARTILLERY PUNCH

- 1 part rum (Bacardi)
- 1 part brandy (Sacred Bond)
- 1 part bourbon (Old Forrester)
- 1 part lemon juice
- 1 part simple syrup (or oleo saccharum)
- If batching, 1 part water or to taste (factor in whether or not you will ice the punch during service).
- 3 parts Champagne or any dry sparkling wine.

For a single drink, combine the first five ingredients in a shaker with ice. Shake well and strain into a tall glass. Top with Champagne.

For batching, combine first five ingredients and water. Either divide into bottles or keep batch whole and refrigerate until service. Add Champagne right before serving.

PROHIBITION EXPEDITION

Savannah has several speakeasy-type establishments, including **220 Congress Street Up** at the **American Prohibition Museum**. The same team that owns the Prohibition bar and restaurant in Charleston owns **Repeal 33**, 125 Martin Luther King Avenue, www.repeal33savannah.com

Mata Hari's Speakeasy operates under the rules of a 1920s joint in that you have to know the daily password to gain admission. It has no website and only a cursory Facebook page, is apparently very hard to find, and that is all by design. The reviews and pictures make this look like a fun place with live music and an authentic Prohibition feel. It even has a small theatre where burlesque shows are staged. I managed to speak to the owner, who said a number of hotels and B&Bs in Savannah are members of Mata Hari (including the **Marshall House**, an historic inn at 123 E. Broughton Street where Leo and I stayed, www.marshallhouse.com) and can provide you with the daily password. Or you could call her up and beg. If you have a particularly good pitch, she might even give the password to you! 912.272.2848.

The U.S. Penitentiary • 601 McDonough Blvd. SE, Atlanta

Unless you are visiting an inmate or are a qualified member of the press, you can't get inside the gates of this medium-security penitentiary, but you can get a look at the grim place in a drive-by or visit the website, https://www.bop.gov/locations/institutions/atl/, for a brief history lesson.

CEMETERY SIDE TRIP

Savannah's Bonaventure Cemetery, made famous by John Berendt's best-selling book *Midnight in the Garden of Good and Evil*, is the resting place of several members of the bootlegging **Haar** family.[134] Their markers are rather plain, but the cemetery is full of gorgeous Victorian memorials and celebrity graves, including that of popular songwriter and composer **Johnny Mercer**. You can walk around on your own using an app provided by the Bonaventure Historical Society (link on the website) or join a tour group. 330 Bonaventure Road. https://www.bonaventurehistorical.org

George Remus is buried in Riverside Cemetery in Falmouth, Kentucky, about two hours from Louisville.[135] Remus died in 1952 at age seventy-nine, having tried unsuccessfully to build a new business empire. According to Kentucky historian Cheri Daniels, who found the grave while "scoundrel hunting" in the cemetery where her grandparents are buried and took the accompanying photo, Remus's is the only one with statuary. His grave is ornamented with a statue of a woman hoisted on the shoulders of two angels. You can see in her photo where the angels' wings were knocked off. U.S. 27 at the intersections with Earle Avenue and Maple Avenue. https://www.countyoffice.org/falmouth-riverside-cemetery-falmouth-ky-415/

George Remus's grave, guarded by a woman hoisted on the shoulders of two wingless angels, is the most ostentatious in Riverside Cemetery. *Courtesy Cheri Daniels*

Bill McCoy died in Martin County, Florida, in 1948. His ashes were scattered at sea. **Gertrude Lythgoe** died in Los Angeles in 1974, but her burial site is unknown.

RECOMMENDED READING

Run the Rum In: South Florida During Prohibition by Sally J. Ling (Charleston: History Press, 2007)

Punch: The Delights (and Dangers) of the Flowing Bowl by David Wondrich (New York: TarcherPedigree, 2010) was recommended by bartender Paul Rabe at the American Prohibition Museum.

CHAPTER NINE

Making Moonshine

ARE THESE WHAT I think they are?

I was standing in the Dawsonville Moonshine Distillery during the Mountain Moonshine Festival in this small Georgia town that claims to be the birthplace of stock car racing, peering into a glass case full of long, curved bones. The label read, "Coon Dicks, $6.54." Coon dicks? The pretty young woman behind the counter told me that yes, that's just what they are, male raccoon genitalia. She explained that they are considered lucky, given to significant others as a sign of affection, and worn in hatbands. While privately reflecting that I would rather be given good jewelry as a sign of affection than a coon dick, I was reminded for the hundredth time that day that I had entered a different world when I traveled down Thunder Road.[136]

For decades before Prohibition and for decades afterward, Dawson County was one of the hotbeds of moonshine-making in the South. Georgia Highway 9, now officially dubbed Thunder Road by the Georgia Department of Transportation, linked the county seat of Dawsonville to Atlanta, sixty miles away. Generations of moonshine makers and fast-driving "trippers" made a precarious living producing and delivering corn "likker" to thirsty customers in the city. Similar markets evolved around mountain hamlets and every city of size in Alabama, Arkansas, the Carolinas,

A display of raccoon genitalia greets
visitors to the Dawsonville Moonshine
Distillery in Dawsonville, Georgia.
Author photo

Georgia, Kentucky, Tennessee, and Virginia, each with their own cast of
bootleggers and Baptists. In Florida and other Southern coastal states,
swamps provided handy cover for stills. Hell Hole Swamp in South Carolina's Berkeley County had been the domain of wealthy rice planters prior to
the Civil War, but afterward it was a desperately poor region whose people
turned to moonshine for the same reason the mountain folk did. When
Prohibition started, "stills sprang up like mushrooms," a local newsman
wrote.[137] But Dawsonville stands alone in its notoriety. With Georgia still
under state-wide prohibition a year after the Eighteenth Amendment was
repealed, nearly a million gallons of the estimated thirty-five million gallons of moonshine produced nationwide came from Dawson County and its
environs.[138] Moonshine flowed from the mountains for decades after Prohibition ended.

Neal Thompson writes in his riveting book *Driving with the Devil: Southern Moonshine, Detroit Wheels and the Birth of NASCAR*, "During Prohibition,
folks had developed a strong taste for the backwoods white lightning, which
offered the added pleasure of thumbing a nose at the federal government
up north. The repeal of Prohibition, therefore, instead of slowing the flow,
actually kicked off a heyday for Southern moonshine that would last until
World War II. It was a period in which a complex, emotional game of cat and
mouse was played out between bootleggers and their pursuers." Although
this "game" has been romanticized and even played for yucks in movies and
television shows, from the 1958 Robert Mitchum drama *Thunder Road* to
the 1979–86 TV sitcom *The Dukes of Hazzard* to today's quasi-reality show

Moonshiners, the illegal moonshine business was a violent one that left death and sorrow in its wake.

Moonshine-making in the mountains of Appalachia and the lowland swamps had pre-dated the Civil War, but it only became illegal after the Confederacy was defeated and the federal government imposed a heavy tax on liquor to help reduce the war debt. During Reconstruction, all-out "Moonshine Wars" erupted between the federal Department of Revenue officials—the hated "revenuers" who were sometimes backed by the military—and the farmers supplementing their pathetic incomes by turning their corn crop into 'shine, mostly keeping it in their own communities for barter or cash.

Once Reconstruction ended and the white Southern voters were electing their own leaders again—many of them former high-ranking officials and military leaders of the Confederacy, such as South Carolina's Governor Wade Hampton—there was a great deal of public sympathy for these self-described "blockaders." One of the most infamous was Lewis Redmond, a native of mountainous Transylvania County, North Carolina, who plied his trade in an area around Greenville County, South Carolina known as the Dark Corner. After shooting dead a U.S. deputy marshal—who had been a friend since childhood—Redmond went on the lam in the South Carolina mountains, becoming known as the King of the Outlaws. Robert Moss writes in his book *Southern Spirits*, "He became the very embodiment of the complex passions, motives, and myths that came to surround illegal liquor in the nineteenth century."[139]

Redmond's crimes included shooting two revenue agents who were trying to take him to jail, surrounding the home of one of the wounded men with a band of ruffians, kidnapping his wife and forcing her to cash a check for him, and then stealing the revenue man's best horse. That caught the attention of the U.S. commissioner of revenue, who declared all-out war on the moonshine makers of the Dark Corner—where it was said stills were "as thick as fleas in a hog pen"[140]—and on Redmond in particular. The outlaw's next caper

The handsome outlaw Lewis Redmond was seen as a folk hero by the poor farmers of South Carolina's "Dark Corner."
Transylvania Heritage

was freeing three of his men in broad daylight from the Pickens County Jail. An admiring reporter from the Charleston *News and Courier* procured an interview and described Redmond as "a man of striking beauty, not more than twenty-three years of age, of slender build, and mild manners," portraying him as a modern-day Robin Hood. The Northern press agreed he was handsome, but painted him as a modern-day pirate, "just the figure for a Bowery drama or a blood-curdling novel."[141]

Redmond was finally captured in Swain County, North Carolina in 1881, taking six bullets in the process. Southerners were outraged, and when he was released from prison in 1884, both former governor Wade Hampton and current governor Johnson Hagood saw him off at the station in Columbia and provided refreshments for his journey home to Pickens County. Not to be outdone, President Grover Cleveland issued him a pardon. Redmond spent the rest of his tumultuous life mostly on the right side of the law as a farmer and superintendent of a government-sanctioned distillery, leaving behind at his death, according to his obituary, "a practical, energetic wife and several children." The inscription on his simple gravestone reads, "He was the sunshine of our home."[142]

While Redmond's story of outlaws vs. lawmen is the more commonly told moonshine tale, violence and death were also doled out by rival moonshiners. In his book about moonshine making in the Dark Corner, *Used to Be a Rough Place in Them Hills*, Joshua Blackwell described a Sunday morning

A modern bumper sticker graces the bumper of a former moonshine runner's car at the Moonshine Festival. *Author photo*

shoot-out at a church in 1891. Church members included two rival clans, the Howards and the Gosnells, members of whom had been involved in a drunken altercation the night before. One of the Howards shot at one of the Gosnells and in seconds the churchyard erupted in gunfire, an estimated fifty rounds of ammunition discharged. When all the dust cleared, one of the Howards was dead, and members of both families had suffered egregious wounds, including a severed tongue. No one was ever charged. When the Greenville County sheriff arrived, "he was welcomed at the border of the community by an armed posse and persuaded to turn back toward his office in Greenville," Blackwell wrote.[143]

The people of Greenville, who were trying to attract northern industry investment and become part of the rising "New South," were horrified and embarrassed by the behavior of the people of the Dark Corner. "The Dark Corner of Greenville County has seceded from the United States of America and is now an independent country," sneered an editorial in the *Greenville Daily News*.[144] In the early twentieth century, the growing influence of the temperance movement—even among some of the churchgoers of the Dark Corner—and the Great War draft that sent young men from isolated communities into the larger world, had its dampening effects on traditional Appalachian life. Up to a point. State and national Prohibition made those snooty Greenvillians and residents of many other Southern cities thirsty for something their mountain cousins were happy to provide. And conveniently, in 1908 Henry Ford—one of the country's most ardent prohibitionists—rolled out his Model T that helped get the moonshine from the mountains and swamps to the cities.

Moonshine production amped up to a tremendous degree and, not surprisingly, the quality suffered. The main ingredient for corn liquor was, of course, corn. But the demands for moonshine were so great that makers began cutting corners. Their main ingredient became sugar, with a handful of corn meal tossed in for flavor. Good moonshine makers knew to throw out the first and last few quarts of a batch—the heads and tails—because they were filled with impurities. Prohibition moonshiners got careless about that. They adulterated their product with chemicals to produce the beading that, when a bottle was shaken, gave "white lightning" its name. They also got sloppy about the stills they made and which revenue agents and local law enforcement were destroying by the hundreds of thousands. They used car parts and lead leached into the hooch. Bad moonshine could get you blind drunk—but it could also leave you blind or severely ill. Some drinkers, in Southern parlance, "woke up dead."[145]

The advent of national Prohibition initiated another moonshine war fought between law enforcement and purveyors of corn liquor and between rival moonshiners. In Florida, a legendary lawman, James Edmund "Pistol Pete" Bowdoin, served as chief of police of the city of Palmetto in the early 1920s. Known for always wearing a fedora hat and a pair of pearl-handled pistols, he famously destroyed eleven stills in one afternoon. Such tenacity and honesty subsequently lost him the election for sheriff; apparently, he had deprived some of the muckety-mucks in town of income and liquid refreshments. At age sixty he became a federal Prohibition agent, serving near Tallahassee. While searching for stills one day, he was shot and killed, one of the 126 such agents who lost their lives while trying to enforce the Volstead Act. His gravestone is inscribed with the words, "Died February 16, 1925 in the service of his country and in the faithful performance of his duty as an officer of the law."

"Pistol Pete" Bowdoin was a fearless enforcer of the Volstead Act until he died in a shoot-out near a Florida still. *Officer Down Memorial Page, odmp.org*

In 1926 down in Berkeley County's Hell Hole Swamp—the same swamp where Francis Marion had bedeviled the British during the American Revolution[146]—feuding moonshiners had a shoot-out worthy of Al Capone's gang (who they were widely rumored to be supplying) on a highway near Moncks Corner. One man was killed and three seriously wounded. An encore engagement left one man dead and one seriously wounded. Incredibly, the federal government decided to intervene by hiring the head man of one of the gangs—whose brother had died in the first shoot-out—to clean up the county. Kingpin Glenn Doward McKnight led a hundred federal agents on a two-day raid that put thirty-three men behind bars and destroyed seventeen stills. Then he resigned and went right back to his life of crime.[147]

McKnight's notorious story was far from over. In 1930, a tubercular World War I veteran he was said to have hired, one W. L. "Sporty" Thornley, shot state Senator Edward J. Dennis on Moncks Corner's Main Street as he was buying a watermelon at a market. The senator died the next day in a Charleston hospital. Even the *New York Times* took notice, blaring in a headline "State Senator Shot in Carolina Feud," and describing the murder as "the latest episode in this county's bloody history of gunfights, ambushes, and assassinations of recent years."[148]

Of course, there are two sides to the story, one that puts Dennis, an attorney, in the "Baptist" camp as a strict enforcer of Prohibition, another that puts him in cahoots with the bootleggers, who he defended in his law practice.[149] Dennis's stature resulted in a massive response by law enforcement, with Thornley and several confederates being arrested and taken to the state prison in Columbia for safe keeping. Thornley soon confessed to the murder and was given a life sentence, but McKnight was acquitted of being an accessory before murder.[150]

Dennis's widow, Ella Mae, who had been defeated in her bid to succeed her husband in the senate less than a month after his murder, sued McKnight for $200,000 in damages and, after a mistrial, settled out of court for an undisclosed amount in 1932. In perhaps the strangest twist of all, the Dennis's son, Rembert, who ultimately claimed his father's senate seat and became one of the most powerful men in the state, led the parade of political worthies who served as McKnight's honorary pall bearers when he died in 1960.[151]

Could this happen anywhere but in South Carolina?

That leads us back to Dawsonville, which not only boasts the Georgia Racing Hall of Fame, flanked by the Dawsonville Moonshine Distillery and the city hall, but also recognizes individuals with its Bootleggers' Hall of Fame awards at the festival. Leo and I spent the night before the festival in Dahlonega, a gentrified town up the road that emphasizes its history as the center of Georgia's gold rush prior to the Civil War. Its lovely town square is surrounded by nice restaurants, upscale shops, and wine-tasting rooms, and Dahlonega is dominated by a large public university. You don't hear much about moonshine there; the Z. Brown Distillery, owned by an Atlanta country and rock band, closed after a short run in 2018 and nothing has taken its place. But Lumpkin County, of which Dahlonega is the county seat, turned out plenty of white lightning.

The leg of Highway 9 connecting Dahlonega and Dawsonville is full of curves and switchbacks, giving some idea of what moonshine trippers encountered decades ago, though the roads they traveled were red-clay lanes "crooked as a roadkill snake," in Neal Thompson's words. The festival was held ten days before the 2020 presidential election and we were clearly in Trump Country, with signs touting the incumbent president in front of residences ranging from shacks to large, handsome homes. A church we passed took no position on the election, its marquee simply urging, "Just Vote Jesus."

We arrived in time for the parade of cars, led by the celebrity grand marshal, recently retired NASCAR driver David Ragan. The opening ceremonies included the induction of three men into the Bootleggers' Hall of Fame. A woman with KARE for Kids, the children's Christmas charity that runs and benefits from the festival, read off the achievements of the inductees, including hijacking sugar trucks, running prodigious numbers of stills, serving prison sentences and, in one case, hauling moonshine for decades without getting caught or even getting a speeding ticket. (An earlier inductee, Simmie Free, began making 'shine at age ten. His granddaughter, Cheryl "Happy" Wood, is the owner of the Dawsonville Moonshine Distillery.) Everyone applauded their achievements, though the daughter of one deceased moonshine laureate said she knew her father would be surprised to be honored for criminal activity he tried to keep on the Q.T.

The festival's main attraction is a classic car show, with a designated covered pavilion for authentic moonshine-hauling cars. There I learned that the 1939 and 1940 Ford sedan and Ford coupe were the preferred vehicles of moonshine trippers. They had powerful V-8 engines, large trunks, were plain-looking, and with black rims and grille and a black paint job, they could easily be hidden from law enforcement. Edsel Ford had also finally convinced his father Henry to install hydraulic brakes in the '39 model, which worked much better than mechanical breaks when you were hurtling down a road at a hundred miles an hour.[152] The Fords were also easy to "soup up" for speed, and when the barrier between the trunk and backseat was taken down, they could haul lots of 'shine.

Although many of the cars on display had been restored to showroom-like perfection, others looked much as they did back in the day. Sherman Woods, owner of a '39 Ford, said he bought the car from someone in Mississippi in 2008 just for the shell, which he painted matte black, and then he replaced the engine to make it drivable. He estimated it could hold eighty gallons

Two Fords, one shiny and restored to mint condition, one unrestored, were displayed at the Moonshine Festival. *Leo Smith photo*

of liquor. Another rustic Ford belonged to Ken Harris, a bristly-haired Alabamian wearing a pair of overalls. He said he got his car for free for restoring another car, and only knew it had hauled moonshine because the bracing had been cut out between the trunk and back seat. The car looked like it belonged on a junk heap, but it ran well enough for Harris to drive it to Dawsonville. He knew nothing of its history but offered that his own grandfather served two prison sentences for making 'shine, once during Prohibition and once after. His still was located just half a mile from the county courthouse.

Elsewhere, the festival featured vendors selling T-shirts, handmade jewelry, and lawn ornaments, plus the obligatory fudge and funnel cake, with a sprinkling of Confederate flag items. The Civitan Club was holding a raffle for guns, with one member energetically waving around a cardboard assault rifle at the booth to get folks' attention. The assault rifle had also

Visitors examine old stills and other moonshine memorabilia in a portable Moonshine Museum at the Moonshine Festival. *Leo Smith photo*

figured prominently on a yard sign for a man running for U.S. Congress.[153] The fellow serving up pulled pork barbecue and Brunswick stew wore a T-shirt with the words "God Family Trump Guns" on it. We stood in line behind a man who had a knife in his hatband. But no coon dicks.

All this outlaw pride doesn't translate into violent crime, however. Dawson County has a violent crime rate lower than the national one and considerably lower than Georgia's as a whole, according to statistics from the FBI and the Georgia Bureau of Investigation.[154] Unfortunately, drug crime, especially the manufacture and sale of methamphetamines, is as common in Dawson County as in the rest of the country.[155] In many rural areas, where unemployment is high and opportunities limited, meth is the moonshine of the twenty-first century.

The Georgia Racing Hall of Fame celebrates the Peach State's stock car racing history. It is stuffed with fast cars, gargantuan trophies, emblem-coated racing uniforms, and historic pictures, with an entire section devoted to local NASCAR hero Bill Elliott—"Awesome Bill from Dawsonville"—and his racing career. (A few weeks after the festival, Bill's son, Chase, won the NASCAR Cup Series, adding more luster to the Elliott crown.) Although spirits at the Dawsonville Moonshine Distillery—moonshine and brandy—are sold under the Bill Elliott brand, his family was never involved in illegal liquor production or tripping.[156] However, young Chase admitted to drinking "maybe forty beers" between his race win on a Sunday and his welcome home celebration the following day. Thousands of cans of Michelob Ultra were consumed at the celebration at the hall of fame, according to volunteer Scott Adams.[157]

The granddaddy of stock car racing in Dawsonville is a man named Raymond Parks, described as a "moonshine baron" in his display in the Hall of Fame and "a micro-Al Capone, without the machine guns or thugs" in Neal Thompson's book. Born to a dirt-poor Dawson County family, he left home in 1928, at age fourteen, to enter the moonshine trade and made a fortune before he was twenty by coordinating deliveries from Dawsonville to Atlanta. Parks drove many loads himself, then began recruiting reckless teens who loved to speed down Thunder Road as his trippers. When some enterprising farmers began laying out rudimentary dirt tracks in cow pastures for auto races, the moonshine trippers combined their night jobs with racing, perhaps picking up a few bucks in prize money. By the time Raymond Parks finished a term in prison for conspiracy in 1937, the stage was set for the first bona fide stock car races in Daytona Beach, Florida and at Lakewood Speedway in Atlanta the following year. The Lakewood racetrack was created by a man from Dahlonega, who leased what had been a horse track circling a lake from the city of Atlanta's Lakewood Fairgrounds. The first auto race was run there in 1917 and Lakewood Speedway eventually came to be called the "Indianapolis of the South."[158]

Parks was in the audience at the 1938 Armistice Day stock car race at Lakewood, along with an astonishing twenty thousand other fans. Two of his moonshine drivers, his younger cousins Lloyd Seay (pronounced See) and "Reckless" Roy Hall, were in the competition, Seay driving with a broken arm. Seay came in first place, Hall in fifth, just behind a driver named Bill France who would go on to found NASCAR. Parks was so enthralled that he decided to form a race team, with Seay and Hall as drivers, and bought them brand new

Raymond Parks, in the fedora, with his drivers Lloyd Seay, left, and Roy Hall, was a pioneer of stock car racing. *Georgia Racing Hall of Fame*

'39 Fords with the names of his (mostly) legitimate businesses painted on the sides as advertisement. In return, he took the lion's share of their winnings. He also brought on board an Atlanta master mechanic named Red Vogt, who knew all sorts of ways to make an engine sing.

In 1939, two brothers from Fort Payne, Alabama, Bob and Fonty Flock, made their debut at Lakewood, driving Ford coupes that they had probably used while running 'shine for their uncle, Peachtree Williams. (Both would intermittently race for Raymond Parks's team.) Roy Hall won that race, but Bob finished third and the Flock family of drivers, which came to include brother Tim and even sister Ethel, would be major stock car winners for two decades. (Ethel, unable to participate in the male-only races, drove in "powder-puff derbies" with other female drivers.) The colorful family, sometimes called the Mad Flocks, were famous for their on-track antics. In 1952, Fonty won the Southern 500 in Darlington, South Carolina while wearing baggy Bermuda shorts and argyle socks, and after the race ended, he climbed on the hood of his car and led the crowd in singing "Dixie." Tim drove in eight races the following year with a pet monkey, Jocko Flocko, as his passenger. According to the *Alabama Encyclopedia*, "In a race in Raleigh, Jocko slipped his leash and began running amok inside the car. Tim had to pull into the pit to get rid of the panicked monkey, likely costing him the race, and Jocko was retired."

Fonty Flock won the 1952 Southern 500 in Darlington wearing Bermuda shorts and argyle socks. *Alabama Encyclopedia*

Another stock car driver who developed his skills in the moonshine trade was North Carolinian Robert Glenn Johnson Jr., better known as Junior Johnson, who became one of NASCAR's most successful drivers and team owners. He was also a frequent guest at the Mountain Moonshine Festival until his death at age eighty-eight in the summer of 2019.[159]

Until Bill Elliott came along in the 1980s, Lloyd Seay and Roy Hall were the towering figures of racing out of Dawsonville. Initially Roy was the most successful, perfecting moves such as driving around corners on two wheels. But his violent temper and habitual law breaking kept getting him thrown into jail; he once won a race in Daytona just hours after being sprung from the local pokey.[160]

There's no telling where Lloyd Seay could have gone. Bill France said he was "the best pure race driver I ever saw" and he was at the top of his game in 1941. A gentle soul, except when he was behind the wheel of his '39 Ford, Seay preferred to start slowly and let the other drivers wreck and burn out, narrowing the field, then surge to the front. In the late summer of 1941, he won three races in fifteen days, beginning with his first coveted win at the Daytona Beach-and-Road Race, then at a dirt-track race in High Point, North Carolina, and finally the Labor Day race at Lakewood, beating Bill France in all three contests. Inexplicably, for his final race Seay had changed the number on his car from lucky seven to unlucky thirteen.

He drove home to Dawsonville, where another cousin, with whom he and his brother Jim operated a still, came calling early the next morning. Woodrow Anderson was angry about a sugar purchase that he said Lloyd had unfairly charged to his account at a general store. That morning, the cousin shot both Jim and Lloyd. Jim survived, but Lloyd, who was just shy of his twenty-second birthday, died with his winnings from the Lakewood race still in his pocket. Anderson helped himself to the money he thought he was owed. He was convicted of murder and served ten years of a life sentence.

Raymond Parks was devastated by the loss of Seay, who was not only his top and most dependable driver but someone he was personally fond of as well. He paid for a four-foot-tall granite marker for Seay's grave in the Dawsonville City Cemetery, ornamented with reliefs of the elaborate Lakewood loving cup and the dead driver's '39 Ford. There is a thumb-sized likeness of Seay, rendered on porcelain, smiling out from the car window. It bears the race number seven.

Raymond Parks paid for Lloyd
Seay's distinctive grave marker.
Author photo

PALMETTO DISTILLERY

Trey Boggs greeted me at the door of his distillery in Anderson, South Carolina early on a cold winter morning, a cup of coffee in his hand. He was
wearing a Palmetto Moonshine knit cap, Palmetto Moonshine T-shirt, Palmetto moonshine biker jacket, boots, and jeans. He had a full beard that is
beginning to grey, and the hat covered a shaved head. His blue eyes twin-
kled behind black square-framed glasses, complementing his wide, friendly
smile. He immediately offered me a cup of coffee, which I gladly accepted.

Palmetto Distillery, the first legal producer of moonshine in South Carolina since Prohibition, has a fun outlaw vibe, with an old blue pickup truck
parked in the middle of the sales floor, trophy heads on the walls, and other
samples of taxidermy scattered about. A vitrine coffee table displays bottles
of the company's products on a bed of shotgun shells.

Trey and his younger brother and business partner, Bryan, are born
entrepreneurs. They began earning money mowing grass—fighting over
who used the mower and who used the weed whacker—before they could
drive. Their mother, Pam, took them to their jobs and read a book in the
car while they worked. When they had earned $1,000, they bought an old

Trey Boggs, left, and brother Bryan opened the first legal moonshine distillery in South Carolina in 2012. Their collection of celebrity signed bottles includes one autographed by Donald Trump while campaigning in Anderson in 2016. *Courtesy Palmetto Distillery*

mill house and fixed it up for rent. That led to more mill houses, apartment buildings, shopping centers, flea markets, and the like. Purchasing the nineteenth century building in downtown Anderson across the street from the county courthouse was just another real estate venture for them. At first.

The state laws governing distilleries in South Carolina changed in 2009 when the state dropped the cost of a distillery license from $50,000 to $2,500 and opened the door for micro-distilleries. The Boggs brothers started mulling over the idea of opening a distillery in the building they had purchased two years before. Their permit was granted in January 2011 and they went looking for someone to build them a still. They eventually found a mountain man—Trey is intentionally vague about where he lived, only asking, "Did you ever see the movie *Deliverance*?"—who was known for his, ahem, "yard art." He agreed to build a thirty-gallon copper still. Then they made connections with three experienced moonshiners who were willing to share their know-how and recipes. "Nobody is born making moonshine," Trey said. "What we thought was going to be a fun hobby turned into a wild run." After about a year and a half of experimentation, they felt their product was good enough to sell to the public—which meant they had to tell their parents.

Pam Boggs grew up in the tiny unincorporated Anderson County community of Possum Kingdom and she and her husband, Arthur, raised their boys as Baptists. "My parents didn't drink, cuss, or hang out with people who did," Trey said. They set the stage for the big reveal by taking their parents out to dinner, then brought them to the building and up into the attic, which they had turned into a giant party room to test their moonshine on willing friends. When their mother saw the still, she said, "Oh my God! Y'all are making moonshine behind the courthouse!" Their father was simply dumbstruck. But once they explained that their products were legal under the new laws and they were paying all the appropriate taxes, his parents were mollified and supportive.

The Boggs brothers went back to the mountain man and asked him what was the biggest still he had ever made. He said 100 gallons. They asked him to try to make a 250-gallon still, which he did, keeping it hidden under a tarp outside his single-wide mobile home. When Trey saw it, he said it was so big it would have been visible from outer space.

Palmetto Distillery opened to the public in 2012. The original product, packaged in Mason jars, included a 105-proof white lightning, a 130-proof "bootlegger" brand, and lower proof moonshine flavored with peach, blackberry, watermelon and apple pie, all suitable for making cocktails. (Apple pie remains the best seller.) The novelty was a drawing card from the start, and they ran their still "eight days a week." They used all kinds of gimmicks to build interest, including hiring two fellows with long grey beards to dress as hillbillies and stand on the busy street between the distillery and the courthouse waving signs. (They had to let one of the "moonshine men" go because, as Trey tactfully puts it, he "became too involved in the brand.") They hired attractive young women who put on Daisy Mae attire to hawk their booze at the store and at special events. They soon had a thousand-gallon still on order, which they continue to use today.

Even going full steam, there was so much buzz, they couldn't keep up. Then a near-disaster raised their profile even more. In May 2012, the still ruptured, causing a flash fire and an explosion that shot its top off. It was a rookie mistake. Trey notes that old-time moonshiners put rocks on the tops of their stills to prevent this from happening; Palmetto Distillery now uses heavy straps. No one was seriously hurt, and Trey grabbed the opportunity to get some positive publicity: "The moonshine industry has exploded in popularity over the past few years, and our 'shine's so good it's on fire . . . " he wrote on the distillery Facebook page. That inspired the headline in the local paper: "'Shine so good it's on fire." They started getting calls from all over the country.

RAGING BULL

Add a shot of Palmetto White Lightning/Bootlegger Proof Moonshine to a glass of Red Bull on ice.

WHITE TRASH LEMONADE (BY THE PITCHER)

- ½ cup of clover honey
- 1 cup hot water
- ½ cup fresh lemon juice (or a full cup for a tarter lemonade)
- ⅛ tsp salt
- 1 cup Palmetto White Lightning Moonshine
- 1 lemon, sliced
- ½ cup cold water
- Ice

In a pitcher, mix the honey and hot water and stir to dissolve. Allow to cool. Add lemon juice, salt, moonshine, and lemon slices. Refrigerate for several hours or overnight. Add cold water. Fill pitcher with ice before serving. Pour into tall tumblers or water glasses filled with ice. Garnish with fresh mint if desired.

—Recipes courtesy Palmetto Distillery

By Christmas, so many people were coming to Palmetto Distillery for gifts that there was a line out the door. "It looked like a soup kitchen," Trey said. When they finally closed at two-thirty Christmas Eve, the staff worn to a nub, they caught people "bootlegging" in the parking lot by selling the moonshine they bought inside for twice its retail price. Two maps at the distillery, one of the United States and the other of the world, are studded with colored pins that show where their visitors have come from. They now operate an auxiliary retail site at the Greenville-Spartanburg Airport to catch passengers looking for an unusual gift to bring an out-of-state friend or for a souvenir. "Of all the gimmicky things you can buy at an airport, I'd much rather have a jar of moonshine," Trey said. "And if someone is traveling back to where they're from, I would want them to bring me a jar of moonshine."[161] (I have been guilty of making such a purchase; my friends in Washington, D.C. were charmed. Or at least they pretended to be!) Palmetto Distillery now ships all over the country and to Canada and even Scotland.

Other moonshine distilleries have opened since the Boggs brothers' venture began, crowding the market, but Trey claims his stuff is still the best. "You can have Betty Crocker's chocolate chip recipe but that doesn't make you Betty Crocker," he said. Plus, the distillery has expanded its offerings with whiskey, introduced in 2015, which they tout as the most-awarded craft whiskey in the state, and developed a Back Stage brand whiskey for country singer Darius Rucker. (The whiskeys are similar in taste but have different proofs.) They are constantly coming out with new twists, including ready-to-pour Bloody Mary mix and even moonshine pickles. Trey said the pickles and moonshine jams and jellies are for nondrinkers who tour their facility, just so they won't leave empty-handed.

Palmetto Distillery • 200 W. Benson Street, Anderson
www.palmettomoonshine.com

PROHIBITION EXPEDITION

The Smith House in Dahlonega has been a hotel for almost a hundred years and is within a block of the heart of town with its gold rush museum, shops, and restaurants. 84 South Chestatee Street. www.smithhouse.com.

Highway 9: You can take Highway 9 from Dahlonega all the way to Atlanta, but you will get a better feel for what the trippers experienced in the Dahlonega to Dawsonville leg.

Mountain Moonshine Festival • Held the third weekend in October
www.kareforkids.org

Georgia Racing Hall of Fame • 415 Georgia Highway 53, Dawsonville
www.georgiaracinghof.com

Dawsonville Moonshine Distillery • 415 Georgia Highway 53, Suite 120
www.dawsonvillemoonshinedistillery.com

Dawsonville Pool Room. Race-themed pool hall and counter service restaurant operated by local racing authority (and former bootlegger) Gordon Pirkle. The center of all Elliott family racing victories in Dawsonville, the Pool Room is open seven days a week and famous for its Bully Burger.

9 Bill Elliott Street • www.dawsonvillepoolroom.com

CEMETERY SIDE TRIP

Lloyd Seay's grave stands out in the city cemetery of Dawsonville, Georgia because of its four-foot-tall monument. 26 Maple Street.[162]

A tiny picture of Lloyd Seay looks out from the driver's window of the car relief on his grave marker. *Author photo*

Lewis Redmond, the King of the Outlaws, is buried in the cemetery of Return Baptist Church in Oconee County, South Carolina. 733 Return Church Road, Seneca.[163]

Senator E.J. Dennis's simple gravestone in the Saint John's Baptist Church cemetery in Berkeley County in inscribed "Father-Leader-Statesman." His widow, who survived him by thirty-eight years, has the unusual inscription "Strength and Honour Are Her Clothing." Sugar Hill Drive, Pinopolis.

Glenn McKnight's gravestone in the Revolutionary War era Biggin Cemetery in Moncks Corner bears the inscription "I Know that My Redeemer Liveth," perhaps an acknowledgement that he was about to face a judge who could not be influenced or bought off![164] Highway 402, Moncks Corner.

RECOMMENDED READING

Driving with the Devil: Southern Moonshine, Detroit Wheels, and the Birth of NASCAR by Neal Thompson (New York: Crown, 2006)

Used to Be a Rough Place in Them Hills: Moonshine, the Dark Corner, and the New South by Joshua Beau Blackwell (Bloomington, IN: Author House, 2006)

CHAPTER TEN

$\mathcal{A}$L $\mathcal{C}$APONE $\mathcal{S}$LEPT $\mathcal{H}$ERE

IT'S AMAZING HOW MANY PEOPLE have an Al Capone story.

A friend told me her mother, who had been a beauty queen in her Michigan hometown of Berrien Springs, had dated one of Capone's henchman when the gangsters were hanging out at their nearby hunting lodge. "He had a nice car," she said, adding unnecessarily, "It was a short-lived relationship." No kidding. Not to mention that working for Al Capone was often a short-term gig.

A woman I met at the ritzy Amelia Island Club in Florida told me her father had gone to Catholic school with Capone's son, Albert, known as Sonny, in Miami Beach. She said Sonny showed her father the trick of throwing a lighted match into a gas tank, then quickly capping it so no oxygen got inside, and the car didn't explode. Fun stuff! To think that my friends merely taught me misinformation about sex.

Although Capone is associated with Chicago more than any other city, he spent the last third of his life—when he wasn't in prison in Atlanta or Alcatraz—at his second home in Miami Beach. His travels through the South for business and pleasure created an entire cottage industry of "Capone Slept Here" hotels. I'll share my own Capone-a-thon in this chapter, but first some background on the most notorious gangster in American history.

Al Capone in 1930 was still styling himself as a businessman just trying to make a living. Florida wasn't having it. *FBI photo*

Alphonse Francis Capone was born in Brooklyn in 1899 and died in Miami Beach forty-eight years later. He entered the world of crime in his teens and came to Chicago in 1920, the protégé and hand-anointed successor of the master gangster Johnny Torrio. When Torrio almost died after an assassination attempt in 1925, he handed his crime organization, called the Outfit, over to Capone, who then spent seven years as the undisputed chief of vice in Chicago. The Outfit had been built on the protection racket, gambling, and prostitution, but was catapulted to empire status by illegal booze sales during Prohibition.

Today "Al Capone" is shorthand for the ultimate gangster and he, more than any other of that breed, is associated with the criminal enterprises that flourished during Prohibition. The Justice Department's Bureau of Investigation, today's FBI, dubbed him Public Enemy No. 1 in 1930. Around that time, it was estimated that the Outfit was raking in at least $105 million a year in illegal gains, most of it from sales of booze, and Capone's personal wealth was estimated at $40 million. (That gross translates into $1.6 billion in current dollars and his personal wealth to $623 million.[165]) The Outfit employed a thousand people, not to mention the thousands of Chicago cops, judges, and elected officials it bribed, and Capone had a personal staff of 185. He told a reporter, "They're all ex-convicts and gunmen, but they are respectable businessmen now, just as respectable as the people who buy my stuff and gamble in my places . . . If you put me out of business, I'll turn every one of those 185 respectable old convicts loose on Chicago."[166]

The notion that Capone had these "respectable businessmen" under control was ludicrous. During the first decade of Prohibition, gang-related murders in Chicago took seven hundred lives, and Capone was said to have ordered or committed more than two hundred of them. While most of the victims were the casualties of inter-gang warfare, others were just people who got in the way, or who tried to vote for a reformer the Outfit didn't want to win office. (One of the casualties was Capone's brother, Frank, killed during an election day riot.) Somehow, no one ever saw anything that would pin a murder on Capone, lest they join the ranks of his victims.

Nevertheless, the public was fascinated by Capone and couldn't get enough news about him. Despite his less-than-svelte figure and a fat, fleshy face marred by a jagged knife scar that was a souvenir of a bar fight—hence his hated nickname "Scarface"—Capone became a fashion icon. He wore bespoke suits in Easter egg colors—yellow, lavender, lime green—diamond-studded stickpins, cuff buttons, and even belt buckles, and a signature pearl-gray fedora. He let it be known he only wore colorful silk underwear. Reporters sought interviews with Capone, who loved the attention and always made good copy. In his interviews, Capone insisted he was merely providing a commodity that people wanted. The most famous line attributed to him was, "When I sell liquor, it's called bootlegging; when my patrons serve it on Lake Shore Drive, it's called hospitality." He had a point. His fellow gangster Enoch "Nucky" Johnson of Atlantic City—he was thinly disguised as Nucky Thompson in the HBO series *Boardwalk Empire*—once said of contraband goods and services, "If the majority of people didn't want them, they wouldn't be profitable and they wouldn't exist."

Al Capone, left, and Enoch Johnson (thinly disguised as Nucky Thompson in the HBO series *Boardwalk Empire*), stroll the boardwalk in Atlantic City. *Wikimedia Commons*

The novelist Sinclair Lewis in his 1922 satirical novel *Babbitt* describes a dinner party that his social-climbing main character George Babbitt gave, beautifully capturing the hypocrisy of Prohibition. Although George is a staunch Republican and supporter of Prohibition, he seeks out a bootlegger in a seedy district of town and grovels to buy a bottle of gin for $12 (that would be almost $200 today). At home he makes a tray of cocktails, though he doesn't own a shaker—that would be "proof of dissipation"—instead improvising "by pouring from an ancient gravy-boat into a handleless pitcher." When he offers his guests their drinks, he asks coyly, "Well, folks, do you think you could stand breaking the law a little?" All gladly partake, including a syndicated writer who has just penned a bit of doggerel supporting Prohibition in his newspaper column: "I'll never miss their poison booze/ whilst I the bubbling spring can use/ that leaves my head at merry morn/ as clear as any babe new-born!" They all agree that Prohibition was not intended for people like themselves, but for the "working classes. Keeps 'em from wasting their money and lowering their productiveness."[167]

To keep the booze flowing to his patrons—wealthy and otherwise—Capone bought from rumrunners up and down the east coast (not to mention numerous suppliers from Canada) and moonshiners all over the South, from the hills of the Carolinas, Georgia, Kentucky, and Tennessee to the lowcountry swamps of South Carolina. That entailed a certain amount of travel. There are so many hotels that claim he was a guest that, as a Chicago reporter once mused, "if Capone frequented even a tenth of the places that he's said to have, the notorious mobster hardly would have had time to build his Chicago crime empire, let alone run the thing."[168]

Capone traveled in an armor-plated Cadillac with two cars full of bodyguards escorting him fore and aft, or took a train from Chicago. He had to sleep somewhere on these trips, and he had 2,550 nights to rest his head during his heyday before he began spending most of his nights in prison cells. So, we shouldn't dismiss these claims that "Al Capone slept here" out-of-hand, even if they are couched in such vague language as, "the story goes" or "old-timers talked about" or "legend has it."

At the height of his notoriety, some chambers of commerce, amazingly, courted Capone as a resident for their cities, reasoning that he could sprinkle the local economy with his fabulous income. Not every city was so enthralled. Looking for a warm weather escape from Chicago's harsh winters and the increasing gang warfare, Capone took a train to Los Angeles in

1927 with his wife, Mae, Sonny, and the usual entourage of thugs. He was met at the station by the chief of police and a cadre of officers who informed him he was not welcome there. "I thought you people liked tourists," he groused. "Whoever heard of anybody being run out of Los Angeles that had money?"[169] Nevertheless, he cut the trip short and returned home to be met with a similar cool greeting in Chicago. Writes biographer Deirdre Bair, "The police chief had called in reporters to proclaim that Capone had only gone to Los Angeles because his force had driven him out of town and would certainly not permit him to return."

Capone was in a fix. Not only were the police standing up to him, but the gang rivalry had become so fierce in Chicago that he was in constant fear for his life, holing up in his headquarters at the Lexington Hotel and eating only food prepared by his personal chef. (He made the chef taste everything he prepared while he watched, just in case.) He sent out feelers to St. Petersburg, Florida—winter home of his old mentor Johnny Torrio— and visited there, allegedly staying at the Vinoy Park and Don CeSar beach hotels, but he didn't get a warm welcome in St. Pete either. His brother Ralph made a trip to New Orleans to case it as a warm-weather home for Al and was thrown into jail when he tried to purchase real estate. Eventually, Al focused on Miami, which was enjoying a land boom and enticing wealthy cold weather escapees, from department store owner J.C. Penney to former Ohio governor James M. Cox, who was the owner of the *Miami Daily News.*

In this vintage postcard touting Miami, the greeting reads, "To Jeer and Gloat May Not Be Nice. I'll Take the Sun . . . You Take the Ice." *Author collection*

Capone was probably not the sort of wealthy Yankee visitor automotive entrepreneur Carl G. Fisher and a group of Southern leaders hoped to attract when they began developing the Dixie Highway in 1915. It was a network of mostly paved two-lane roads linking Chicago to Miami, where Fisher had real estate investments.[170] By 1926, the system was composed of 5,786 miles of roads and Capone and his retinue of bodyguards and hangers-on could travel south through Louisville—remember the stories from the Seelbach Hotel there?—and on through Tennessee and Georgia. When Al traveled over the Georgia line, he could continue through central Florida or make a beeline to the east coast, where he had some dealings in Jacksonville with the bootlegging Hysler family and was said to have slept at the city's Casa Marina Hotel, then head on down to Miami. It's a twenty-hour trip on major highways today, so we can only imagine how long it took to make the trip on the Dixie Highway.

Leo and I undertook a Capone-a-thon through Georgia and Florida looking for places associated with the gangster, sometimes following Dixie Highway roads. In Americus, Georgia, a local visionary in 1892 built a tremendous red brick European-style hotel, with a turret and a tower, and ornamented with gorgeous hand-carved oak woodwork and exuberant brass and glass chandeliers. The Windsor Hotel had a hundred rooms in its heyday, boasted guests such as the celebrated French actress Sarah Bernhardt, and was the setting for an address to the chamber of commerce by Franklin Delano Roosevelt in 1928.

At the Windsor, now a beautifully restored Best Western Plus hotel, we went on a brief tour led by a friendly fellow from the town's visitors' bureau. Steve Short told us about the chamber maid who was pushed down an elevator shaft and now haunts the hotel, then he took us up the narrow stairway to the bridal suite, located in the turret on the third floor. Former President and Mrs. Jimmy Carter really did sleep there—his hometown of Plains is nearby—and the story goes that Al Capone did too, stopping off in Americus during a train trip south.

It would be a safe refuge for a nervous gangster. The round room's multiple windows give a panoramic view of the streets, enabling his bodyguards' eagle eyes to watch for enemies outside the hotel, and the private staircase could be easily defended by a thug with a tommy gun should anyone breach security and get inside. The Windsor's Capone story has the usual details:

The Windsor Hotel in Americus, Georgia is one of the many places Al Capone was said to have been a guest. The private staircase leads to the tower bedroom. *Leo Smith photos*

The tower bedroom has windows all around, offering look-out posts for Capone's bodyguards.

a series of escape tunnels underneath, plus the titillating addition of a local woman who was supposedly his mistress, and even an illegitimate son.

Did he really stay there? Who knows! But it was a beautiful place to visit, and we made a quick trip to Plains to see President Carter's church. The county's other claim to fame—a sobering one—is the notorious Confederate prison at Andersonville, now home to the National POW Museum and a national cemetery.

The flat peanut and cotton fields of south Georgia are worlds away from the sun-washed shores of Miami Beach, where we headed to explore

Al Capone's documented stomping grounds. When Capone zeroed in on Miami in 1927, he so charmed the mayor, John N. Lummus Jr., and Parker Henderson, the manager of the city's fanciest hotel, that they acted as "straw men" to purchase a home for him. Henderson, who leased the top story of his Ponce de Leon Hotel in downtown Miami to Capone as a business office, went a step further, buying guns for him. Authorities traced one of them to the murder of one of the gangster's main rivals, Frankie Yale, in the summer of 1928. While the Ponce de Leon fell victim to the wrecking ball, another luxury lodging place with a Capone legend is very much in business. The Biltmore Hotel in the tony Coral Gables suburb has a thirteenth-floor luxury suite where,

PONCE DE LEON HOTEL, MIAMI, FLA.

The Ponce de Leon Hotel was Miami's fanciest. Its manager rented the top floor to Capone and purchased guns for his use. *Author collection*

it is rumored, Capone ran an illegal gambling room and speakeasy. Its official name is the Everglades Suite, but it is better known, of course, as the Al Capone Suite.

The home Capone bought in 1928 was on Palm Island. It is one of a group of man-made islands in Biscayne Bay, the largest of which is Miami Beach, created in the early twentieth century on a large sand bar augmented with thousands of tons of swamp land dredged out of the bay. Miami has a separate government from Miami Beach, which has jurisdiction over the islands. By the time the good people of Miami got wind that Capone and his extended family had set up housekeeping at 93 Palm Avenue, there wasn't much anyone could do about it, though everyone from the governor of Florida down to the Miami police chief tried to run him out of the state. His neighbors were horrified that their property values would decline, and the Miami City Council was mightily miffed that the mayor had not only welcomed the gangster to town but had accepted a commission on the real estate transaction.

Capone promised that he was retiring from his life of crime and coming to Miami Beach to restore Sonny's precarious health and have some fun in the sun. He bought a cabin cruiser and a motorboat, had the largest private swimming pool in Florida built in his back yard, and played golf at the Bayshore Golf Course, today's Miami Beach Golf Club.[171] He was photographed beside his pool in a black one-piece bathing suit and fishing off his cabin cruiser wearing a striped bathrobe, a long stogie poking out of his mouth. Of course, he had no intention of retiring from his lucrative career. Miami was a convenient base for managing rum-running to fuel his booze business and he was said to have invested money in local enterprises from a dog racing track in Hialeah to a speakeasy in Deerfield Beach.[172]

This is an aerial view of the 93 Palm Island property after Capone bought and "improved" it in 1928. *State Archives of Florida*

Capone was often photographed fishing in a striped robe over his pajamas and slippers. *Alamy photo*

In 1920, Miami Beach and neighboring islands had just 644 residents, though that number increased ten-fold in the following decade.[173] Today, it is a bustling city of more than 90,000 full-time residents, attracting millions of visitors each year.[174] South Beach is famous for its nightlife, restored art deco district, and topless sunbathing. I had to admit to feeling like an old woman clutching my purse as I passed voluptuous young things in wildly colored Spandex leggings and string bikinis strolling down the sidewalks. I recalled the diplomatic words of the desk clerk at our hotel, who had said it was best to visit South Beach early in the day because later it became a sort of "Pandora's box." We heeded her advice.

The Miami Beach of the 1920s was a much quieter place. It had some fine hotels and a really good restaurant founded in 1913 by a Hungarian immigrant couple, Joe and Jennie Weiss. Begun as a lunch counter that served fish sandwiches, it is still in business today as Joe's Stone Crab, but its in-house dining in the original restaurant is limited to "the season" which runs from October to May, so I didn't get to partake.[175] Al Capone often did, however. The restaurant's website said he would arrive with a carload of "associates" at about 5 p.m. to beat the dinner crowd, eat heartily of stone crabs and cole slaw, and tip well. He used an alias, Al Brown,

Lummus Park and Miami Beach in Capone's day, as shown in this vintage postcard, were much more staid places than they are today. *Author collection*

and Mrs. Weiss, who oversaw the dining room and did not put up with any nonsense, thought he was okay. "Mr. Brown," she told him, "if I don't like somebody, I don't allow them to come in here, but you've always been a gentleman and anytime you want to come into this restaurant, you can." On Mother's Day he sent her a horse-shoe shaped wreath with the message "Good Luck Mother Joe."[176]

The Capones spread money around the Miami area with a trowel as they made their new house a home. Mae bought expensive furnishings and carpets for the 6,100-square-foot, two-story Spanish-style house, which had seven bedrooms, five baths, and two half-baths, including a gold-and-black tile powder room. (Between Al's goons and his extended family, they had a lot of company.) Improvements at 93 Palm included a tall wall around the property and a twenty-five-foot-long dock extending into the bay, both of which enraged neighbors, who said he was violating island building restrictions.[177] Al paid top wages to workman who added a rock garden and fountains to the property, even providing them with lavish lunches each day. He also shopped at a ritzy men's store and was so impressed with the owner's customer service that he presented him one of his diamond-studded belt buckles.

The couple enrolled Sonny at St. Patrick Catholic Church School, where his classmates included Desi Arnaz, Jr., son of the former mayor of Havana, Cuba and future husband of Lucille Ball. Mae attended mass daily at the church, built in the Mediterranean Revival style that was popular at the time of its dedication in 1929. The founder, an Irish priest named William Barry, was very solicitous of Mae and would give Al last rites, though he was denied a funeral mass in a Catholic church.

During our visit to Miami Beach, Leo and I drove over to see St. Patrick Church, which the Trappist monk and writer Thomas Merton once described as "one of the nicest churches in America."[178] The church doors are flanked with stone carvings of mother pelicans and their young—I was reminded, absurdly, of the clay pelicans roosting in the rathskeller of the Seelbach Hotel in Louisville—but these pelicans had Christian symbolism.[179] Gorgeous leaded stained glass windows commemorating saints, many of them Irish, line the walls of the sanctuary, and its two rose windows are as impressive as those found in many a cathedral in Europe. In the parking lot, parishioners were cheerfully handing out groceries to a

Capone's wife, Mae, was a daily worshipper at St. Patrick Catholic Church and their son attended the day school there. *Leo Smith photo*

bedraggled group of people, something I was told they did every Saturday. It reminded me of the murderous Capone's "softer" side. He carried wads of cash with him and was a sucker for a sad story. Once the Depression got a grip on Chicago in 1930, he funded a soup kitchen that fed 2,200 people a day.[180]

THE CAPONE

Deirdre Capone, Al Capone's great-niece and author of the book *Uncle Al Capone: The Untold Story from Inside his Family*, insisted that Templeton rye was his favorite liquor. Templeton is a small town in Iowa whose bootleggers turned out an illegal product known as "The Good Stuff" that was supposedly sold by Capone in Chicago. This drink was demonstrated by one of the modern Templeton Rye Spirits company's brand managers, Michael Killmer, on a YouTube video. https://www.youtube.com/watch?v=7D6yFmynMTk

- 2 oz. Templeton Rye whiskey
- ¾ oz. Grand Marnier
- 2 dashes Angostura bitters
- 1 oz. Champagne

Pour ingredients into a cocktail shaker with ice and shake vigorously. Strain and pour into a chilled cocktail glass. Twist a slice of lemon rind over the drink to express oils, and then top with Champagne.

—Templeton Rye Spirits

The next stop on our Capone-a-thon was a speedboat tour of Biscayne Bay and a look at his waterfront home on Palm Island. Captain Mike Lynch welcomed us aboard his spotless little boat at the dock across the street from the Eden Roc and Fontainebleau hotels—they call it the Fountain Blue in Miami Beach. Mike has been a tour guide in Miami for many years, and until the Covid-19 shutdown most of his clients were from abroad. He said they like to know about the celebrities who have homes on Miami Beach and the other man-made islands, people like Jennifer Lopez and Alex Rodriguez, who recently bought a mansion on Star Island. But Mike, born in Arizona, admitted that what attracted him to Miami some years ago was the television series *Miami Vice*, the stylish crime drama which aired on NBC for six seasons beginning in 1984. They did a lot of location shooting in Miami Beach.

As we surveyed the shoreline of Miami, Mike proclaimed it "the city cocaine built," and we had a lively discussion comparing the effects of Prohibition and rum-running of the 1920s to the "cocaine cowboy" days that began with a drug gang shoot-out at a Miami shopping mall in 1979 and continuing into the late 1980s. At that time, Miami had so many drug-related murders and deaths that the city morgue ran out of space and had to store bodies in refrigerated trucks. In 1983 director Brian DePalma remade the 1932 movie *Scarface*, loosely based on the life of Al Capone, with Al Pacino playing Tony Camonte, a cokehead drug lord in Miami. Mike's point was that cocaine sales generated huge amounts of money, some of which was legitimately invested in Miami's skyscrapers and other real estate. The same thing happened, of course, during Prohibition.

A photo souvenir from a glass bottom boat tour company in the 1940s is evidence that Capone's home always attracted thrill seekers. *Author collection*

The water view of Capone's home is blocked by foliage and the two-story pool house he had built. *Leo Smith photo*

We tooled around the various islands, with Mike pointing out celebrity homes, former celebrity homes, places where episodes of *Miami Vice* were shot, and an elderly billionaire working in his waterfront garden. (He was Phillip Frost, who made his fortune in pharmaceuticals, and is one of Miami's leading philanthropists.) Mike told us about Stiltsville, a group of twenty-six houses on stilts located at the edge of Biscayne Bay, where all sorts of good times, legal and illegal, were had in the 1940s to 1960s. He described it as sort of a low-rent Las Vegas hovering above water. Finally, we pulled up alongside the Capone property.

Capone wanted privacy at 93 Palm, and the property still has it today. All you can see from the water is the two-story pool house he had built and a smidgen of the main stucco-over-wood house, which is mostly hidden by tropical foliage. When Leo and I drove onto Palm Island the next morning, we could see even less. Thick foliage and a large gatehouse with heavy wooden doors obscure vision from the road.

It is possible to get a good view of the Capone home on-line at the website www.93palm.com, which was apparently set up to market the newly renovated property a few years ago. It was offered for sale in 2018 for $14.9 million, was knocked down to $12.9 million in in 2019, and taken off the market in July of 2020. Zillow.com now estimates its value at $11 million.[181]

Capone's good times at 93 Palm did not last long. If Miamians were upset to learn he had taken up residence in 1928, they were outraged after February 14, 1929, when six members of the Bugs Moran gang in Chicago were lured into a warehouse and executed, along with a gang mechanic who happened to be repairing a tire, by four men, two of them dressed in police

A photo provided by a Florida realty shows the pool and pool house, looking out toward the water. *Wikimedia Commons*

uniforms. The St. Valentine's Day Massacre electrified the nation because of the brutal escalation of gang violence it represented, and Capone was widely believed to be its architect. But he insisted on complete innocence, not only pointing out that he was in Miami on Valentine's Day, but that he was being questioned by the Dade County prosecutor at the same time the massacre occurred. No one was ever charged with the crime, but from then on Capone was a marked man. Writes biographer Deirdre Bair, "Al Capone became firmly fixed in the legal sights of different governmental agencies and the several [citizens] groups that sprang up around them." Rival gangs smelled blood and ramped up their efforts to horn in on the Outfit's businesses. And that was just in Chicago. He had also gotten the attention of two important men named Hoover: the director of the FBI, J. Edgar Hoover, and the president of the United States, Herbert Hoover, who took office three weeks after the massacre.

Capone took a page out of his mentor Johnny Torrio's playbook, figuring the wisest action was to bow out for a while. He contrived to have himself arrested for carrying a gun in Philadelphia, expecting a short prison sentence where he would be safe until things cooled down. Instead, he was sentenced to a year at the Eastern State Penitentiary in Philadelphia. Naturally, he comfortably feathered his nest behind bars with posh furniture, an expensive radio, thick rugs, and other homely touches. The warden allowed him unlimited visitors, and he frequently used the warden's phone to keep up with the Outfit's dealings.[182]

When Capone was released on St. Patrick's Day, 1930, he returned to Chicago, keeping a low profile. It did no good. Mabel Walker Willebrandt, the assistant attorney general for Prohibition enforcement, had left the federal government for a private law practice by then, but her brilliant idea to prosecute for nonpayment of taxes on illegal income—so successful against the Savannah Four—was being used in a case against Capone. The U.S. attorney in Chicago was developing it, aided by a crackerjack team of Department of Revenue accountants who had gotten hold of some of Capone's financial records. (Although the bean counters were more important in putting Capone behind bars, people prefer to remember the work of the dashing and handsome soon-to-be-famous Treasury agent Elliot Ness and his squad of incorruptible associates known as "the Untouchables," who were busting into the Outfit's warehouses of beer and liquor and putting a hurting on income.)

To add to Capone's woes, the governor of Florida sent a telegram to every sheriff in the state ordering them to arrest Capone on the spot if he dared try to return home. The governor's order was struck down by a judge, but when Capone got to Miami, he was harassed by the local police on a charge of vagrancy, which was interpreted to apply to any known criminal or person "dangerous to public safety or peace of the city." The Miami judge who heard the case ruled against the city, and Capone was again able to enjoy the pleasures of Palm Island with his family. He mounted "charm offensives" in both Chicago and Miami Beach. He and Mae threw many lavish parties in the summer of 1930. Prominent Miamians were happy to attend, but they did not return the invitations. Late that fall in Chicago, thousands of hungry people lined up for a different kind of hospitality at Capone's soup kitchen.

Meanwhile, the federal case against him moved forward. In June 1931, a federal grand jury indicted the gangster on twenty-four counts of nonpayment of taxes. A year later, he pleaded guilty, entering a plea bargain in which he would serve two and a half years in prison and pay a $10,000 fine. Instead, the judge refused to accept the agreement and the case went to trial. Among those testifying to Capone's lavish lifestyle were leading businessmen from Miami, who had enjoyed the fine food and free-flowing liquor at 93 Palm Island. He was convicted on five counts of tax evasion and on October 24, 1931, the judge sentenced him to eleven years in prison and fined him $50,000, plus court costs. Appeals exhausted, on May 4, 1932, he returned south in a train car on the *Dixie Flyer*, this time handcuffed to a terrified young car thief and sitting on a hard, wooden bench. (Among his

As the Great Depression set in, Capone polished his Robin Hood image by feeding the hungry at a Chicago soup kitchen. *National Archives*

escorts to the station from the Cook County Jail was Elliot Ness.) The next day, he entered the federal penitentiary in Atlanta.

The Atlanta pen where George Remus and Willie Haas had lived in ease and comfort was no more. Remember that Mabel Walker Willebrandt, whose federal bailiwick included federal prisons, had gotten the corrupt warden appointed by President Harding not only fired but locked up in his own prison. The new warden was a no-nonsense fellow who extended no special privileges to Prisoner No. 40866. Capone would do hard time there.

His body began to turn on him too. He had contracted syphilis in his teens and had passed the disease on to Mae and countless other women. Now, the effects of nontreatment were uncovered during his admission physical in Atlanta. The syphilis was so advanced that it began affecting his behavior, leading to uncontrollable outbursts. He was the target of other prisoners' taunting and violence and forced to meet with VIPs, from members of Congress to other thrill-seekers favored by J. Edgar Hoover. Reporters hung around the prison gates, getting interviews from newly released prisoners about what it was like for Capone behind bars, and they wrote highly colored and mostly false reports about it. Writes biographer Deirdre Bair, "Capone's daily life was one humiliation after another for the man who had once held the same sort of ultimate power to humiliate." Then it got worse.

MELVIN PURVIS

Many of the episodes of the TV series *The Untouchables* gave Elliot Ness credit for crime fighting he never did, including the gunning down of Ma Barker and her son Fred in 1935. Ness's squad was disbanded after Prohibition and though he had a long career in law enforcement, he did not work for the FBI, which was leading the war on crime in the 1930s.

Handsome and personable, Melvin Purvis was J. Edgar Hoover's darling—until he wasn't. *FBI photo*

The real gangbuster after Capone went to prison was the special agent in charge of the FBI in Chicago, a South Carolinian named Melvin Purvis. Born in Timmonsville, Purvis earned a law degree at the University of South Carolina and joined the Bureau of Investigation in 1926. He was just twenty-nine years old when he became Chicago's SAC, arriving in the city with a palomino horse, a Pierce Arrow automobile and an African American man servant named President. The slender and attractive Purvis was at first J. Edgar Hoover's fair-haired boy; he jokingly called him "the Clark Gable of the service."

Although Purvis was responsible for many blunders in his attempts to find, capture and/or kill the big gang members of the early 1930s, he was

Kids all over America wanted to be a G-Man like Melvin Purvis. Post cereals gave them the opportunity to play cops and robbers by sending in box tops for badges like this one. *Author collection*

integrally involved in the cases of Pretty Boyd Floyd, Baby Face Nelson, and, most significantly, John Dillinger. Writes historian Richard Gid Powers, "The country seized on Melvin Purvis, with his squeaky voice and diminutive build, as a kind of Frank Capra hero, proof that ordinary citizens, provided they stuck together, could lick anything and anybody, even John Dillinger, the age's chosen symbol of social disintegration."[183]

The exploits of Purvis and other FBI "G-Men" was celebrated in movies in the 1930s, and Post Toasties Cereals offered

Purvis premiums for children who sent in box tops. Writes Ted Hakes, an authority on character toy collectibles, "As the embodiment of law and order and the implacable enemy of criminals, Purvis was heavily promoted in the 1930s by Post cereals in newspapers, on cereal boxes, and in magazine advertising . His 'Junior G-Man Corps and Law and Order Patrol' enlisted kids by the thousands with a profusion of premiums—badges, ID cards, rings, flashlights, knives, fingerprint kits, manuals, pen and pencil sets, even separate badges for members of the Girls Division."[184]

FBI Director Hoover turned on Purvis when his popularity acceded Hoover's own. *FBI photo*

All the attention soured Hoover's opinion of his once-favored agent. He began denigrating him and downplaying his role in bringing down the gangsters. Purvis resigned from the FBI in 1935, a year after Dillinger's death, and eventually returned to South Carolina, where he married an old sweetheart and had three sons. He served in the Army during World War II, obtaining the rank of colonel, and was an investigator for the Nuremberg Trials after the war. On February 29, 1960, Purvis was found dead of a gunshot wound to the head at his Florence home. He was fifty-six. Whether he shot himself by accident or on purpose was not determined, though Hoover immediately issued a press release describing it as a suicide. Hoover never sent his condolences to the family, and Purvis's widow rebuked the director in a short note. "We are honored that you ignored Melvin's death," she wrote. "Your jealousy hurt him very much but until the end I think he loved you."[185]

The Florence County History Museum has a permanent exhibit about Purvis. He is buried in the Mount Hope Cemetery under a marker carved with Latin words that translate to "I was often afraid, but I never ran."[186]

Florence County History Museum

111 W. Cheves Street, Florence, South Carolina • www.flocomuseum.org

Mount Hope Cemetery

100 Cherokee Road, Florence, South Carolina • www.mthopeflorence.com

Franklin Delano Roosevelt took office in March 1933 and appointed Homer S. Cummings as his attorney general. That summer brought a wave of spectacular crimes—kidnappings, bank robberies, a shoot-out in Kansas City that killed four law enforcement agents—and Cummings and J. Edgar Hoover declared war. In a little over two years, outlaws from "Machine Gun" Kelly to George "Baby Face" Nelson to John Dillinger were either gunned down or put in prison, and Cummings dreamed of opening a prison fit for the worst of the worst prisoners. He got his wish in August 1934, when the Federal Bureau of Prisons took control of Alcatraz Island in San Francisco Bay. Among the grim prison's first inmates was Al Capone. During his eight years there, the harshness of the conditions and the advance of his disease broke him completely. By the time he was released, he had the mental age of a seven-year-old child, and, in today's lingo, a seven-year-old with ADHD, prone to violent outbursts and tantrums that required burly men to subdue.

Mae and Sonny had stayed in Miami Beach throughout Al's incarceration, supported in a greatly reduced manner by the Outfit and Al's brother, Ralph. In early 1940, a much-diminished Public Enemy No. 1 joined them and stayed there until his death from a stroke and pneumonia on

Capone, right, and an unidentified man leave St. Patrick Church following Sonny Capone's wedding. *State Archives of Florida*

January 25, 1947. He had just turned forty-eight years old. He made a rare appearance in December 1941, a few weeks after Pearl Harbor, when he attended Sonny's wedding at St. Patrick Catholic Church. Capone stayed close to home during the last years of his life, spending time with family, including four grandchildren and a young great-niece, Deirdre Marie Capone, who became one of his greatest defenders. Many years later, she published a memoir called *Uncle Al Capone: The Untold Story from Inside His Family* that presented her view of a loving *paterfamilias* who also happened to be a master criminal. It included recipes.[187]

There was no funeral mass for Al Capone. His visitation was held at a mortuary on Dade Avenue in Miami, where an employee of the funeral home stealthily took pictures of him in his coffin.[188] *Miami Daily News* publisher James M. Cox ordered his obituary to be handled like any other dead person's, telling his editors, "I don't want that son of a bitch on my front page." His coffin and his family returned to Chicago, where a graveside service was held on February 4, 1947.

With Capone's death, life got much harder for his widow and son. Mae kept the Palm Island home until 1952 when she could no longer afford to pay for its upkeep. She moved to Hollywood, Florida to be near a sister and died there at age eighty-nine. Sonny's marriage fell apart and to escape living under his father's dark shadow he legally changed his name to Albert Francis. In 1959 Sonny's former classmate Desi Arnaz, Jr., co-star with his wife Lucille Ball of the popular *I Love Lucy* television show and one of the most influential producers in Hollywood, developed a television series based on Elliot Ness's war on Al Capone and other gangsters called *The Untouchables*. Sonny, Mae, and Al Capone's sister Mafalda filed a lawsuit seeking millions of dollars in damages for invasion of privacy. The case was dismissed with the judge's conclusion that a deceased person had no privacy to invade.[189] The series, starring Robert Stack as Eliot Ness, ran for five seasons and was remade into a 1987 Brian DePalma movie of the same name starring Kevin Costner as Ness and Robert DeNiro as Al Capone.

In January 2015, Deirdre Capone threw a posthumous 116th birthday for her Uncle Al at the Seminole Casino in Coconut Creek, Florida. Tickets to the sumptuous four-course meal cost $125 each and included a signature cocktail called the Chicago Typewriter, slang for a Thompson submachine gun.[190]

HOT SPRINGS, ARKANSAS

The other Southern destination that has documented evidence of Al Capone's visits is Hot Springs, Arkansas. Once a respectable resort where well-to-do Victorians came to enjoy the supposed curative powers of its hot mineral springs, by Capone's day it had become a sort of Magic Kingdom for gangsters. In his highly readable book *Public Enemies: America's Greatest Crime Wave and the Birth of the FBI, 1933–34*, Bryan Burroughs describes the town divided by its Central Avenue. "On one side stretched seven ornate bathhouses. On the other was a line of pool halls and taverns that ended at two casinos, the Belvedere and the Southern Club. Brothels and cabarets dotted the surrounding houses. It was illegal, of course, but everyone, from the governor of Arkansas on down, looked the other way. The mayor and local police ran it all like a corporation, taking their cut from every whore, blackjack dealer, and pool shark."[191]

Just the sort of spot to take your wife and kiddie for a little relaxation, right? In fact, Capone did just that on at least one occasion, bringing his family to his favorite Arlington Hotel and having several pictures made during their stay. One of these was at Happy Hollow, a touristy photo studio specializing in "rustic and comic photos," where customers could pose in front of mock-ups of wild west saloons and the like. There are several such photos of Capone and his cronies there, and one of young Sonny standing behind the saloon bar pouring a "drink" for his mother.[192]

Not all visits were so congenial. According to Leigh Phillip, author of *The Devil's Town: Hot Springs During the Gangster Era*, Capone grew angry after a bad streak at cards in the Southern Club and stalked out without paying his debt. The intervention of the police chief, who informed Capone that a welsher would not be welcome in the future, persuaded him to ante up.[193] ■

A vintage postcard shows the Maurice Bath House, one of the ornate facilities in Hot Springs. *Author collection*

PROHIBITION EXPEDITION IN HOT SPRINGS

While Hot Springs is no longer a gangster's paradise, a visitor can get a flavor of those times by staying at the luxurious 500-room rebranded Arlington Resort Hotel and Spa (Al often rented the entire fourth floor), visiting the historic bath houses, and taking in the Gangster Museum of America, with its own Al Capone Gallery.

Arlington Resort Hotel and Spa • 239 Central Avenue, Hot Springs
www.arlingtonhotel.com

Gangster Museum of America • 510 Central Avenue, Hot Springs
www.tgmoa.com

Bathhouse Row in downtown Hot Springs is a National Historic Landmark administered by the National Park Service. It consists of eight bathhouses—two of which offer bath and/or spa services—a park, and twenty-six miles of hiking trails. www.nps.gov/hosp/learn/historyculture/bathhouse-row-today.

GEORGIA-FLORIDA CAPONE-A-THON PROHIBITION EXPEDITION

Windsor Hotel • 125 W. Lamar Street, Americus, Georgia
www.windsor-americus.com

Biltmore Hotel • 1200 Anastasia Avenue, Coral Gables, Florida
www.biltmorehotel.com

93 Palm Island. Although you won't be able to see much of the house, you can drive onto the island or take a tour by water. We booked a private tour with Captain Mike Lynch's service, www.speedboattours.com.

Miami Beach Golf Club. You can play on the course that Capone and his goons knew as the Bayshore Golf Club or have a meal or a drink at the club restaurant. 2301 Alton Road, Miami Beach. www.miamibeachgolfclub.com

Joe's Stone Crab, 11 Washington Avenue, Miami Beach. www.joesstonecrab.com. The large restaurant that Capone dined in is not open year-round, but a smaller Joe's Take Away is, and the company ships crab claws nationwide.

St. Patrick Catholic Church • 3716 Garden Avenue, Miami Beach
www.stpatrickmiamibeach.com

Cemetery Side Trip

Miami's Caballero Rivero Woodlawn North Park Cemetery, founded in 1913, is the resting place of the two men who helped Al Capone buy his home on Palm Island, former mayor **John N. Lummus, Jr.** and hotel manager **Parker Henderson**.[194] More interestingly, its residents include two former presidents of Cuba and one of Nicaragua—all deposed and exiled, of course—and **Manuel Artime**, leader of the Bay of Pigs invasion. 3262 S.W. 8th Street, Miami. www.caballeroriverowoodlawn.com.

In Georgia, Andersonville is the home of the most notorious of the Civil War prisons, now a National Historic Site operated by the National Park Service. A national cemetery, the prison site, and the National Prisoner of War Museum are on the grounds, which are about ten miles from Americus. This has nothing to do with Prohibition, but while you're in the neighborhood . . . 760 POW Road, Andersonville. www.nps.gov/ande/planyourvisit

Recommended Reading

Al Capone in Miami: Paradise or Purgatory by Sally J. Ling (Deerfield Beach, FL: Flamingo Press, 2016)

Capone: His Life, Legacy, and Legend by Deirdre Bair (New York: Doubleday, 2016)

The Vendetta: Special Agent Mel Purvis, John Dillinger, and Hoover's FBI in the Age of Gangsters by Alston Purvis and Alex Tresniowski (New York: Public Affairs, 2005)

The Devil's Town: Hot Springs During the Gangster Era by Philip Leigh (Columbia, SC: Shotwell Press, 2018)

CHAPTER ELEVEN

$\mathcal{R}$EPEAL

WE'VE MOVED BACK AND FORTH in time during our Baptists and Bootleggers Prohibition Expedition, from the legal and illegal distillers and temperance leaders of the post-Civil War era to the moonshine runners-turned-stock-car-drivers and "revenuers" of the twentieth century. On the way, we learned that the prohibition of alcohol (with a small p) wasn't limited to the thirteen-year big-P Prohibition period when the Eighteenth Amendment and the Volstead Act were the law of the land. But let's now home in on the year 1928.

Prohibition had been in effect for more than eight years. Al Capone was still the big cheese in Chicago, where his henchman enforced his will with intimidation and tommy guns. That year, there were 527 murders in the city of four million; New York, with more than six million residents and its own problems with gangs, registered 337 murders.[195] (One of them was the notorious racketeer Arnold Rothstein.) It was said that sixty percent of the Chicago police were on the take.

Other gangs were at work in cities large and small across the country, where they had largely taken over the rum-running trade. Future NASCAR drivers were hurtling down the mountains and through the swamps of the South with loads of moonshine in their Ford cars. Anyone in America who wanted a drink could get one from a bootlegger or at a speakeasy or blind tiger or the well-stocked cellar of their private club or mansion wine cellar. Isidore "Izzy" Einstein, one of the few truly honest Prohibition agents in the government, said the shortest wait he had for an offer of a drink was in New Orleans, where a cab driver offered him a bottle thirty-five seconds after picking him up at the railroad station.[196] Scofflaws included members of Congress and other elected officials who bellowed their support of Prohibition in public and drank in private. The president of the American Bar Association identified the bootlegger as "the spider in the center of the American web of crime."[197]

On the national stage, the Anti-Saloon League had suffered a terrible blow with the death of its ruthless leader, Wayne B. Wheeler, at age fifty-seven, following a vacation from hell in which his wife burned to death and her father had a fatal heart attack when he saw her in flames. Nevertheless, Wheeler seemed able to control Congress from the grave—for now. The ASL's female counterpart, the Women's Christian Temperance Union, was still active; its president was Ella A. Boole, the sanctimonious widow of a Methodist minister in Brooklyn, who claimed in a hearing before

Ella Boole, a Methodist minister's widow from Brooklyn, was the president of the WCTU. *Library of Congress*

Isidore "Izzy" Einstein was offered booze thirty-five seconds after arriving in New Orleans. *National Archives*

Congress to speak for the women of America and their desire to keep Prohibition in effect.[198]

President Calvin Coolidge had decided not to run for re-election and his very able and popular secretary of commerce, Herbert Hoover, won the Republican nomination. Hoover liked to stop in at the Belgian embassy for a cocktail on his way home from work—embassies were exempt from Prohibition laws—but in his acceptance speech at the GOP convention he called Prohibition "a great social and economic experiment, noble in motive and far-reaching in purpose."[199] Ever since, he has been credited as the author of the phrase "a noble experiment."

Assistant Attorney General Mabel Walker Willebrandt, still fighting a losing battle over Prohibition enforcement but hoping to be appointed attorney general or to the federal bench should Hoover win, was making campaign speeches on his behalf. She assured gatherings of Methodist ministers that Hoover would continue the dry crusade and told them to urge their church members from the pulpit to vote for Hoover.

The Democrats had nominated Alfred E. Smith, the four-term governor of New York. Al Smith, a creature of New York City's Tammany Hall Democratic Party machine, but a very effective politician, was the first person of the Catholic faith nominated by any major party for the presidency—there would not be another until John F. Kennedy in 1960—and an avowed wet. Even though both parties called for better enforcement of Prohibition in their platforms, Smith's well-known disdain for the Volstead Act, combined with the long-running "Coolidge Prosperity," his religion, and his city slicker background, put him far behind the rather colorless Hoover in the race for president.

Al Smith, the "wet" governor of New York, was the Democratic nominee for president in 1928. Herbert Hoover headed the Republican ticket. *Both photos Library of Congress.*

Down in Warm Springs, Georgia, Franklin Delano Roosevelt was operating a rehabilitation center for polio survivors in a broken-down hotel and a scattering of ramshackle cottages beside pools fed with mineral water. He had first come to the Meriwether Inn four years before after hearing of another polio patient who recovered the ability to walk after exercising in the warm, buoyant water. Against the advice of his wife, Eleanor, and his political guru, Louis Howe, he bought the place and set up a foundation to fund its operations. Polio patients from all over the country were coming there for rehabilitation and redemption, and "Old Doc" Roosevelt was reveling in his new role. His chief assistant and official hostess was again his faithful secretary, Missy LeHand, who had never stopped believing that he would walk again and return to political life.[200] There were reasons to be hopeful. Recently he had given the nominating speech for Smith at the Democratic National Convention and he had staggered across the living room of his Warm Springs cottage in heavily braced legs.

The swimming pool wasn't the only place FDR liked to get wet. Though he was cagey about his public stance on Prohibition—he sometimes described himself as "damp"—he and LeHand jointly hosted a cocktail hour every afternoon at the cottage they shared.[201] FDR's popularity in his adopted state of Georgia helped him secure endorsements for Smith, including that of the nearby *Manchester Mercury*. But the efforts of the GOP to smear Smith as a man who would allow the Pope to rule America—a charge Kennedy would later face—took hold of voters' imaginations. A Georgia woman asked FDR if Smith's election would annul all non-Catholic marriages and make her children illegitimate. It was a common perception.

FDR loved swimming in the warm mineral pools in Warm Springs, Georgia. He also enjoyed his daily cocktail hour in his cottage. *FDR Presidential Library and Museum*

The Rev. Bob Jones, an Alabama evangelist second in popularity only to Billy Sunday on the revival circuit, announced, "I would rather see a saloon on every corner than a Catholic in the White House." He also said he would prefer an African American president to Al Smith, except he didn't use such a respectful descriptor.[202]

With three strikes against him in the conservative South—religion, rum, and Tammany—Smith was nervous about not only losing the South—even with its innate hatred of the Party of Lincoln dating from the Civil War—but also the state where he was the sitting governor. New York had the largest population of any state in the country and the Democrats had not yet nominated a candidate for governor. Roosevelt's name was being widely mentioned. In late September, from his hotel suite at the New York Democratic Party convention in Albany, Smith began haranguing Roosevelt to run, using every tool from telegrams to surrogates. Finally, FDR caved. To the dismay of Eleanor, Louis Howe, and, especially, Missy LeHand, he threw his hat in the ring.

On the Republican side, Willebrandt's efforts to elect Hoover were joined by those of another prominent woman. Pauline Morton Sabin, a patrician, politically astute socialite, and wife of an ultra-wealthy New York banker, had been active in Republican politics for a decade. She was the first woman elected to the Republican National Committee and was a formidable fundraiser, presiding over huge, gala events at her English manor-style estate in the Hamptons, Bayberry Land. Initially, she had favored Prohibition, thinking it would be good for her teen-aged sons, but the realities of Prohibition had soured her. Like many wealthy people, she had well-stocked liquor cabinets and wine cellars in her homes, but she was disgusted when "drinking-dry" politicians came to visit and guzzled her booze. When she heard Ella Boole declare, "I speak for the women of America," Sabin thought, "Well, lady, not this woman you don't."

The WCTU had been motivated to defend the home, especially children, from the evils of alcohol. Remember Carry Nation's self-proclaimed title as "Your Loving Home Defender"? Sabin felt it had all backfired, and the speakeasy culture had made liquor more accessible to young people rather than less. "Today in any speakeasy in the United States you can find boys and girls in their teens drinking liquor, and this situation has become so acute that the mothers of this country feel something must be done to protect their children," she said.

An election cartoon in 1928 presented Al Smith's "gang": the wet crowd, Romanism, and the Tammany Hall tiger. *Library of Congress*

Hail! Hail! The Gang's All Here!

Sabin's husband, Charles, was a Democrat and a founding member of the Association Against the Prohibition Amendment, started in 1918. AAPA was looked at somewhat askance, however, because it was comprised of wealthy men who seemed most concerned about having to pay higher income taxes to make up for the lost alcohol excise tax revenue. Although she adored her husband, Sabin was a rock-ribbed Republican and dutifully marched to the GOP drumbeat. In 1928, she held out hope that, because of Hoover's wishy-washy statement about the "noble experiment" (and perhaps his frequent "happy hours" with the Belgian ambassador) he would be willing to take a hard look at Prohibition.

On November 6, Smith lost in a landslide, carrying only Massachusetts and six Southern states. But he also *lost* four Southern states—Florida, North Carolina, Tennessee and Kentucky, as well as Texas—that had been reliably democratic for two generations. He even lost New York, where Franklin Roosevelt won the governorship by such a narrow margin that his victory was not declared until the next day.

So, let's move on to 1929. FDR was inaugurated as governor of New York on January 1. Hoover's inauguration was set for March 4. Two days prior to that, Congress, emboldened by Smith's historic loss and misreading it as support for Prohibition, passed the Jones Act, an amendment to the Volstead Act. It converted most alcohol violations, which had been misdemeanors, into felonies, greatly increased the top penalties for Volstead violations and,

for the first time, made it a crime for citizens to *purchase* illegal alcohol—
activity that was not even forbidden under the Eighteenth Amendment.
Furthermore, anyone who was aware of illegal alcohol activity and didn't
squeal to law enforcement could be convicted of a felony themselves. In
effect, this made it a crime *not* to snitch on your neighbors. Among the violators caught up in the net was a twelve-year-old girl in Greenville, South
Carolina who was arrested for carrying a bottle of liquor across the street.
She appeared in court without legal counsel (or any adult support, for that
matter) and was sentenced to a month in jail.[203]

In a series of newspaper articles that were collected into a book called
The Inside of Prohibition, Mabel Walker Willebrandt expressed approval of
the new law "because there is such a thing as being too lenient and 'easy'
with the criminal," no matter how minor the offense. Throughout her
book, she harped on the lack of honest revenue agents, insisting America
could indeed go dry if only the government would put the resources behind
law enforcement and find 4,000 men "who cannot be bought" to serve as
agents. In fact, the cost of enforcing Prohibition had been climbing steadily,
from $6.35 million in 1921 to $8.5 million in 1925. By 1932, the cost would
exceed $16 million.[204] Finding the honest men was much harder. Seven
hundred-fifty agents had been dismissed for delinquency or misconduct in
the first six years of Prohibition, many for violating the very laws they were
hired to enforce.[205]

Mabel Walker Willebrandt,
working at her desk in
Washington, continued to
insist the country could go
dry with proper enforce-
ment of the Volstead Act.
Library of Congress

Now, let's bring Al Capone and his "frenemies" back into the picture for a moment. In May 1929, New York gangster Meyer Lansky called the first organized crime conference in American history, hosted in Atlantic City by its criminal overlord Nucky Johnson. Lucky Luciano was there, as was Bugsy Siegel. So was Capone, who shortly after got arrested for carrying a gun in Philadelphia and spent a year in prison. At the conference, Lansky presented a plan to create a national crime syndicate, with territories for each major gang and an organizational structure for gang "families." The idea was to reduce the inter-gang wars that were taking up so much time and energy, and focus on the business of getting rich. An outgrowth of this was a professional hit arm called Murder, Inc. Thus, was formed the modern Mafia, which controlled drug trafficking, prostitution, gambling, and some unions well into the 1960s.[206]

At Hoover's inauguration, held on a miserably cold and rainy day, he scolded all the violators of the Volstead Act, from criminal bootleggers to the citizen scofflaws who bought their products. He announced his plan "to appoint a national commission for a searching investigation of the whole structure of our Federal system of jurisprudence, to include the method of enforcement of the Eighteenth Amendment and the causes of abuse under it." His words on the failure of the criminal justice system and the enforcement of Prohibition were the only ones in his short speech that drew cheers from the shivering audience, except when he recognized outgoing President Calvin Coolidge.

Not every Republican was thrilled by Hoover's promise. Pauline Sabin had been under the impression that the commission would focus solely on the Volstead Act and find enforcement so impossible that repeal would be recommended. The day after the inauguration, Sabin sent her resignation to the Republican National Committee. A month later, speaking at a Women's National Republican Club luncheon, she shocked the room by sharing her resignation and her commitment to work for repeal.[207] She was inundated with letters and even donations. "Coming out against Prohibition I found I had spoken for thousands of other women," she said. "There was a large group ready to be organized, wanting to be organized. And the road that lay before me was so plainly indicated I could not turn back from it."[208] She quickly gathered some of her well-heeled and similarly disenchanted Republican lady friends and formed the Women's Organization for National Prohibition Reform, or WONPR.

Sabin's action was headlined in newspapers across the country. "Mrs. Sabin Out to Battle Drys!" one said. In today's terms, what she did might be comparable to Democratic U.S. House Speaker Nancy Pelosi resigning to focus all her attention on striking down *Roe v. Wade* or former South Carolina GOP Governor Nikki Haley recanting all the nice things she had said about Donald Trump and announcing she planned to run for president as a Democrat.

As a practiced political hand and a high-profile socialite with a network of wealthy friends, Sabin soon got WONPR humming. Attractive, well-spoken, and always beautifully dressed—"Thank God, a pretty woman in politics at last," sighed an unnamed senator—she was a natural in the media, and she found an especially welcoming platform for her views in the press empire of William Randolph Hearst. He turned against Prohibition in 1929 and influenced many other newspaper publishers to do the same. Although Sabin took some pages out of the WCTU playbook in building an army of female agitators, she wisely recruited women from all economic and social levels. The WCTU was a resolutely middle-class organization that looked down on the working classes (especially immigrants) *and* the elite. WONPR welcomed all women. Its largest constituency was housewives, but the working women members had occupations ranging from nurse to factory worker.

Sabin's wealthy friends contributed the money needed to fuel the organization's activities, and there was no membership fee to join, though many women sent in donations of nickels and dimes wrapped in toilet paper. This meant women of modest means could join just as easily as a Park Avenue heiress.

The WCTU was not the least bit ready to concede its role as the representative for American womanhood. Dr. Mary Armor, president of the Georgia chapter, lashed out, "As to Mrs. Sabin and her cocktail-drinking women, we will outlive them, out-fight them, out-talk them, out-pray them and out-vote them." But the ranks of WONPR's membership grew as

An unexpected activist, Pauline Morton Sabin's patrician beauty was captured in this portrait by Phillip Alexius Laszlo. *National Portrait Gallery* the WCTU's lagged, and even Armor had to admit that her organization's support of the Republican Hoover had hurt membership in the South.[209] To bolster their membership rolls, the groups set up rival booths at county fairs and flower shows. In Kentucky, a WONPR coordinator boasted, "the WCTU met with very little success in winning people away from the WONPR booth because our women were more amiable and laughed with the crowds instead of preaching to them." It took a thick skin to work for repeal in Kentucky. A dry newspaper said the typical "repealist" woman in the state was either a drunkard, had an immoral home life, or planned "to get into the liquor business when and if it is again legalized." Such accusations were expressed in lurid language in print and over the radio waves across the country.

WONPR wasn't the only organization agitating for reform or repeal. Charles Sabin's Association Against the Prohibition Amendment attracted new, prominent members of the business community as well, and the two organizations often worked hand-in-hand. But Sabin and his capitalist buddies were overshadowed by his wife and her "Sabine Women." Their job was made easier when Bishop James Cannon, who had succeeded Wayne B. Wheeler as leader of the Anti-Saloon League and ridiculed Al Smith as "the cocktail president," was accused of stock speculation, adultery, and campaign finance irregularities. Although he was eventually exonerated, the charges ruined his reputation, embarrassed the Methodist Church, and damaged the ASL.[210]

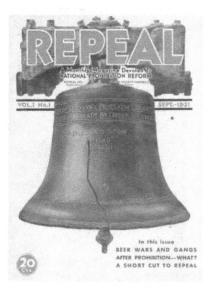

Meanwhile, Mabel Walker Willebrandt discovered she had fallen on her sword for Herbert Hoover and gotten nothing for it but a fatal wound. Rather than appoint her attorney general, Hoover asked her to recommend other nominees for the post. She swallowed her pride and did so, and then resigned to go into private practice. One of her first clients was Fruit Industries Ltd., a California grape growers' consortium that produced a concentrate called

The first issue of *Repeal* Magazine was published in September 1931. *Courtesy Steven Lomazow, M.D.*

Vine-Glo, sold door-to-door and at grocery stores and pharmacies. She helped the company get millions of dollars in federal farm loans, testifying that the concentrate was "a strictly legal product." It was, but when yeast and water were added, it turned into wine. To make sure the customer was satisfied, Fruit Industries even provided helpful follow-up visits by employees who would bottle the finished product. A court battle over Vine-Glo resulted in it being found in violation of the Volstead Act and Fruit Industries discontinuing it in 1931. The *Baltimore Evening Sun* wrote an editorial chiding Willebrandt that it headlined simply, "Back to Gin."[211]

Photographer Dorothea Lange's portrait "Migrant Mother" is one of the most searing depictions of the toll of the Great Depression on Americans. *Library of Congress*

Of course, the news overshadowing all events in 1929 was the crash of the stock market on October 24 and the start of the Great Depression. I could quote all sorts of statistics here about unemployment, bank failures, homeless people living in Hoovervilles, dust storms, hoboes riding the rails, children being abandoned to orphanages, etc. etc., but we all know the Depression was just awful and it lasted for a long time. Herbert Hoover, who had been lauded as "the great humanitarian" for his relief work during World War I, seemingly could not think outside the GOP box of limited national government. He kept insisting recovery was right around the corner, despite all evidence to the contrary. Worse, as federal revenues fell, Hoover was determined to cut spending to balance the budget. His face became more and more dour; it was said that if you put a rose in Hoover's hand it would wilt.

With their tremendous wealth, the Sabins and most of their friends were insulated from the harshest effects of the Depression, so for her it was full steam ahead with WONPR. Her women researched Prohibition issues—she emphasized facts, not emotions—lobbied legislators, generated publicity, and became accomplished public speakers. When the worst of the Depression became evident and Al Capone was finally being brought to justice, WONPR cleverly linked Prohibition reform to the financial crisis as well as crime with flyers like the one headlined, "DO YOU WANT TO . . . PUT THE CRIMINAL OUT OF BUSINESS? HELP THE UNEMPLOYED?" Membership—remember, it was free—had reached 100,000 by the time the first national WONPR convention was held in 1930. It had tripled by the 1931 convention and reached 620,000 by 1932, with branches in thirty-four states.

Although the greatest membership concentrations were in New York, other Northeastern states, and the Midwest—notably Michigan—Sabin was not daunted by the challenges of the traditionally dry South. Southern states were slower to establish chapters, but the efforts got a boost when a WONPR member in Kentucky, looking for pewter in an antique shop, came upon an album of old newspaper clippings. In one of them, Jefferson Davis, the president of the Confederacy, had defended his opposition to prohibition. The "effect throughout the Southern states was most favorable to the Repeal cause," wrote Grace Root in her official history of WONPR.

In New Orleans, Elizabeth Thomas Werlein volunteered to lead the Louisiana branch. A free spirit if there ever was one, this daughter of a Michigan dynamite manufacturer "hunted tigers in India, shot big game in Africa, had lunch in a submerged submarine, was one of the first three women in the country to go up in a hot air balloon, broke stallions on the Steppes of Russia, and flew in the Wright Brothers' plane in Paris." After marrying a wealthy New Orleans businessman, she founded the first League of Women Voters in Louisiana and then headed off to China "to study ants." Veteran of many community improvement committees, she was a natural for WONPR.[212]

In 1930, Pauline and Charles Sabin bought a plantation in South Carolina's Berkeley County near Charleston called The Oaks, established in colonial times by a planter from Barbados. In buying a former plantation, the Sabins were joining thousands of wealthy Northerners who established hunting preserves in the South which they used primarily as winter homes. From her Southern base, Sabin enlisted two socially prominent Charleston women, Mrs. Cesare A. Andreini (née Eliza Huger Dunkin) and Mrs. Simons Vanderhorst Waring (née Louisa Anna Johnson), as the chair and vice-chair for the state WONPR.

ELIZA HUGER DUNKIN ANDREINI SIMONS KAMMERER

Eliza Andreini, the daughter of William
and Eunice Dunkin, was a leading light
of Charleston culture for most of her life,
being actively involved in the preservation
movement, the Charleston Poetry Society
and the Gibbes Museum of Art.

In the matter of husbands, Eliza just
had plain bad luck.[213]

At the time she became involved
in WONPR, Eliza was in her early for-
ties and living with her parents at the
Branford-Horry House, a colonial landmark
house at 59 Meeting Street that is now on
the National Register of Historic Places.
Eliza had been married at age twenty-nine
to Cesare Andreini, a British subject, in
Kobe, Japan. Andreini died shortly afterward and Eliza, who had renounced her

This miniature portrait of Eliza Andreini
done by her friend Leila Waring in 1923
was donated by Eliza to the Gibbes
Museum of Art. *Gibbes Museum*

American citizenship when she married, came home to Charleston and petitioned for reinstatement as an American citizen. She spent the rest of her life
in the city of her birth.

A gifted organizer, Eliza headed up the arrangements in Charleston for
the WONPR executive committee meeting in February 1932 and was an
active voice in the WONPR movement throughout the repeal process, being
repeatedly elected state president. The South Carolina division had hoped for
ratification of the Twenty-First Amendment here, but were, of course, disap-
pointed, and legal sale of alcohol in South Carolina did not begin until 1935.

Eliza married for a second time, in 1934, to Aiken Simons of Wilmington,
Delaware, an electrical engineer, who had formerly worked in Charleston for
DuPont. They turned their attention to the restoration of her family home,
which *National Geographic* magazine mentioned favorably in a 1939 article
titled "Charleston: Where Mellow Past and Present Meet." Unfortunately,
Simons died of a brain hemorrhage in 1939 at age 59.

continues on next page

continued from previous page

When World War II began, Eliza joined the Charleston Committee of the Friends of France and turned over part of her home to war relief activities. Neighborhood women met at 59 Meeting Street to knit and sew clothing for French refugee children. She also housed Navy captains and their families during the war, which may be how she met her third husband, the Rev. Dr. Percy Kammerer, an Episcopal minister who had come to Charleston to work with the British War Relief Society. His first wife had divorced him in Reno in 1941 and he married Eliza in 1942. During a trip to Maryland in 1946, he died unexpectedly of a heart attack the day before his sixtieth birthday, was cremated, and his ashes were interred in a cemetery plot in that state. His ex-wife, who died in a plane crash many years later, was buried beside him. Eliza died in 1962 and is buried in Charleston beside Aiken Simons. (Surely there's a story there, but I don't know what it is.) Inscribed on her gravestone are words from *Hamlet*, "To sleep perchance to dream." ■

In February 1932, Sabin called a meeting of the national executive committee and seventy-five members from all over the country traveled to Charleston. In between social activities at The Oaks and the homes of Charleston hostesses and tours of the gardens of Middleton Place and Magnolia Plantation, the women presented what the *News and Courier* called "the largest anti-prohibition demonstration ever held in South Carolina." They also got down to serious legislative business, voting to send telegrams to all members of Congress urging them to support a recently introduced resolution which would require each state to either reaffirm or denounce its support of Prohibition.[214]

At about the same time the WONPR women were touring Charleston's plantation gardens, Franklin Delano Roosevelt launched his run for the presidency and gave his full support to the repeal of the Eighteenth Amendment. Although he was considered the frontrunner for the office, there were others who had a longer history of being wet, including Al Smith, who wanted another shot at the presidency.

Both of the national political conventions were held in Chicago that June, with the Republicans gathering first. WONPR banded with other repeal groups to form the United Repeal Council and presented their case

Campaign items such as this license tag and pin emphasized the "wet" stance of FDR and his running mate John Nance Garner. *Both, FDR Presidential Library and Museum*

to both convention platform committees. The GOP committee listened to them stone-faced and issued a muddy plank that tried to appease both sides by giving the states the option to allow alcohol but leaving regulation and distribution under federal control. That made both the wets and the drys mad. The Democrats invited the United Repeal Council members into their platform meetings with open arms and later issued a recommendation for full repeal of the Eighteenth Amendment.

You would have thought that the worsening economic situation would have gotten the Democrats the most riled up in Chicago, where the dire nature of the Great Depression was evidenced by the Hoovervilles planted throughout the city. But you'd be wrong. The most riveting issue at the convention was Prohibition. When the platform committee's recommendation was made, the response was sensational. Grace Root wrote, "There was an uproar. The delegates jumped to their feet, gathered their banners, and started to parade around the convention hall. The organ played 'Happy Days are Here Again' and the noise was pandemonium."

Sabin was photographed at the Democratic convention laughing it up with Al Smith, the man she had worked so hard to defeat just four years before but had come to value and admire. Smith's hopes of being renominated were dashed by the maneuvers of Louis Howe and the rest of FDR's team, plus the party's realization that even the dour Hoover could likely beat the Catholic Smith. The drafting of wringing wet Speaker of the House John Nance Garner of Texas as vice president clinched the crucial endorsement of William Randolph Hearst. On July 2, Roosevelt flew to Chicago to accept the nomination in person—an unheard of feat. Two weeks later Pauline Morton Sabin wound up on the cover of TIME Magazine.

Using the Anti-Saloon League's own tactics to destroy it, Sabin instructed all the WONPR members to work for wet candidates up and down the ballot, no matter their party affiliation, and the organization endorsed Franklin Roosevelt for president. The endorsement wasn't universally popular; in fact, it resulted in 150 resignations—but also 137,000 new members. Enthused and mobilized, Sabin and her women helped deliver a landslide for Roosevelt, who carried all but six states and won 472 electoral votes to Hoover's 59. He reclaimed the South for his party—South Carolinians gave him 98 percent of their vote—which would keep the Southern states in the Democratic fold for another thirty years. Focusing on one issue and disregarding everything else a candidate brings to the table has its risks. In North Carolina, wet Democrat Robert R. Reynolds was elected to the Senate. In addition to a wet, he turned out to be rabidly isolationist—he wanted to build a wall around the entire United States, not just the Mexican border—anti-Semitic, and an apologist for Hitler. By 1944 the party had enough of him and nominated another candidate for Senate.[215]

The winter of 1933 was cold, miserable, and terrifying. But with commanding Democratic majorities in both houses—along with the White House, the party picked up ninety-seven seats in the House and twelve in the Senate—and with more than a few wet Republicans, Congress swiftly passed the Twenty-First Amendment, repealing the Eighteenth and turning the regulation of alcohol over to the individual states and territories. Then it was up to the states to ratify. WONPR researched various alcohol control systems in other countries, presenting numerous options for regulating alcohol. Quite a few members got appointed to the state commissions that would propose licensing and control measures.

A WONPR member proudly displays one of the organization's posters. *Library of Congress*

By the time FDR took office on March 4, 1933, every bank in the country had been closed by governors' order. Unemployment was at 25 percent. The situation was so dire that the new president swore in his cabinet that afternoon and skipped the inaugural balls. What followed was a period in American politics never seen before or since, the fabled Hundred Days. Fifteen major pieces of legislation, addressing everything from reorganizing and saving the banking system to providing emergency relief for the destitute, rolled through Congress. Among the less crucial but more popular pieces of New Deal legislation was the Beer-Wine Revenue Act, which legalized "non-intoxicating" 3.2 percent beer and light wine. Upon signing it on April 7, the president famously said, "I think this would be a good time for a beer."[216] The Anheuser-Busch brewery in St. Louis was happy to oblige, delivering a case of beer to the White House in a wagon pulled by the soon-to-be world-famous Clydesdale horse team.[217] It was hardly the first drop of alcohol the new president had enjoyed. Upon moving into the White House, FDR started the custom of a daily cocktail gathering, the "Children's Hour," with his immediate staff. Eleanor Roosevelt, who frowned on drinking and was a late convert to repeal, seldom joined them; Missy LeHand was his happy hour hostess.

The Beer-Wine Revenue Act resuscitated an industry that had once legally employed an estimated 500,000 people and sent excise tax dollars streaming into the treasury. Free-wheeling Louisiana, which had never voted itself dry before national Prohibition and, as its Governor Huey Long said, didn't do a "damn thing" to police it, was ready to act immediately. More than 900 beer licenses were issued in New Orleans the first week of the revenue act. [218]

Meanwhile, the Twenty-First Amendment was coming up for votes in the states, mostly by especially called constitutional conventions. Michigan was the first state to ratify, on April 10. The first Southern states to ratify were Arkansas, Alabama, and Tennessee, all in August, followed by Virginia in October and Florida and Kentucky in November. North Carolina held a referendum and voters chose not to consider the issue, and South Carolina voters rejected the amendment on December 4. The following day, with Utah voting in favor—Mormon Utah, for goodness sake!—the amendment was ratified. Georgia, Louisiana, and Mississippi had not taken action by that date. In fact, Mississippi became the last state in the country to ratify—in 1966!—proving a prediction made by the hayseed comedian Will

Rogers. He had said Mississippi was the one state that was going to vote dry as long as voters could stagger to the polls. [219]

The euphoria of victory was dimmed for Pauline Sabin by heartbreak. In early October, while she was making a speech in Pennsylvania, her husband was dining alone at Bayberry Land and suffered a stroke. He died at the dinner table. In October, she announced WONPR would fold as soon as ratification was accomplished, its work done. She remained politically active throughout her life, which included a third marriage in 1936. Among her accomplishments was serving as director of volunteer services for the American Red Cross during World War II. She sold both The Oaks and Bayberry Land and settled in Washington, where she was a popular hostess and advised President Truman on interior decoration of the renovated White House.

You can Google "Repeal Day" and find hundreds of pictures of happy people guzzling beer and drinking liquor, but the truth was that prohibition—the little-P kind—kept its grip on much of the country for years. It was 1935 before Georgia and South Carolina opened the door a crack and allowed counties and municipalities to pass local option ordinances. This practice was followed in most states, creating a bewildering patchwork quilt of rules and regulations. For example, until quite recently in the county where I live, I could buy beer on Sunday at a chain grocery store in one town but not at the same chain grocery store in the county seat.

Daniel Okrent, whose book *Last Call* I have cited numerous times, summarizes the situation nicely. Repeal, he wrote, replaced "the almost anything-goes ethos with a series of state-by-state codes, regulations, and enforcement procedures. Now there were closing hours and age limits and Sunday blue laws, as well as a collection of geographic proscriptions that kept bars or package stores distant from schools, churches, or hospitals. State licensing requirements forced legal sellers to live by the code, and in many instances, statutes created penalties for buyers as well. Just as Prohibition did not prohibit, making drink legal did not make drink entirely available."

The Bible Belt mentality—or tradition or whatever you want to call it—that had Baptists and bootleggers working for the same outcome but for different reasons persisted in the South. North Carolina opened up alcohol sales in 1937, but it created a state monopoly on liquor, which is to this day sold only in state-operated retail stores. Residents complain that the stores are overpriced, poorly stocked and give poor customer service. You would think that Charlotte, the seat of the financial industry in the state and a city we perceive as being forward-thinking and sophisticated today, would have been at the front of the line when it came to local option, but you'd be wrong. Charlotte went dry in 1905, three years before the state did, and didn't allow liquor stores until 1947. It was 1978 before liquor-by-the-drink could be served in North Carolina restaurants and bars, if allowed by local option. Passing that option was considered a landmark event in Mecklenburg County, leading to Charlotte's business and cultural renaissance.[220]

Down in Mount Pleasant, South Carolina, Louise Jefferson Brown, a widowed African American woman who worked at the cigar factory in Charleston, supported her family by operating a speakeasy out of her home. Well into the 1960s, she supplemented her cigar factory earnings by "inviting guests in after work to buy beer and stay awhile," according to her great-granddaughter Johnny Caldwell. Obviously, the blind tigers were still lurking in Charleston![221]

South Carolina, which always seems to vie with Mississippi and Alabama for the worst of everything, finally allowed serving liquor-by-the-drink with its 1973 mini-bottle law. It required bars and restaurants to use tiny one-serving bottles for drink-making. Although the bottles were cute and handy for smuggling a shot of booze in your purse or pocket their use severely restricted creativity in drink-making so that bars were pretty much reduced to two or three-ingredient concoctions. The repeal of the mini-bottle law in 2005 paved the way for the craft cocktail bar, like The Gin Joint in Charleston. Naturally, South Carolina was the last state to abolish the practice of mini-bottles in favor of free pours, which forced a new generation of bartenders to learn how to measure and pour from a full-size bottle.

The practice of making and selling moonshine persisted in the South for decades after Prohibition ended, especially in states that kept the most restrictive laws. In North Carolina, according to Daniel S. Pierce, author of *Tar Heel Lightnin'*, the profit margin on moonshine was such that "if North Carolina has ever held the distinction of being number one nationally in anything, it is moonshine production."[222] Pierce, an authority on NASCAR, subtitled his book *How Secret Stills and Fast Cars Made North Carolina the Moonshine Capital of the World*. Twenty-seven current NASCAR drivers call North Carolina home, more than any other state.[223] It's not for nothing that Charlotte eventually became the home of the NASCAR Hall of Fame.

In my own Anderson County, Jim Williams, who was the sheriff in the late 1960s and early 1970s, blamed 97 percent of the crime, from murders to domestic violence, on illegal liquor. He and his deputies were busting up three or four stills a month, and in May 1970 set a record when they seized over a thousand gallons of liquor in one weekend raid. Still, that dwarfed the moonshine production of Northeast Georgia, which supplied border counties like Anderson. A federal ATF agent operating out of Northeast Georgia said at that time that his men had raided twenty-five stills in two weeks. Like the swill made during Prohibition, the moonshine of these more recent years was not for the faint of heart. "If people who drink that moonshine whiskey could go around and see where it is made and the filth from the stills, I'm sure they would change their drinking habits," Sheriff Williams said. He had found dead squirrels, muskrats, and possums in the open barrels of mash beside moonshine stills.[224]

When it came to legal drinking, especially in public, American culture had traveled light years from the days of the early temperance movement, and in at least one regard, Wayne B. Wheeler and Frances Willard were successful. There were no more saloons. The speakeasy bartenders, who had learned to disguise bad liquor with fruit juice and other flavors and pour it into pretty glasses, had welcomed women customers. When the speaks gave way to legal bars (sometimes in the same venue!) the women became their customers too. Oh, sure there were still (and still are today) some bars where a woman wouldn't feel especially welcome. Probably the most famous example was the Roosevelt Hotel's Main Bar in New Orleans, which

Although the "Storming of the Sazerac" was actually a publicity stunt, it marked the first time women in New Orleans were welcome in the Roosevelt Hotel's bar.

opened in 1933. Women were only allowed there during Fat Tuesday, the day of Mardi Gras. In 1949, Seymour Weiss, the hotel owner, decided to open a new, more elegant bar in the hotel that would be coeducational, so to speak. This Sazerac Bar, lined with murals by artist Paul Ninas, was set to open September 26, and Weiss orchestrated publicity by inviting pretty, stylish young women who worked at a downtown department store to be the first customers. Word quickly got around. The event was a huge hit, with women three-deep at the bar. The so-called "Storming of the Sazerac" is reenacted each year, with women dressing up in period finery for a drink, a luncheon, and a fashion show—at $69 a pop.[225]

PROHIBITION EXPEDITION

NEW ORLEANS • There are so many Prohibition-related places to go in the Big Easy that, to paraphrase Carry Nation, you would drop from exhaustion before walking a block. Two deserve special mention.

The **Sazerac Bar** at the Roosevelt Hotel is a truly spectacular bar, beautifully restored. Check out the website for information about the Storming of the Sazerac ladies' tea. 130 Roosevelt Way. www.therooseveltneworleans.com. Refer back to the introduction for the drink Huey Long favored at the Roosevelt Hotel's bar, the Ramos Gin Fizz.

The **Museum of the American Cocktail**, located inside the Southern Food & Beverage Museum, 1504 Oretha C. Haley Blvd., is full of interesting displays, including WCTU posters and the largest collection of absinthe and absinthe artifacts in the country. Check out the website, southernfood.org/cocktail-museum, for a visual "aperitif."

For a cemetery side trip, visit the grave of WONPR leader **Elizabeth Thomas Werlein** in the historic Metairie Cemetery, 5100 Pontchartrain Boulevard. Others resting there are jazz musicians Al Hirt and Pete Fountain, numerous former mayors and governors, and Éve Curie, an author best known as the daughter of scientists Pierre and Marie Curie. It is full of fascinating tombs, all above ground because of the high water table in New Orleans, and intriguing statuary. https://www.findagrave.com/cemetery/68207/metairie-cemetery

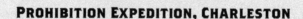

PROHIBITION EXPEDITION, CHARLESTON

You can trace the travels of the executive committee members of WONPR during their February 1932 meeting in Charleston.

Pauline Sabin held a luncheon and policy meetings at her home, **The Oaks**, a historic plantation property Charles had purchased in 1930. The Oaks is no more, having been demolished in July 2020. When I visited it shortly before its demolition, a pair of ornamental eagles sat on brick columns on either side of the driveway, looking a bit sheepish about what they were guarding. The once-impressive avenue of oaks leading to its gates was diseased and dying and the house was hemmed in by a subdivision of modest homes. Its last iteration was as a golf club, which went out of business in 2019. You can see what's left at 130 The Oaks Avenue, Goose Creek.

These photographs of The Oaks were taken in the final days before its demolition in the summer of 2020. *Author photos*

Happily, Mrs. Andreini's home at **59 Meeting Street** is in fine shape and is a regular stop on carriage tours around the city. You can find lots of pictures of the interior on-line as well. A short video from the William Means Real Estate firm, which listed the house for sale in 2018, can be viewed at https://www.charlestonrealestate.com/blog/featured-listing-branford-horry-house/

The Branford-Horry House, where Eliza Andreini lived, is one of Charleston's many jewels of historic preservation. *Author photo*

The wet rally, with Sen. Millard E. Tydings of Maryland as the headliner, was held in Charleston's **Hibernian Hall**, 105 Meeting Street. The building, circa 1840, was packed to the rafters and responded favorably to Tydings' address, which combined appeals to states' rights and quotes from the Bible.

WONPR members took a number of garden tours, both at private homes and at historic Magnolia Plantation and Gardens and Middleton Place. Both are open to the public year-round.

Magnolia Plantation and Gardens • 3550 Ashley River Road, Charleston
www.magnoliaplantation.com

Middleton Place • 4300 Ashley River Road, Charleston
www.middletonplace.com

PORTIA'S PUNCH AND IMPROVED PORTIA'S PUNCH

Mabel Walker Willebrandt offered "Portia's Punch," a recipe for a non-alcoholic fruit punch, to *Prohibition Punches: A Book of Beverages*, compiled by Roxana B. Doran, the wife of James M. Doran, President Hoover's commissioner of prohibition in 1930.[226] In his cocktail recipe book *Noble Experiments by Judge Jr.* the author, very tongue-in-cheek—his foreword is shaped like a cocktail shaker—included a section on "improved temperance drinks." Of Portia's Punch, he said, "A concoction of Mrs. Mabel Walker Willebrandt which can be made surprisingly palatable by adding one pint of New Jersey pure concentrated apple jack and half a cup of Jamaica rum:

To one small bottle of Red Concord California pure concentrated grape juice add two bottles of light-colored ginger ale and one lemon sliced thin, and half a cup of chopped mint leaves. Serve very cold."[227]

Since I doubt any of you will try this recipe—assuming you could even decide what constitutes a "small" bottle of grape juice or what size bottles of ginger ale to use—here is the recipe for the signature cocktail served at the Roosevelt Hotel's Sazerac Bar in New Orleans:

SAZERAC

- 1 sugar cube
- 3 dashes Peychaud's bitters
- 2 oz. Sazerac six-year rye (the original recipe called for cognac)
- Herbsaint (the original recipe called for absinthe)
- Lemon peel

Fill an old-fashioned glass with ice to chill. Muddle a sugar cube with three dashes of Peychaud's Bitters in a mixing glass. Add two ounces of rye. Fill mixing glass with ice and stir 35 times. Empty ice from the old-fashioned glass and, using an atomizer, spray the inside of the glass with Herbsaint. Strain the rye and Peychaud's mixture into the glass and garnish with a lemon twist.[228]

CEMETERY SIDE TRIP

The two women who led the repeal movement for WONPR in South Carolina, **Eliza Huger Dunkin Andreini Simons Kammerer** and **Louisa Anna Johnson Waring**, are buried in Charleston's Magnolia Cemetery.[229] (You may remember from Chapter 4 that Magnolia Cemetery is also the resting place of the early WCTU leader **Sallie F. Chapin**. Let's hope her grave is not close to those cocktail-swilling Sabine Women.)

Bishop James Cannon Jr., the disgraced leader of the Anti-Saloon League, is buried in Hollywood Cemetery in Richmond, Virginia.[230] It was established in 1847 in the "garden" style so popular with Victorians. His neighbors include more dead Confederates than you can shake a stick at, including Jefferson Davis, whose anti-Prohibition views stoked the repeal fire in Kentucky. 412 S. Cherry Street. https://www.hollywoodcemetery.org/

RECOMMENDED READING

For more details about the role of women on both sides of the Prohibition issue, check out *Liberated Sprits: Two Women Who Battled Over Prohibition* by Hugh Ambrose and John Schuttler (New York: Berkley, 2018) and *American Women and the Repeal of Prohibition* by Kenneth D. Rose (New York: New York University Press, 1996).

Louise Jefferson Brown's great-granddaughter is half of a duo known as the Cocktail Bandits. Johnny Caldwell and her co-author Taneka Reeves introduce readers to Charleston culture through alcohol in their book *Holy Spirits! Charleston Culture Through Cocktails* (Charleston: Evening Post Books, 2018). And yes, they offer lots of recipes!

*E*PILOGUE

WHEN I STARTED WRITING this book in January 2020, the words "novel coronavirus" and "Covid-19" were just coming into the world's vocabulary. The coronavirus was something going on in a province of China that was causing many deaths. By the end of the month, it had spread to eighteen countries, with the United States reporting its first case in Washington state. New Orleans held its Mardi Gras as planned in late February, but it would be the last large gathering in the country for some time. By the end of February, the World Health Organization warned we were headed for an international pandemic.

About that time, Leo and I were visiting Knoxville, enjoying drinks at the Peter Kern Library speakeasy, and Louisville, where Fred and Linda Ruffenach described the Prohibition centennial bash the Whisky Chicks and Bourbon Brotherhood had hosted a few weeks before in the Rathskellar of the Seelbach Hotel. We went on tours of bourbon distilleries and had cocktails at the Hell or High Water speakeasy. Within a month, the bars would be closed, and the tours discontinued until further notice because of Covid-19. Then Louisville was rocked by riots and unrest over the death of Breonna Taylor, a young African American woman killed during a misdirected raid by Louisville police. Eventually the city would announce a $12 million settlement with her estate.[231]

I still managed to take the historic tour of Charleston's liquor hotspots with Valerie Stow the weekend before St. Patrick's Day, but Savannah had canceled its legendary, green beer-soaked celebration and by March 16, the lockdowns and sheltering-in-place orders were becoming ubiquitous under the slogan "Fifteen Days to Slow the Spread."[232] College athletics canceled March Madness and the NBA called off its playoffs. Concert tours were postponed, and movie theaters shuttered. By March 28, Covid deaths in the United States totaled 2,000; by April 5, nearly 10 million people had applied for unemployment.[233]

My datebook, usually crowded with meetings, speaking engagements, and appointments, was blank except for a meeting here and there on the Zoom platform I had scarcely been aware of the month before. Zoom was soon linking people to work, school, and social events, including Zoom happy hours. The Kentucky Derby was postponed from May until the fall, but the Whisky Chicks put on their fancy Derby Day hats anyway and had a Zoom meeting with a bourbon company representative.

With no federal directive other than suggested guidelines, governors in March had begun issuing stay-at-home orders and shutting down restaurants, bars, and non-essential retail businesses, as well as schools, and even churches. Curiously, in most states liquor stores were classified as essential. However, churches adapted like every other entity. Some held online services. Others required masks and spaced worshippers six feet apart. The tiny country church in South Carolina where the outlaw bootlegger Lewis Redmond is buried held drive-in services in the parking lot.

The mayor of Denver tried to close liquor stores; it caused such an uproar that he reversed himself in a day. Pennsylvania's governor reopened its state-owned stores when it became obvious people were simply driving to adjoining states to buy booze. No such nonsense went on in the South. In North Carolina, even with negative sales to restaurants and bars—they were allowed to return unsold inventory—the state-run liquor stores set a new record for the fiscal year ending in June, with a 17 percent sales increase.[234] In Alabama, patrons were banned from the stores, but curbside pick-up was instituted, with limits; apparently officials feared a rebirth of the blind tiger. An emergency order in Arkansas allowed liquor stores to make deliveries.[235] The man who owns the ABC store I patronize in Anderson told me his sales from April to June tripled over the year before. (A cartoon in the *Wall Street Journal* had a man asking of a liquor store clerk, "What goes well with the evening news?"[236]) In July, a scientific committee advising the federal government on nutrition guidelines recommended lowering the number of alcoholic drinks an adult male could safely consume in one day from two to one. It didn't seem to have much of an impact.[237]

As hand sanitizer disappeared from grocery store shelves, the craft distilleries sprang into action. They had the raw ingredient—ethyl alcohol—that could be combined with hydrogen peroxide and glycerin or aloe vera to make sanitizer. Trey and Bryan Boggs at Palmetto Distillery in Anderson made some for their family and friends, then requests started pouring in for more. They were soon supplying a twelve-hospital health system, BMW and Michelin manufacturing plants, and the state Department of Transportation. "We had to hire twelve people to keep up with the production," said Trey. "It has been a good thing and a terrible situation." Distilleries all over the South did the same.

On the beer scene, Covid-19 sent many suds-lovers back to the tried-and-true brands of the big beer companies and struck a blow to craft breweries. Because about half the beer produced by these small breweries is consumed on-site and restrictions either closed the taprooms or spooked customers, an industry spokesman said in November that sales were down 8 percent from the year before.[238] As people focused more on eating and drinking at home, they tended to head to the grocery store and buy cases of dependable Budweiser and Coors. Even sales of Corona, as unfortunate a brand name as can be imagined during a coronavirus pandemic, held steady.[239]

Like most everyone else who could, I stayed at home from mid-March to mid-May. I got out my sewing machine, and constructed cloth masks by the dozen, the Centers for Disease Control having recommended their use in early April. I ordered a T-shirt from the Life is Good company that had a cocktail glass on it and the word "Quarantini." Then I sewed a bunch of dresses to match my masks. Once the sheltering-in-place restrictions were relaxed and I wore them out in public, they caused a sensation wherever I went.

In May, the Labor Department announced that 20.5 million jobs had been lost, bringing the unemployment rate to 14.7 percent.[240]

The lockdowns, closings, and the severe limitations on indoor gatherings and large outdoor spectator events affected my plans for the book. I had hoped to attend a race at Darlington Raceway, one of the oldest stock car racing tracks in the South. After putting the season on hold for two months, NASCAR held its Real Heroes and Coca-Cola 600 races there in May, but without spectators. Leo and I did manage to get inside the gates of "the track too tough to tame" as the Real Heroes race was being set up—it's amazing what people will allow you to do when you say the magic words, "I'm writing a book"—but it was hard to imagine the color and sound of a live race while looking at the empty stands and vacant track. By September, a limited number of tickets to Darlington's Southern 500 were distributed to previous ticketholders but there were no tickets sold to the general public.

By June, with Covid-19 cases leveling off and restrictions being lifted, Leo and I went on the road again. In Charleston, The Gin Joint had reopened but the Prohibition bar and restaurant was still closed. The Museum of American Prohibition in Savannah welcomed customers again, with signs everywhere cautioning about social distancing and mandating masks. Our cocktail-making class there was limited to us and one other couple rather than the twenty or more students that was typical. That had its advantages; we got lots of attention and free old-fashioned glasses. Georgia had been the first state to re-open restaurants, with reduced capacity, in late April.

Most states followed. It was then believed that Covid wouldn't spread as easily during hot weather.

A second wave of Covid cases began in the mid-summer, but by then the country was becoming tremendously divided about closures. Really, it was the Baptists and bootleggers story all over again, except with the Democratic governors and mayors taking the role of the morally righteous scolds and the Republican governors reluctant to tighten up again because they felt the damage to the economy was as serious as the threat to life. Or else they wanted to follow the lead of President Trump, who kept saying, Herbert Hoover-like, that the problem would soon disappear on its own. The economy had begun to recover, but by mid-July the total deaths had reached 140,000, with another thousand added each day.[241]

George Floyd's death at the hands of Minneapolis police ignited a summer of protest, violence, and soul-searching as the Black Lives Matter movement took off. At The Villages in Florida, a video made during a Trump rally, which the president re-Tweeted, included someone yelling, "White power!" Trump later deleted the video from his Twitter feed.[242] Democrats complained that the Trump rallies spread Covid, and Republicans complained that the protest marches spread Covid. The twin issues highlighted the stark divisions between the supporters of the incumbent and his challenger, Joe Biden. (Interestingly, Trump and Biden are both teetotalers!)[243]

Despite all this misery—or perhaps because of it—people continued to find ways to gather and drink. While reading former President Obama's memoir *A Promised Land*, I was struck by his admission that he not only enjoyed martinis but also smoked a handful of cigarettes a day. He wrote, "Sometimes you were just screwed and the best you could do was have a stiff drink—and light up a cigarette."[244] During the warm months, many cities relaxed their restrictions on sidewalks, allowing restaurants to set up temporary tables for outdoor dining. Florida was one of the least restrictive states, though some of its municipalities passed stricter ordinances.[245] When we arrived in Miami in mid-September on the trail of Al Capone, the sidewalks of South Beach were packed with tables and thronged with people, some in masks, many using them as "chin diapers" or hanging them in useless places such as on one ear or an elbow. Some of the iconic old hotels in Miami Beach, including the art deco Delano South Beach Club, had closed.[246] The Frenchman who owned a darling little bakery where we breakfasted said he was barely hanging on. A 10 p.m. curfew had greatly curtailed the legendary party scene.

One of the Al Capone-related places I had hoped to tour, the federal penitentiary in Atlanta, was now out of the question. I don't know what the Covid-19 infection rate was there, but a news report in December said one out of every five state and federal prisoners in the country had tested positive for Covid-19 and more than 1,700 had died.[247]

Leo and I were quite surprised that Dawsonville, Georgia still planned to hold its October moonshine festival, because surrounding towns had canceled festivals celebrating apples and the Georgia gold rush, but since it was an outdoor event, we decided to take our chances and go. Most of the people we encountered were mask-less and not bothering with social distancing, an indication to us that the "outlaw culture" that had made Dawson County a moonshine hotspot for a century was still a fact of life. When hometown boy Chase Elliott won NASCAR's Cup Series a few weeks later, the Dawsonville Pool Room was packed shoulder-to-shoulder. By then Joe Biden had been elected president, in large part because of the Trump administration's perceived mishandling of the coronavirus pandemic.

As I write, at the end of January 2021, Covid-19 deaths in the United States top 440,000, with three to four thousand added each day. Hospitals are reaching capacity country-wide, and the South is one of the hardest-hit regions with hospitalizations tripling since October 1.[248] A more contagious variant arose in South Africa and the first two cases in the United States were diagnosed in South Carolina. More than 110,000 restaurants and bars have either closed permanently or "fallen dormant," according to the National Restaurant Association. That represents a 17 percent shrinkage from before the pandemic.[249] On the positive side, vaccines made by Pfizer and Moderna have been approved and are being distributed around the country, with the first shots going to health care workers and elderly people. The number of new cases is starting to fall. Oh, and Congress in December passed a new Covid relief package that included enhanced unemployment benefits, direct cash payments to most families, and a return of the three-martini lunch. The last, championed by South Carolina Sen. Tim Scott, was supposed to boost the restaurant business, but the real beneficiaries will be corporations that can write off the full cost of business meals at white-tablecloth restaurants.[250] And their clients, who will no doubt include many members of Congress.

I've often been struck this year about the parallels between the Prohibition years and the pandemic year of 2020. In both cases, the restrictions imposed by the government were supposed to be for the good of the public. Rampant drunkenness is bad for society. Recklessly spreading a deadly disease is bad for society too. But in both cases, the methods of reducing bad behavior fell far short of the goals. The temperance movement had already made a tremendous impact on alcohol use by 1918. If the WCTU and ASL leaders had continued to push responsibility and moderation, perhaps the overreach of the Eighteenth Amendment could have been avoided, and with it all the excesses that followed: a permanent organized crime system, youthful drinking, and a general disdain for the law among the citizenry and lawmakers alike.

The "gotcha" moments under Covid-19 remind me a lot of the "dry-drinkers" who so disgusted Pauline Morton Sabin. The most touted example was California governor Gavin Newsom who, after imposing some of the tightest restrictions in the nation, was caught skirting his own stay-at-home orders by dining out in a crowded restaurant without a mask. Newsom, observed a columnist in the *Wall Street Journal*, "instantly became the poster boy for the 'Do as I Say, Not as I Do' crowd."[251] His Southern counterpart may be South Carolina governor Henry McMaster. Though he imposed far fewer restrictions on his state and rolled them back much faster, during a press conference prior to the holidays he urged South Carolinians to wear masks, limit the size of their gatherings, and hold as many events outdoors as possible. "We have to be careful, we have to be smart," he said. McMaster and his wife, Peggy, both 73 and thus in a high-risk category, came down with Covid a week after attending an indoor Christmas party at the White House.[252]

In concluding their own book on *Bootleggers & Baptists*—which I remind you is written by my economist father, Bruce Yandle, and son, Adam C. Smith—there will always be incentives for Bootlegger and Baptist behavior. The Bootleggers are after cash and the Baptists are after moral superiority and control: "We are all each a little bit Bootlegger, a little bit Baptist—which means as long as we remain human, the story of Bootleggers and Baptists will continue."

So, excuse me while I remove my mask and enjoy a martini. Join me if you like.

FDR MARTINI

- 1 oz. gin
- ½ oz. dry vermouth
- 1 tsp. olive brine
- Lemon twist
- Cocktail olive

Rub the lemon twist around the rim of a chilled cocktail glass and discard the peel. Combine gin, vermouth, and olive brine in a cocktail shaker with cracked ice and shake well. Strain into chilled glass and garnish with olive.

—Courtesy Swank Martini Company

MISSY MARTINI

In honor of FDR's loyal secretary and cocktail hour hostess Missy LeHand, my son-in-law Nick Dowling developed this lovely drink. (Nick is co-owner of Daps Breakfast + Imbibe in Charleston.)

- 1 oz. botanical gin
- ¼ oz. St. Germain Elderflower
- ¼ oz. Cointreau
- ¼ oz. fresh lemon juice
- 2 dashes orange bitters
- Champagne to top

Put in a shaker with ice, shake until very cold, strain into a cocktail glass or Champagne coupe, top with Brut Champagne and garnish with an orange peel.

RECOMMENDED READING

Bootleggers & Baptists: How Economic Forces and Moral Persuasion Interact to Shape Regulatory Politics by Adam Smith and Bruce Yandle (Washington: Cato Institute, 2014)

*N*OTES

INTRODUCTION

1. In choosing which states constitute "the South" for this book, I am following the lead of Ann Barrett Batson, author of *Having It Y'All: An Insider's Guide to Life Southern Style* (Nashville: Rutledge Hill Press, 1988). Batson designated the Southern states, based on their culture, as Virginia, the Carolinas, Georgia, Alabama, Mississippi, Louisiana, Kentucky, Tennessee, Arkansas, and Florida. In fact, she specified *northern* Florida, "due to the irreversible effects of the New York migration and the Cuban occupation." During the time I am covering, there was relatively little influence from those quarters, so I am including the entire state.

2. Neal Thompson, *Driving with the Devil: Southern Moonshine, Detroit Wheels, and the Birth of NASCAR* (New York: Crown, 2006), map showing major racetracks of the 1930s and 1940s.

3. Letter from Keith Johnson, St. Charles, Illinois, in the *Wall Street Journal*, April 14, 2020.

4. Mario J. Rizzo and Glen Whitman, *Escaping Paternalism: Rationality, Behavioral Economics, and Public Policy* (Cambridge, England: Cambridge University Press, 2019), 328.

5. Adam Smith and Bruce Yandle, *Bootleggers and Baptists: How Economic Forces and Moral Persuasion Interact to Shape Regulatory Politic,* (Washington: Cato Institute, 2014). Bruce Yandle is also featured in a cartoon explanation of Bootleggers and Baptists, which can be viewed at https://www.youtube.com/watch?v=msQ_khFmKtU

CHAPTER ONE

6. Richard F. Hamm, *Shaping the Eighteenth Amendment* (Chapel Hill: UNC Press, 1995), 46.

7. Robert F. Moss, *Southern Spirits: Four Hundred Years of Drinking in the American South, with Recipes* (Berkeley: Ten Speed Press, 2016), 56–67.

8. John Elflein, "Alcohol consumption per capita from all beverages (in gallons of ethanol) in the U.S. from 1850 to 2018," statista.com, https://www.statista.com/statistics/442818/per-capita-alcohol-consumption-of-all-beverages-in-the-us/

9. Phillip Kenneth Huggins, *The South Carolina Dispensary: A Bottle Collector's Atlas and History of the System* (Orangeburg, SC: Sandlapper Publishing, 1997), 108–9.

10. Andrew J. Glass, "Tennessee enacted the nation's first prohibition law, Jan. 26, 1838," Politico, January 26, 2012, https://www.politico.com/story/2012/01/this-day-in-politics-071959

11. Moss, *Southern Spirits*, 143.

12. Ben Perrone, "How Mini-Bottles Shaped Charleston's Cocktail Culture," Carolinas Eater, October 16, 2015, https://carolinas.eater.com/21515859/mini-bottles-charleston

CHAPTER TWO

13. In the South, black women like the trio standing at the Burn Memorial that cold day were locked out of voting until the Civil Rights Act was passed some four decades later.

14. Debra Michals, "Carrie Chapman Catt (1859–1947)," National Women's History Museum, https://www.womenshistory.org/education-resources/biographies/carrie-chapman-catt

15. Glass, "Tennessee enacted the nation's first prohibition law."

16. William Thayer Smith, *The Human Body and Its Health: A Textbook for Schools, Having Special Reference to the Effects of Stimulants and Narcotics on the Human System* (New York: Ivison, Blakeman & Company, 1884).

17. Frances E. Willard, *Woman and Temperance: The Work and Workers of the Women's Christian Temperance Union* (Hartford, CT: Park Publishing Co., 1883).

18. Anita S. Goodstein, "Lide Smith Meriwether," Tennessee Encyclopedia, https://tennesseeencyclopedia.net/entries/lide-smith-meriwether/

19. Bennard B. Perlman and Arthur Bowen Davies, *The Lives, Loves and Art of Arthur B. Davies* (Albany: SUNY Press, 1998). Alas, Virginia's problems with men did not end with her first marriage. After her second husband died, she discovered he had another wife and children.

20. The account of Kid Curry's time in Knoxville, including the quote from a contemporary newspaper, the *Journal and Tribune*, are from *Harvey Logan in Knoxville* by Sylvia Lynch (College Station, TX: Creative Publishing, 1998).

21. "Harvey Logan, aka 'Kid Curry'—The Wildest of the Wild Bunch," Legends of America, https://www.legendsofamerica.com/we-harveylogan/2/; and "Harvey Logan—Wildest of the Wild Bunch," historynet, https://www.historynet.com/harvey-logan-wildest-of-the-wild-bunch.htm

22. W. Calvin Dickinson, "Temperance," Tennessee Encyclopedia, https://tennesseeencyclopedia.net/entries/temperance/

23. Tanner Hancock, "History of Alcohol: University of Tennessee," UT *Daily Beacon*, March 25, 2013.

24. "January 1903: Lt. Gov. shoots newspaper owner in front of State House," WIS-TV, August 4, 2014, https://www.wistv.com/story/26185030/gov-ben-tillman-shoots-ng-gonzales-the-state-near-the-state-house/

25. "Dens of Vice Breeding Crime," *Nashville Globe*, November 11, 1908, https://chroniclingamerica.loc.gov/lccn/sn86064259/1908-11-13/ed-1/seq-1/

26. Timothy P. Ezell, "Duncan Brown Cooper," Tennessee Encyclopedia, https://tennesseeencyclopedia.net/entries/duncan-brown-cooper/

27. "Prohibition in East Tennessee," https://www.knoxlib.org/sites/default/files/prohibition_in_east_tn.pdf

28. Erik Schelzig,"Should toppled Carmack statue be repaired at Tennessee Capitol?," *Tennessee Journal*, June 1, 2020, http://onthehill.tnjournal.net/should-toppled-carmack-statue-be-repaired-at-tennessee-capitol/

29. Timothy P. Ezzell, "Edward W. Carmack," Tennessee Encyclopedia, https://tennesseeencyclopedia.net/entries/edward-ward-carmack/; "Edward W. Carmack," Wikipedia, https://en.wikipedia.org/wiki/Edward_W._Carmack; and Gallatin Public Library website, https://www2.youseemore.com/gallatinPL/

30. Lynn Tolley, "Jack Daniel Distillery," Tennessee Encyclopedia, https://tennesseeencyclopedia.net/entries/jack-daniel-distillery/

31. Moss, *Southern Spirits*, 153–57.

32. Peter Kern Library bar menu, https://www.theoliverhotel.com/eat-drink

33. "The Hairy History of Sideburns," Merriam-Webster, https://www.merriam-webster.com/words-at-play/sideburns-meaning-origin

34. "A Slice of History from Knoxville," https://www.experiencekernsbakery.com/history/

35. Richard Hamm, *Shaping the Eighteenth Amendment: Temperance Reform, Legal Culture, and the Polity, 1880-1920* (Chapel Hill: University of North Carolina Press, 1995), 33.; and "Temperance," Tennessee Encyclopedia, previously cited.

36. Hamm, *Shaping*, 33.

37. www.cityofharriman.net

38. Patrick D. Reagan, "Harriman Hosiery Mills Strike of 1933-34," Tennessee Encyclopedia, https://tennesseeencyclopedia.net/entries/harriman-hosiery-mills-strike-of-1933-34/

39. "Harriman, Tennessee," Wikipedia, https://en.wikipedia.org/wiki/Harriman,_Tennessee

40. Find-a-grave.com

CHAPTER THREE

41. Robert Lewis Taylor, *Vessel of Wrath: The Life and Times of Carry Nation* (New York: New American Library, 1966), 1.

42. Carry A. Nation, *The Use and Need of the Life of Carry A. Nation*, (Topeka, KS: F.M. Steves & Sons, 1905), 40.

43. Taylor, *Vessel*, 5.

44. The pins may have been cheap at one point, but they are highly collectible today. I paid $100 for the pictured brooch with Nation's photograph.

45. Nation, *Use*, 10–12.

46. The account of the remainder of Nation's life is derived from Taylor, 4, 6, 18, 37–46, 50–52, 56, 61, 72, 84–95, 92, 121, 124, 133–34, 141–43, 155–56, 230, 297–98, and 361; and Nation's autobiography, 10–12, 17, 19, 30, 34–36, 57, 62–63, 105, and 136. Fran Grace in her academic biography *Carry A. Nation: Retelling the Life* (Bloomington: Indiana

University Press, 2001) disputes some of the wilder statements about Nation, including the insistence that her mother, Mary Moore, believed she was Queen Victoria. She also says Nation's height was a mere five feet and that eastern press accounts inaccurately picture her "as a hyperthyroid Amazon." In her preface she asks, "How did male-biased negative accounts of Carry Nation become historical 'fact'?"

47. The information on the height of men in Nation's time is from https://ourworldindata.org/human-height

CHAPTER FOUR

48. Willard, *Woman and Temperance*, 540 and 541.

49. Helen Glenn Smith, "The Red Tape Cocktail: Charleston's Reaction to the South Carolina Dispensary System," *Chrestomathy: Annual Review of Undergraduate Research, School of Humanities and Social Sciences*, College of Charleston, Vol. 4, 2005, 195–217.

50. Lewis, *The Coming of Prohibition*, 5. Lewis says 913 Southern counties voted themselves dry during the local option period, while 117 counties opted for legal liquor sales.

51. Jones, *South Carolina*, 568.

52. Huggins, *The SC Dispensary*, 118.

53. "Pitchfork" Ben Tillman, South Carolina Information Highway, https://www.sciway.net/hist/governors/tillman.html

54. Benjamin Ryan Tillman, Clemson University website, https://www.clemson.edu/about/history/bios/ben-tillman.html#_ftn18

55. Will Moredock, *Charleston City Paper*, February 5, 2014.

56. Adam Benson, "Columbia Pair Accused of Trying to Blow Up Tillman Statue on SC Statehouse Grounds," *Post and Courier*, July 2, 2020.

57. *Yorkville Enquirer*, July 19, 1893.

58. Jones, *South Carolina*, 572. Tillman's solution was echoed in the 1933 film *Gabriel Over the White House*, in which the president of the United States adjourns Congress and declares war on bootlegging crime boss Nick Diamond by setting up a dispensary system. The first store is ransacked by the mob within an hour of opening, and an assassination attempt is made in a drive-by shooting. The president then designates a special unit of the Army to go after Diamond and his gang. They are captured, courts-martialed and executed at dawn. Wouldn't Tillman have loved to have had that kind of power?

59. In addition to Valerie Stow's tour and the contemporary newspaper accounts, Mark Jones's *Wicked Charleston Volume 2: Prostitutes, Politics and Prohibition* (Charleston: History Press, 2006), 54–59, informed this section. Jones's entertaining book includes stories of other bootleggers and also activities in Hellhole Swamp in Berkeley County.

60. *Yorkville Enquirer*, July 19, 1893.

61. George Eastman's camera for the masses was introduced in 1888. "Original Kodak Camera, Serial #540," National Museum of American History. https://americanhistory.si.edu/collections/search/object/nmah_760118

62. *Lancaster Ledger*, July 10, 1901.

63. "Token of the Month # 24, Vincent Chicco and His Blind Tiger," http://www.angelfire.com/sc2/tokenofthemonth/token024/

64. Palmetto Distillery makes an even higher-proof product, Bootlegger Proof. At 130-proof, it pulled double duty during the coronavirus outbreak as the main ingredient for Palmetto Distillery Hand Sanitizer. Cost: $29.75 a gallon. https://shop.palmettodistillery.com/collections/hand-sanitizer

65. Restaurant website, https://blindtigerchs.com/

66. Interview with Robert F. Moss, plus his article "From hooch to haute cuisine," *Post and Courier*, December 8, 2015.

67. Traci Rylands, "Adventures in Cemetery Hopping" blog, https://adventuresincemeteryhopping.com/2018/04/06/saint-lawrence-cemetery/, and author visit.

68. www.hunley.org and www.magnoliacemetery.net/

69. Excellent photos of the cemetery monuments, including Brandon Coffey's shot of Rosalie Raymond's bassinet-shaped grave, can be viewed at https://www.scpictureproject.org/charleston-county/magnolia-cemetery.html

70. Find-a-grave.com

CHAPTER FIVE

71. Paul S. George, "A Cyclone Hits Miami: Carrie Nation's Visit to 'The Wicked City'," *Florida Historical Quarterly*, 58, no. 2 (October 1979).

72. "A Brief History of Alcohol and Government in Leon County," Responsible Tallahassee website, https://www.responsibletallahassee.com/leon-county-history

73. If Sanford rings a bell, it may because of the murder of unarmed black teenager Trayvon Martin there in 2012 by a neighborhood watch coordinator, thereby launching the Black Lives Matter movement.

74. Kathryn Smith, *Gertie: The Fabulous Life of Gertrude Sanford Legendre, Heiress, Explorer, Socialite, Spy* (Charleston: Evening Post Books, 2019), numerous examples.

75. The information on Sanford's wet-dry history comes from an interview with Sanford Museum curator Brigitte Stephenson and her slide presentation "You Can Ship it to Savannah," which she generously shared.

76. Daniel Okrent, *Last Call: The Rise and Fall of Prohibition* (New York: Scribner, 2010), 25.

77. "Joseph and the Zapfs flooded Florida—with Bottles" from the blog Those Pre-Pro Whiskey Men. www.pre-prowhiskeymen.blogspot.com/2019/11/joseph-and-zapfs-flooded-florida-with.html

78. Information and observations on The Villages are derived from a personal visit; Solomon Gustavo, "Golf cart protests intensify in the Villages, as one anti-Trump Florida man receives threat," *Orlando Weekly*, January 31, 2020; Meta Minton, "Woman in wrong-way golf cart arrested on DUI charge at town square," www.villages.news.com, February 10, 2020; Mike Czeczot, "The Villages in Florida—How it became a Haven for Relocating Retirees," www.southeastdiscovery.com/blog/2017/05/the-villages-in-florida-how-it-became-a-haven-for-relocating-retirees/; www.thevillages.com; and Ryan Erisman's blog www.insidethebubble.net. The AA meeting information is from the website https://www.sober.com/meetings/state/city/aa?state=Florida&city=The%20Villages

79. The quote is from an information board at Brownwood Paddock Recreation Center in The Villages.

CHAPTER SIX

80. Gregory Mixon, "Atlanta Race Riot of 1906," New Georgia Encyclopedia, https://www.georgiaencyclopedia.org/articles/history-archaeology/atlanta-race-riot-1906

81. Lewis, *Coming*, 243.

82. Jackson Lears, *Rebirth of a Nation: The Making of Modern America, 1877–1920* (New York: HarperCollins, 2009), 102–3.

83. "Map: States Grant Women the Right to Vote," https://constitutioncenter.org/timeline/html/cw08_12159.html

84. Martha Quillin, "Statue of Josephus Daniels, publisher and white supremacist, removed from Raleigh square," *Raleigh News and Observer*, June 16, 2020. Like Tennessee's Edwin Carmack, Daniels was a newspaper publisher and a white supremacist who used his newspaper, the *Raleigh News and Observer*, to foment racial strife. The larger-than-life statue of him in Raleigh was removed at the request of his family following weeks of Black Lives Matter demonstrations, and the Wake County school board voted to rename Daniels Middle School to Oberlin Middle School, honoring a community founded by former slaves.

85. Okrent, *Last Call*, 224.

86. Okrent, *Last Call*, 27.

87. Kelli R. Kerbawy, "Knights in White Satin: Women of the KKK," master's thesis, Marshall University, 2007.

88. Okrent, *Last Call*, 54.

89. Okrent, *Last Call*, 53, 57.

90. Jennifer M. Murray, "Richmond Pearson Hobson," Encyclopedia of Alabama, http://encyclopediaofalabama.org/article/h-3235. It is interesting to note that Hobson had an enlightened view of racial equality for his time and state, which is what cost him re-election. He was also a supporter of women's suffrage.

91. Okrent, *Last Call*, 57.

92. Mabel Walker Willebrandt, *The Inside of Prohibition* (Indianapolis: Bobbs-Merrill Company, 1929), 27.

93. Karen Abbott, *The Ghosts of Eden Park: The Bootleg King, the Women Who Pursued Him and the Murder that Shocked Jazz-Age America* (New York: Crown, 2019), 25.

94. Moss, *Southern Spirits*, 236.

95. Okrent, *Last Call*, 118.

96. Clay and Stewart did not come from the same mold. A generation older than Stewart, Clay opposed the so-called Anthony Amendment because she believed it interfered with state's rights; she supported a state-by-state approach to women's suffrage. By 1928, she had given up on temperance and supported New York "wet" Al Smith for president against Herbert Hoover. Stewart later convinced President Hoover to form the first Presidential Advisory Committee on Illiteracy. Clay biography under Laura Clay Papers, https://exploreuk.uky.edu/fa/findingaid/?id=xt70rx937t9n; Stewart bio from "Cora Wilson Stewart," https://www.readinghalloffame.org/node/711

97. "Our History: The USS *Hobson*, a Lowcountry Ship," https://www.northcharleston.org/news/our-history-the-uss-hobson-a-lowcountry-ship/

98. "Temperance Fountain, Washington, D.C., a much-maligned monument to teetotalism," https://www.atlasobscura.com/places/temperance-fountain-of-washington-dc

99. Both graves were located through find-a-grave.com.

CHAPTER SEVEN

100. Rebecca Rolfes, "Drunk at the Seelbach Hotel," The Bitter Southerner, https://bittersoutherner.com/f-scott-fitzgerald-at-the-seelbach

101. Rolfes, "Drunk."

102. Interview with Linda and George Ruffenbach and Linda's book, *How to be a Bourbon Badass* (Bloomington, IN, Red Lightning Books, 2018). Both Whisky Chicks and Bourbon Badass are registered trademarks.

103. https://kybourbontrail.com/distilleries/; The Whiskey Row statistic was posted on signage at Old Forester distillery.

104. Many thanks to my son-in-law Nick Dowling, a founder and director of the Charleston Brown Water Society, for clarifying my understanding of the fine points of bourbon making.

105. Jim Warren, "Revisiting Prohibition: Kentucky was ahead of the times," *Lexington Herald-Leader*, October 18, 2011.

106. Brown-Forman is one of the largest and oldest spirit and wine companies in the United States still controlled by its founding family. Evan Williams is a brand of Heaven Hill in Bardstown, Kentucky, also family-owned, but founded after Prohibition. Bulleit is part of the international Diageo conglomerate based in London, and Rabbit Hole is owned by the French Pernod Ricard corporation.

107. Willebrandt, *Inside*, 151.

108. Willebrandt, *Inside*, 68; "Katherine Gudson Langley," Biographical Directory of the U.S. Congress, https://history.house.gov/People/Detail/16680; Okrent, *Last Call*, 275. Langley served less than a year and was ultimately pardoned by President Coolidge, one of the conditions being that he would not run for office again.

109. Bullock's book is available in several editions, including Kindle, but a beautiful hardcover facsimile edition was published by www.cocktailkingdom.com and is available on the company website.

110. Find-a-grave.com

CHAPTER EIGHT

111. Ian Lendler, *Alcoholica Esoterica: A Collection of Useful and Useless Information As It Relates to the History and Consumption of All Manner of Booze* (New York: Penguin Books, 2005), 87.

112. Okrent, *Last Call*, 160.

113. H. De Winton Wigley, *With the Whiskey Smugglers*, (London: Daily News Ltd., 1923) republished in *The Bahama Queen: Prohibition's Daring Beauty* (Mystic, CT: Flat Hammock Press, 2007), 20.

114. Wigley, *Whiskey*, 24.

115. Lythgoe, Gertrude. *The Bahama Queen: Prohibition's Daring Beauty* (originally published 1964, republished by Flat Hammock Press, Mystic, CT, 2007.)

116. Ann Dermody, "The Real McCoy," *Boat U.S.*, June 2015. https://www.boatus.com/magazine/2015/june/the-real-mccoy.asp

117. Okrent, *Last Call*, 165.

118. Willebrandt, *Inside*, 252–53.

119. Okrent, *Last Call*, 170.

120. Lythgoe, *Bahama*. The publisher's afterword in the reprint stated that Gertrude was the inspiration for the lead female character in the 1975 movie *Lucky Lady*, starring Liza Minnelli, Burt Reynolds, and Gene Hackman.

121. Sarah Baird, "Meet the Swashbuckling Female Rumrunners Who Ran Prohibition," saveur.com, July 2015, https://www.saveur.com/rumrunners/

122. Willebrandt, *Inside*, 224–29.

123. Robert Carse, *Rum Row: The Liquor that Fueled the Roaring Twenties*, (Mystic, CT: Flat Hammock Press, 2007, originally published in 1959), 131.

124. Carse, *Rum Row*, 181.

125. Willebrandt, *Inside*, 147.

126. Chase, Karen. *FDR on His Houseboat, the Larooco Log, 1924–26* (Albany, NY: State University of NY Press, 2016), 153.

127. Becky Billingsley, *Lost Myrtle Beach* (Charleston: History Press, 2014). https://www.scribd.com/book/266858404/Lost-Myrtle-Beach

128. Willebrandt, *Inside*, 126.

129. J. E. McTeer, *High Sheriff of the Low Country* (Beaufort, SC: Beaufort Book Company, 1970), 7–8.

130. McTeer, *High*, 16–17.

131. Abbott, *Ghosts*, 87; prison "celebrity" inmate list from "United States Penitentiary, Atlanta," Wikipedia, https://en.wikipedia.org/wiki/United_States_Penitentiary,_Atlanta

132. Abbott, *Ghosts*, 99.

133. Thelma Combes, "Thelma Terry (1901-1966), Syncopated Times website, https://syncopatedtimes.com/thelma-terry-1901-1966/

134. Find-a-grave.com.

135. Find-a-grave.com and e-mail from Cheri Daniels.

CHAPTER NINE

136. As it turns out, Gogo Jewelry out of St. Simon's Island, Georgia sells sterling silver and 14 kt gold "Raccoon Pecker" rings and earrings cast from, well, you know. www.gogojewely.com

137. Suzanna Smith Miles, "Moonshine Over Hell Hole Swamp," *Charleston Magazine*, December 2015, https://charlestonmag.com/features/moonshine_over_hell_hole_swamp

138. Thompson, *Driving*, 60. Georgia rolled back its state prohibition in 1935, but many of its counties remained dry.

139. Moss, *Southern Spirits*, 149–59.

140. Joshua Beau Blackwell, *Used to Be a Rough Place in Them Hills: Moonshine, the Dark Corner, and the New South* (Bloomington, IN: Author House, 2009), 67. The quote is from a Spartanburg newspaper in 1898.

141. Moss, *Southern Spirits*, 149–53.

142. Moss, *Southern Spirits*, 158–59; Lewis Richard "Major" Redmond, https://www.findagrave.com/memorial/45715392/lewis-richard-redmond; author visit to cemetery.

143. Blackwell, *Rough*, xv–xvii.

144. Blackwell, *Rough*, 65.

145. Thompson, *Driving*, 19–21, gives the most succinct and understandable description of moonshine making I have read. On page 65 he states that federal agents seized 340,000 stills and arrested almost a million people during the thirteen years of Prohibition. Thanks also to Robert F. Moss for further clarification on the issue of "heads" and "tails."

146. Hell Hole Swamp was said to have gotten its name from Francis Marion's British adversary, General Cornwallis, who described the place as "one hell of a hole of a swamp," according to the S.C. Picture Project entry on the swamp. The community has held a Hell Hole Swamp festival annually since 1971, though it was disrupted in 2020 by Covid-19. https://www.scpictureproject.org/berkeley-county/hell-hole-swamp-festival.html

147. Miles, "Moonshine Over Hell Hole Swamp."

148. *New York Times*, July 25, 1930.

149. Shamira McCray, "Booze for Al Capone: Archaeologists study SC illegal moonshine sites near Charleston," Charleston *Post and Courier*, February 8, 2021. Berkeley County Sheriff Duane Lewis, who has researched this case, gave me important insights during a telephone interview May 1, 2021. He said Al Capone had been spotted in Moncks Corner, staying at the McKnight home across the street from the courthouse, but bought from both rival gangs in Berkeley County. Lewis said heroin is the biggest source of contraband headaches for law enforcement in Berkeley County today.

150. Charleston *News and Courier*, March 4, 1932.

151. Charleston *News and Courier*, May 25, 1960.

152. Many thanks to my classic car expert Jameson Moreau for the nugget of information about the hydraulic brakes.

153. Andrew Clyde, a gun store owner from Athens, won the open seat with almost 80 percent of the district's vote. His top issues were gun rights, standing up to big government, and dismantling the IRS. www.clyde4congress.com

154. The most recent GBI report was for 2017. Dawson County, population 23,860, had no murders, seven rapes, three robberies, and 26 aggravated assaults. The national average per 100,000 population that year was 5.3 murders, 41.7 rapes, 30.7 robberies, and 98 aggravated assaults.

155. Matt Aiken, "Jail shakedown leads to drug bust," *Dahlonega Nugget*, October 7, 2020. Numerous other stories of drug busts and raids were reported in the *Dawson County News*, www.dawsonnews.com.

156. Georgia Racing Hall of Fame signage.

157. Interview with Scott Adams, board member of the Hall of Fame, and John Newby, "NASCAR Cup Series Champ Chase Elliott Says He's Had 'Maybe 40' Celebratory Beers Since Phoenix Race," www.popculture.com, November 12, 20202.

158. Interview with Scott Adams and "Lakewood Speedway" on Wikipedia, https://en.wikipedia.org/wiki/Lakewood_Speedway

159. Zack Albert, "Junior Johnson, moonshiner turned NASCAR legend, dies at 88," December 20, 2019, www.nascar.com.

160. Roy wasn't as lucky in 1946, when he was sentenced to six years in prison for bank robbery. Thompson, *Driving*, 191.

161. Quote from www.palmettomoonshine.com

162. Author visit.

163. Find-a-grave.com and author visit.

164. Information on both graves found at find-a-grave.com.

CHAPTER TEN

165. Figures from www.usinflationcalculator.com

166. Deirdre Bair, *Al Capone: His Life, Legacy, and Legend* (New York: Doubleday, 2016), provides the basic narrative for Capone's life followed in this chapter, 67–68, 74, 93–94, 108, 112, 115–16, 135, 136, 138, 161, 191, 209, 235, 259, 286, 303, 306.

167. Sinclair Lewis, *Babbitt* (New York: Harcourt, Brace & Co., 1922), 96–103.

168. Dave Wischnowsky, "Where in the world WASN'T Al Capone?" (Kankakee, Illinois) *Daily Journal*, August 10, 2012.

169. William K. Klingaman, *1929: The Year of the Great Crash* (New York: Harper & Row, 1989), 132.

170. Paul Moon, "What was the Dixie Highway, anyway?" *Asheville Citizen-Times*, December 11, 2020. Carl Fisher's developments included Fisher Island, the most exclusive of the man-made islands in Biscayne Bay.

171. Sally J. Ling, *Al Capone's Miami: Paradise or Purgatory?* (Deerfield Beach, FL: Flamingo Press, 2016), 79.

172. Ling, *Miami*, 25–26.

173. James J. Carney, "Population Growth in Miami and Dade County, Florida," Tequesta, 1946, 50–55, http://digitalcollections.fiu.edu/tequesta/files/1946/46_1_06.pdf

174. Ashley Protera, "2018 was a record-breaking year for Miami tourism. 2019 could be even better," www.bizjournals.com, May 3, 2019.

175. Joe's Take Away, which has seating for eighty, operates year-round, and the restaurant also ships stone crab claws nationwide.

176. https://www.joesstonecrab.com/about-joes. Ian Fleming thinly disguised Joe's as Bill's on the Beach in his 1959 novel *Goldfinger*.

177. Ling, *Miami*, 45.

178. The Merton quote is on a plaque inside the church. He made the remark in April 1940.

179. According to Father William Saunders in "The Symbolism of the Pelican," posted on catholiceducation.org, the mother pelican represents Christ because in times of famine she will tear open her own breast to feed blood to her young so they won't starve.

180. Christopher Klein, "Mobster Al Capone Ran a Soup Kitchen During the Great Depression," www.history.com, April 5, 2019.

181. I received no responses to emails and telephone calls I made to the contacts on the website 93Palm.com. My descriptions are gleaned from the pictures on the website and the appendix of Ling's book *Al Capone in Miami,* in which she describes what she saw on a tour of the house.

182. The Eastern State Penitentiary in Philadelphia has been turned into a museum, where visitors can see Capone's cell, restored to resemble its appearance in 1929. You can take a virtual tour at https://www.easternstate.org/explore/exhibits/al-capones-cell.

183. Bryan Burrough, *Public Enemies* (New York, Penguin Books, 2005), 544.

184. Ted Hake, *The Official Hake's Price Guide to Character Toys, Sixth Edition* (House of Collectibles, an imprint of Random House Information Group/Gemstone Publishing, 2006).

185. Burrough, *Public Enemies*, 546.

186. Alston Purvis and Alex Tresniowski, *The Vendetta: Special Agent Melvin Purvis, John Dillinger, and Hoover's FBI in the Age of Gansters* (New York: Public Affairs, 2005).

187. Deirdre Marie Capone, *Uncle Al Capone: The Untold Story from Inside His Family* (ReCap LLC, 2010).

188. The photos of Capone in his coffin are displayed on the website www.myalcaponemuseum.com, operated by Mario Gomes.

189. Maritote v. Desilu Productions, https://law.justia.com/cases/federal/district-courts/FSupp/230/721/1413083/

190. David Minsky, "Al Capone's Niece to Host Templeton Whiskey Dinner at the Seminole Casino January 17," Broward Palm Beach *New Times*, January 14, 2015.

191. Burrough, *Public Enemies*, 40–41. Actually, there were eight bathhouses built between 1892 and 1923. The Buckstaff has been offering hot baths for more than a century.

192. The Hot Springs photos are displayed on myalcaponemuseum.com.

193. Phillip Leigh, *The Devil's Town: Hot Springs During the Gangster Era* (Columbia, SC: Shotwell Publishing LLC, 2018), 25.

194. Find-a-grave.com and cemetery website.

CHAPTER ELEVEN

195. Klingaman, *1929*, 128, and U.S. Census data for 1930. Chicago in our time is held up as the poster child for gun violence and murder. Metro Chicago, which has a population of 9.4 million—twice what it had in 1928—had 774 murders in 2020, according to the *Chicago Sun-Times*. New York in 2020 had 447 murders, according to the *New York Times*. New York's metro population is now 18.8 million, three times what it was in 1928. Both of those cities had huge crime increases in 2020 over 2019 statistics—but they are still significantly less than the murder rates in 1928.

196. Okrent, *Last Call*, 258.

197. Okrent, *Last Call*, 131.

198. You have to admit it. Ella Boole looks a lot like The Church Lady portrayed by Dana Carvey on *Saturday Night Live*.

199. Kenneth Whyte, *Hoover: An Extraordinary Life in Extraordinary Times* (New York: Knopf, 2017), 350.

200. Kathryn Smith, *The Gatekeeper: Missy LeHand, FDR and the Untold Story of the Partnership that Defined a Presidency* (New York: Atria, 2016), 80–81.

201. Smith, *Gatekeeper*, 70. On one famous occasion, LeHand was coming out of the kitchen with a tray of martinis when there came a knock on the door. "Come in, come in!" FDR boomed, expecting one of their guests. It was, instead, a Baptist preacher. LeHand quickly about-faced into the kitchen, where several guests found an excuse to join her, and when the preacher finally departed, they were all agonized with laughter.

202. Okrent, *Last Call*, 305. Jones founded a Christian college in Florida that relocated in 1947 to Greenville, South Carolina. It is called Bob Jones University and is now lead by Jones's great-grandson, Dr. Stephen Jones. www.bju.edu

203. Okrent, *Last Call*, 318.

204. Rose, Kenneth D., *American Women and the Repeal of Prohibition* (New York: New York University Press, 1996), 47.

205. Willebrandt, *Inside*, 121.

206. "The American Mafia: A World of Violence and Intrigue Revealed," a History Channel publication, Meredith Special Interest Media, 2020.

207. Rose, *American Women*, 77.

208. Root, Grace C., *Women and Repeal: The Story of the Women's Organization for National Prohibition Reform* (New York: Harper & Brothers, 1934) is the source of the activities of WONPR in this chapter, except when otherwise cited, 4, 26, 27, 62, 80, 97, 98–99, 110, 133.

209. Rose, *American Women*, 97.

210. Rose, *American Women*, 62.

211. Brown, Dorothy M., *Mabel Walker Willebrandt: A Study of Power, Loyalty and Law* (Knoxville: University of Tennessee Press, 1984), 180–87. Willebrandt's more successful private sector clients including MGM Studios and several airlines.

212. Ned Hémard, "Prohibition in New Orleans," https://www.neworleansbar.org/uploads/files/Prohibition%20in%20New%20Orleans_1-8.pdf

213. Information on Eliza Andreini's life was found on ancestry.com, including city directories, her petition for reinstatement of her citizenship, newspaper accounts of her marriages and the deaths of her three husbands, and find-a-grave.com. Also, "Friends of France Open Supply Room," *News and Courier*, March 6, 1940; and William Means Real Estate PDF about 59 Meeting Street. Thanks to Josephine Humphreys and other members of the Facebook page "Charleston History Before 1945" for their assistance.

214. Rose, *American Women*, 98–99.

215. Sarah Wildman, "Meet Robert Reynolds, the senator who wanted to 'build a wall' 70 years before Trump," Vox.com, April 14, 2017. https://www.vox.com/world/2017/4/4/15022190/robert-reynolds-isolationism-nativism-refugees-wwii-trump-holocaust-america-first

216. April 7 is National Beer Day.

217. "Toasting the Repeal of Prohibition," www.anheuser-busch.com, March 31, 2016. The company also delivered a case of beer to Al Smith in New York.

218. Samuel C. Hyde, "Prohibition," https://64parishes.org/entry/prohibition

219. "Twenty-First Amendment of the American Constitution," Wikipedia, https://en.wikipedia.org/wiki/Twenty-first_Amendment_to_the_United_States_Constitution. The Will Rogers quote is from Root, *Women and Repeal*, 132.

220. Alistair Williams, "Exploring the impact of legislation on the development of craft beer," *Beverages* 3, no. 2 (2017), 18; Ben Steelman, "North Carolina has complex history with liquor," *Wilmington Star News*, March 6, 2010; Chuck McShane, "How Charlotte got liquored up," Charlotte Magazine, October 24, 2017.

221. Johnny Caldwell is half of the Cocktail Bandits duo, authors of *Holy Spirits! Charleston Culture Through Cocktails* (Charleston: Evening Post Books, 2018). The other "bandit" is Taneka Reaves.

222. Daniel S. Pierce, *Tar Heel Lightnin': How Secret Stills and Fast Cars Made North Carolina the Moonshine Capital of the World* (Chapel Hill: University of North Carolina Press, 2019), 3.

223. NASCAR drivers by state of residence, https://www.nascarreference.com/driver/drvstates.php

224. Thanks to Lisa Glenn Silvestri, granddaughter of Sheriff Jim Williams, for sharing news clippings about the stills and raids in Anderson County.

225. Rebecca Treon, "Storming of the Sazerac: Feminist Cocktail History is Alive Today," wine4food.com, https://www.wine4food.com/featured/storming-of-the-sazerac/ #:~:text=The%20women%20who%20stormed%20the,(legally)%20consumed% 20without%20care; and "The Roosevelt New Orleans A Waldorf Astoria Hotel announces date of 70th Anniversary of 'Stormin' of the Sazerac,'" www.MyNewOrleans.com, April 14, 2019.

226. Doran, Roxana B., *Prohibition Punches* (Philadelphia: Dorrance & Company, 1930).

227. Judge Jr., *Noble Experiments* (New York: John Day Company, 1930).

228. Todd A. Price, "Sazerac cocktail recipe," www.nola.com, October 27, 2014. Price shared a recipe demonstrated by a bartender at the Roosevelt Hotel.

229. Find-a-grave.com

230. Find-a-grave.com

EPILOGUE

231. Scott Calvert, "Louisville Settles for $12 Million Over Raid," *Wall Street Journal*, September 16, 2020.

232. Bob Woodward, *Rage* (New York: Simon & Schuster 2020) informs my Covid-19 timeline for this chapter.

233. Woodward, *Rage*, 293 and 301.

234. Paul Woolvertson, "Cheers! Pandemic drove N.C. liquor sales to new heights," Asheville *Citizen-Times*, July 27, 2020.

235. Jelisa Catrodale, "Why Liquor Stores Should Be Considered 'Essential Businesses' During Quarantine," Vice.com, March 25, 2020.

236. Gottschalk cartoon in "Pepper . . . And Salt," *Wall Street Journal*, January 8, 2021.

237. Indeed, the U.S. Department of Agriculture and Health and Human Services disregarded the recommendation when the final version of the dietary guidelines were issued in December, saying there was insufficient evidence to recommend it. Andrea Petersen, "New U.S. Dietary Guidelines Reject Recommendation to Cut Sugar, Alcohol Intake Limit," *Wall Street Journal*, December 29, 2020.

238. Barbara Harfmann, "Craft beer focus shifts during Covid-19," Beverage Industry, November 18, 2020. https://www.bevindustry.com/articles/93572-craft-beer-focus-shifts-during-covid-19

239. Jennifer Maloney, "Pandemic Boosts Big Beer Brands," *Wall Street Journal*, May 19, 2020; and Nat Ives, "Corona Beer's Brand Name Keeps Buzz Amid Covid-19," *Wall Street Journal*, December 22, 2020.

240. Woodward, *Rage*, 328.

241. Woodward, *Rage*, 380.

242. Nick Timraos, "Trump Retweets, Deletes Video of Racist Supporters," *Wall Street Journal*, June 29, 2020.

243. Adam Nagourney, "The Teetotaler Campaign: Two Dissimilar Candidates Share Aversion to Alcohol," *New York Times*, October 31, 2020.

244. Barack Obama, *A Promised Land* (New York: Crown Publishing Group, 2020), 295.

245. Arian Campo-Flores, "As Covid-19 Surges, Florida Sticks to No Statewide Restrictions," *Wall Street Journal*, November 24, 2020.

246. Matthew Arrojas, "SEB sells Delano South Beach hotel to Eldridge, South Florida Business Journal, November 24, 2020, https://www.bizjournals.com/southflorida/ news/2020/11/24/delano-south-beach-hotel-sold-to-eldridge.html. The hotel is expected to reopen after a refurbishment.

247. Barbara Schwartzapfel, Kate Park and Andrew DeMillo, "1 in 5 Prisoners in U.S. Has Had Covid-19," themarshallproject.org, December 18, 2020. https://www. themarshallproject.org/2020/12/18/1-in-5-prisoners-in-the-u-s-has-had-covid-19. As it turned out, the report gave Georgia the best marks in the South, with just one in 22 prisoners affected compared to numbers more like the national average in the other Southern states.

248. Talal Ansari, "Hospitalizations Rise in South, West," *Wall Street Journal*, December 30, 2020. The United States marked 500,000 Covid-19 deaths on February 22, 2021. President Biden pointed out that this represents more American deaths than both World Wars and the Vietnam War combined. Talal Ansari, "Virus Toll Hits Half a Million," *Wall Street Journal*, February 23, 2021.

249. Heather Haddon and Julie Wernau, "Restaurants Say Safety Net Frays as Winter Sets In," *Wall Street Journal*, December 21, 2020.

250. Editorial Staff, "The Martini Lunch Tax Code," *Wall Street Journal*, December 22, 2020. In this case of Bootlegger and Baptist behavior, the restaurant lobby uses the moral cover of wanting to help small businesses recover and hire back staff, while the biggest beneficiaries are corporations which can now write off all their meal expenses rather than just half, as has been the case since the tax law was changed in the 1980s. The losers, of course, are other taxpayers who pick up the revenue loss or see the federal deficit enlarged.

251. William McGurn, "A Heap of Thanksgiving Hypocrisy," *Wall Street Journal*, November 24, 2020.

252. Governor's Press Conference, November 19, 2020, https://www.youtube.com/ watch?v=NlWSFGbfpk0; and Seanna Adcox, "S.C. Gov. Henry McMaster tests positive for COVID-19, undergoing antibody treatment," Charleston *Post and Courier*, December 22, 2020.

DETAIL ON WIKIMEDIA COMMONS PHOTOS

Ida B. Wells, photographed by Mary Garrity, 1893. Public Domain.

The Wild Bunch, 1890. Public Domain.

Edward W. Carmack statue, photographed October 19, 2019 by Nancy Cox-McCormack. https://creativecommons.org/licenses/by-sa/4.0/deed.en

Harrington Temperance Building, photographed March 6, 2010 by Brian Stansberry. https://creativecommons.org/licenses/by/3.0/deed.en

The Villages, Trump Rally, October 23, 2020. https://creativecommons.org/licenses/ by-sa/4.0/deed.en

The Villages, Golf Cart Parade, November 20, 2020. https://en.wikipedia.org/wiki/ Creative_Commons

KKK cartoon, published in "The Ku Klux Klan in Prophecy," 1925. Public Domain.

New York Times, "Nation Voted Dry," January 17, 1919. Public Domain.

Richmond P. Hobson, portrait from *Famous Americans* by B.J. Falk, 1898. Public Domain.

Seelbach Hotel, both pictures taken September 17, 2010. https://creativecommons.org/licenses/by-sa/3.0/deed.en

Nucky Johnson and Al Capone, https://creativecommons.org/licenses/by-sa/3.0/deed.en

Al Capone's Miami Beach pool, photographed April 25, 2013, Jills/Coldwell Banker Real Estate. https://commons.wikimedia.org/wiki/File:Al_Capone%27s_Miami_Beach_Home_-_View_of_the_Pool.jpg

ᛁNDEX

213

ABOUT THE AUTHOR

 **Kathryn Smith** is an American history writer. Her non-fiction books include *The Gatekeeper: Missy LeHand, FDR, and the Untold Story of the Partnership that Defined a Presidency* and *Gertie: The Fabulous Life of Gertrude Sanford Legendre, Heiress, Explorer, Socialite, Spy*, which won the Benjamin Franklin Gold Award in biography from the Independent Book Publishers Association She also co-authors the Missy LeHand Mystery series with Kelly Durham, which features LeHand as the Nancy Drew of the New Deal. Smith speaks widely on her books at venues that have included the FDR Presidential Library and Museum in Hyde Park, New York and the National World War II Museum in New Orleans, as well as to book club, civic club, library and history museum audiences. She and her husband Leo live in Anderson, South Carolina.

CPSIA information can be obtained
at www.ICGtesting.com
Printed in the USA
JSHW021733050622
26648JS00003B/9